Praise for
Sweet, Savory & Free

"I have a big, loud, Italian family, and we love to eat. I also have a daughter and nephew with food allergies, so it can be tricky. Debbie Adler has found a way to make everybody happy. *Sweet, Savory, and Free* allows you to make everything from condiments to pizza to cookies, without using any of the eight top food allergens. The genius part? It's all delicious. My family doesn't know the difference, because believe me, if they did, I'd hear about it. Thank you, Debbie!"

—Ray Romano

"The way we eat has a profound effect on our health, and the health of the planet. *Sweet, Savory, and Free* is filled with recipes that will keep you (and our Mother Earth) from going into cardiac arrest . . . and did I mention that they're all delicious!"

—Ed Begley, Jr., Emmy- and Golden Globe–award nominated actor and environmentalist

"*Sweet, Savory, and Free* could easily qualify as an optimum health book, with an eye toward making tasty dishes. Your kitchen would not be complete without this book. Debbie Adler's personal motivation for this book is compelling."

—T. Colin Campbell, PhD, coauthor of *The China Study* and the *New York Times* bestselling *Whole*

"*Sweet, Savory, and Free* proves that allergen-free, healthful plant-based cooking can be delicious—and fun! Debbie Adler makes it possible to prepare wonderful worry-free dishes for anyone, anytime."

—JJ Virgin, celebrity nutrition and fitness expert, and author of the *New York Times* bestselling books *The Virgin Diet* and *Sugar Impact Diet*

"Debbie makes living plant-based and allergy-free delicious and fun with her super tasty and nutritious recipes. This book is an incredible resource for any family wanting to eat healthy."

—**Tess Masters, author of *The Blender Girl*, *The Blender Girl Smoothies*, and *The Perfect Blend***

Sweet, Savory & Free

Sweet, Savory & Free

INSANELY DELICIOUS PLANT-BASED RECIPES
WITHOUT ANY OF THE TOP 8 FOOD ALLERGENS

Debbie Adler

PHOTOGRAPHY BY CARL KRAVATS

BENBELLA BOOKS, INC.
DALLAS, TX

BenBella Books, Inc.
10440 N. Central Expressway, Suite 800
Dallas, TX 75231
www.benbellabooks.com
Send feedback to feedback@benbellabooks.com

Printed in the United States of America
10 9 8 7 6 5 4 3 2 1

Library of Congress Cataloging-in-Publication Data
Names: Adler, Debbie, author. | Kravats, Carl, photographer.
Title: Sweet, savory, and free : insanely delicious plant-based recipes
    without any of the top 8 food allergens / Debbie Adler ; photography by
    Carl Kravats.
Description: Dallas, TX : BenBella Books, Inc., [2017] | Includes
    bibliographical references and index.
Identifiers: LCCN 2016047875 (print) | LCCN 2016054061 (ebook) | ISBN
    9781944648046 (trade paper : alk. paper) | ISBN 9781944648053
(electronic)
Subjects: LCSH: Cooking (Natural foods) | Nutrition. | Vegan cooking. | Food
    Allergy—Diet therapy—Recipes. | LCGFT: Cookbooks.
Classification: LCC TX741 .A27 2017 (print) | LCC TX741 (ebook) | DDC
    641.3/02—dc23
LC record available at https://lccn.loc.gov/2016047875

Editing by Karen Levy
Copyediting by Scott Calamar
Proofreading by Kim Broderick
Indexing by WordCo Indexing
    Services, Inc.

Full cover and text design by Sarah
    Avinger
Text composition by Aaron Edmiston
Front cover by Kit Sweeney
Printed by Versa Press

Distributed by Perseus Distribution
www.perseusdistribution.com

To place orders through Perseus Distribution:
Tel: (800) 343-4499
Fax: (800) 351-5073
E-mail: orderentry@perseusbooks.com

**Special discounts for bulk sales (minimum of 25 copies) are
available. Please contact Aida Herrera at aida@benbellabooks.com.**

To my son, Shahn,
who teaches me every day
how to live insatiably,
laugh recklessly, and love
ferociously.

Contents

Introduction

There are some people who are blessed with a preordained drive to pursue a specific goal, which they set out to achieve the minute they're conceived in the womb. Then as soon as they're born, they pursue their life's purpose with the same precision and tactical exactitude of an Army Rangers operation. I'm totally like that. But the opposite.

My career path has been anything but linear and methodical. In fact, when I sat down to think about it, I realized that I have had jobs beginning with practically every letter of the alphabet. I did not do particularly well at any of these vocations, and I have twenty-six capital and lowercase failures on my resume to prove it.

But something happened in 2009 that set me on a course that I have not deviated from since. My son was one year old, and I gave him a taste of frozen yogurt for the very first time. About twenty minutes later he was vomiting profusely, and soon lay unconscious on the floor, barely breathing. While I dialed 911, my husband hovered over my son, ready to administer CPR. Luckily, the paramedics came in time to revive my son and take us to the hospital.

It turns out my son had a severe allergic reaction to the milk protein in the yogurt, called casein. After further testing and several months and anaphylactic reactions later, we found out that my son has life-threatening allergies to most of the top eight food allergens, which include dairy, eggs, tree nuts, peanuts, wheat, shellfish, fish, and soy.

As I got more and more involved in the food allergy community, I learned that there are eighteen million people in the United States alone with the same allergies as my son. This knowledge propelled me on a mission to learn how to create allergy-free meals and desserts that would accommodate this particular population.

It was at this time that I decided to revamp my already-thriving, sugar-free bakery, Sweet Debbie's Organic Cupcakes in Los Angeles, into one that was completely free of the top eight food allergens, in addition to gluten, sesame (which is fast becoming a top nine food allergen), and, as always, refined sugar. I never wanted to use refined sugar in my baked goods due to its detrimental health effects, including the rise of insulin levels, causing weight gain and inflammation, and the fact that it depletes the body of essential nutrients.

Instead, I use coconut nectar and stevia, both of which are low-glycemic, all-natural sweeteners that do not spike your blood sugar and insulin levels as refined sugar does.

In 2010, my newly revamped bakery became a safe haven to anyone with food allergies, intolerances, celiac disease, diabetes, or any other dietary restrictions. They could indulge in my baked goods without worry. Business quadrupled in the first year of this transformation and continues to grow due to the continuous rise of these diseases as well as the amount of people who just want healthy and delicious treats.

My research about which ingredients to substitute for the allergenic ones led me to information that further changed the course of my life. I learned, loud and clear, that the foods America and the world have come to know and love, such as cow's milk, soy, animal protein, and eggs, are not all they're cracked up to be. In other words, all humans, whether allergic or not, would probably be better off not eating them.

And then, all the information I cultivated from various sources throughout my research was corroborated when I read *The China Study*, by Dr. T. Colin Campbell and his son, Thomas. This groundbreaking scientific study proved that eating animal protein can lead to the diseases we have grown to expect as we age, such as heart disease, diabetes, and cancer. The animal protein they used to conduct the study was casein, which, as I mentioned earlier, is what caused my son's anaphylaxis. The conclusions of the study suggest that if you want to experience optimal health, eat plants, not animals.

That book catapulted me into the land of plant-based cooking and eating. That same year, I attended the International Plant-Based Nutrition Healthcare Conference and met Dr. Campbell in person. After hearing him and other prominent doctors, such as Dr. Michael Greger, Dr. Dean Ornish, and Dr. Caldwell

Esselstyn, Jr., talk about the life-changing and lifesaving health benefits of a whole-foods, plant-based diet, I knew I couldn't look back.

My first book, *Sweet Debbie's Organic Treats: Allergy-Free & Vegan Recipes from the Famous Los Angeles Bakery*, is a compilation of the gluten-free, sugar-free, vegan baked goods recipes from my popular West Coast bakery. When I put out a feeler to my customers, social media followers, and people I met at the conferences where I spoke, and asked them what they would like to see in my second cookbook, they almost unanimously requested that I write a plant-based cookbook of savory recipes (with some sweets thrown in for good measure) that are free of oil, gluten, refined sugar, and the top eight food allergens. When I did some research to point them in the direction of a cookbook they could get their hands on before I finished my own, I came up short. A cookbook like this didn't exist at the time.

My quest became clear. I wanted to create the most exquisite and delicious, safe and nutritious, allergy-free/plant-based/gluten-free/sugar-free/oil-free meals this side of the Yangtze River.

And so it is within these pages that I bring you simple-to-prepare Asian, Indian, Greek, Italian, Mediterranean, Eastern European, Middle Eastern, and American cuisine that I created in my dreams and then in my kitchen. These include but are not limited to my down-home Spanakopita Enchiladas, naan-dipping-good Palak Paneer and Coriander Dal, golden-crusted Margherita Pizza Wheels, mellow Sweet Miso Forbidden Rice Ramen Noodle Bowl, luxurious Asian Fusion Noodle Kugel, and creamy Herb-Stuffed Grape Leaves Casserole with Mushroom Béchamel. As for the sweets, you're in for a treat with scrumptious Caramel Macchiato Sandwich Cookies, raw and rad Chocolate Pudding Pie with Seed Crust, nostalgic Candy Bar Cookies, mouthwatering Tiramisu Cupcakes, and rustic Rosemary & Fig Galette-lets.

And because processed substitution foods, such as mock meats, add an allergy risk as well as unnecessary chemicals, preservatives, and sodium, I figured out a way to use whole foods as expert impersonators. Roasted shiitake mushrooms, for instance, transform impeccably into fakiin bacon. Creamed cannellini beans are masters of disguise as mayonnaise, hemp tofu morphs miraculously into ricotta cheese, and a mixture of ground sunflower, pumpkin, and hemp seeds with a touch of nooch (nutritional yeast) perform for your taste buds as "Parmesan."

If you're not familiar with plant-based cooking, you may scan these recipes and start to wonder where the oil is. The biggest shock for me came when I found out that oil, any oil, even some you may deem as "healthy oils," are a no-no in a plant-based diet. This is because all oils, even olive oil and coconut oil, in addition to being highly processed, highly caloric, and void of any nutritional value, can cause damage in your endothelial cells and create cardiovascular disease. There is a lot of misinformation out there that says coconut oil is healthy. Maybe on your skin it is, but in your body, it raises "bad" cholesterol (LDL), which eventually forms plaque and blocks arteries. Scientific study after scientific study has proved this.

Wow. That blew me away and scared me all at the same time. I thought, "How am I going to do a Mediterranean meal without using extra-virgin olive oil? What will make my baked goods moist? What will become of my creamy salad dressings?" I had a LOT of questions. But once I started to tinker with plant-based, whole-food alternatives, the answers revealed themselves one by one.

I was amazed at the spectacular results of using coconut aminos or vegetable broth, instead of oil, for sautéing, adding fruit purees for moistness in muffins, and substituting pureed cannellini beans instead of mayonnaise in dressings. And I found that the extraordinary bonus of all this, in addition to being healthier with fewer fat calories, is that it's better to cook and bake without the oil because it eliminates the allergen and cross-contamination issues that many oils bring with them. It's a win-win all around.

The ultimate testing ground for this new way of preparing food was to try it out on unsuspecting dinner guests. I would have an Italian- or Asian-themed party, let's say, and make the recipes that ultimately landed in this book. It was almost like a double-blind, randomized, placebo-controlled trial. Nobody, except me, knew what the ingredients were. I watched and waited as everyone sat and ate their food. Were they pushing it around on their plates or into their mouths with gusto? Were they looking at their watches aching to pull a grab-and-go at the nearest In-N-Out Burger, or wiping their plates clean? The consensus was unanimous. Everybody was eating with relish. They asked for seconds and then for thirds and then requested the recipes. When I told everyone that they were eating a plant-based meal that contains no dairy, eggs, animal protein, soy, gluten, or refined sugar, they were stunned. Then they asked to be invited back to the next trial.

My point is that nobody missed what wasn't in the food. It was satiating, tasty, and appealing to people who eat unrestricted diets every single day. And for those who need customized meals due to allergies, sensitivities, or other dietary restraints, these recipes provide a way to make the things everyone loves to eat without ever feeling deprived.

So I urge you to create your shopping list, buy your ingredients, give those ingredients a pep talk, and start cooking. Soon you'll be gratified with delicious food that you'll think of as a true friend you can always count on to lift your spirits, give you sustenance, and nourish your soul. What better purpose can food have than that? And what better purpose can I have than to show you the way? Follow me.

CHAPTER 1

Just Haves

I know the scenario all too well. You're super excited about trying a new recipe from a cookbook you just purchased. You gather all the foodstuffs you just bought at the grocery store and online and now it's time to . . . wait. You realize you're missing one key ingredient that precludes you from making the recipe right here and now. The thought of schlepping back to the store gives you a spasm of despair. You ditch the idea of cooking and make popcorn.

I've been there, I've done that, and I'm here to help you prevent it from happening ever again (at least with this cookbook). I'm giving you the list of things you should JUST HAVE in your pantry, fridge, freezer, cupboard, and handbag (you never know).

In the Resources section (see page 258), I provide a list of trusted companies whose manufacturing practices limit the chances of cross-contamination when allergic reactions are a concern. You should always call the company yourself (you can usually find the contact information on the packaging) if you have any questions.

It may be tempting to buy some of these ingredients in bulk to save money, but I urge you not to do so because of the high risk of cross-contamination. If food allergies aren't a concern, then by all means, buy in bulk.

Herbs and Spices

Basil – Crushed, sun-dried basil, used mostly in the Italian recipes in this book, is a member of the mint family.

Chipotle Chili Powder – This is a pure blend of dried chipotle chilis, which are smoked, dried jalapeños. This spice is used mostly in Mexican dishes and sometimes to turn up the heat in chocolate. If you are allergic to any kind of sweet or hot pepper, you should not use this ingredient.

Cinnamon – This warm, aromatic spice comes from the curly bark of a variety of trees. It is used in both savory and sweet recipes.

Coriander – Before coriander is dried into seeds to make the spice, coriander leaves are also known as cilantro. Coriander as a spice has a lemony/lime essence and is very fragrant.

Cumin – A member of the parsley family, cumin has a nutty/peppery fragrance and taste, and is used in a variety of cuisines, including Mexican, Indian, and Tex-Mex.

Curry Powder – This powder mix usually contains a combination of coriander, turmeric, cumin, fenugreek, and chili peppers. Curry powder is used in rice, curries, soups, and sauces. Since there is flexibility, you can easily blend your own medley of curry powder spices depending on your preference and allergies. In the Resources section, I give you the names of companies whose curry spices I love and trust due to their meticulous manufacturing practices.

Dill – This herb is related to celery. The fernlike leaves of dill can be freeze-dried and used as an aromatic addition to soups, potatoes, and many other dishes. My favorite use of fresh dill is snipping the fronds into Matzo Ball Soup (page 58) and my Spanakopita Enchiladas (page 140).

Garlic Powder – This is dehydrated garlic that is ground into a powder. It is most commonly used in Italian dishes.

Nutmeg – Poor Meg. She's really a seed, but because of the unfortunate name her parents gave her, people think she's a nut. She is a warm, pungent spice that you can add to sweet dishes that contain pumpkin, and savory ones that include creamy greens.

Onion Powder – This is onion that is made into a powder using dehydration or freeze-drying methods. It is generally used in sauces, soups, and pasta dishes or anywhere you want onion flavor without hunks of onion.

Oregano – Part of the mint family and a second cousin to marjoram, this aromatic, pungent herb is generally used in Italian dishes.

Red Pepper Flakes – This is also called crushed red pepper and is made from dried red chili peppers, usually cayenne. If you are allergic to any kind of chili peppers you should not use red pepper flakes.

Smoked Paprika – If paprika is made from crushed dried chilis, then smoked paprika is made from smoked, dried chilis. The effect is dramatic and the flavor of the smoked variety is more full-bodied. If you have an allergy to any kind of bell, jalapeño, or other pepper, not including black pepper, you should not use paprika of any sort.

Thyme – A close relative of oregano, thyme has a rustic profile and is a wonderful addition to vegetable and pasta dishes.

Turmeric – Related to the ginger family, turmeric has a warm, peppery flavor and fragrance. It is most famous for its use in curries. Turmeric has the potential to create hives on contact, but that is rare.

Condiments

Chickpea Miso Paste – Since soy is considered one of the top eight allergens, I choose to use chickpea miso instead of conventional miso, which contains soybeans. This is the perfect substitute as it is just as flavorful and can be used exactly the same way as the original. I am so grateful some clever companies thought to do this. I use Miso Master. See Resources for more information.

Coconut Aminos – These aminos are your amigos. They are the perfect swap for soy sauce as they are free of soy and gluten. The coconut sap from which these are derived is high in amino acids, which are key components to building protein. If you are worried that they come from coconut, please note that coconuts

are not tree nuts. They are drupes, or, in other words, fruits with a big, fat pit in the middle. Almost every savory recipe in this cookbook uses coconut aminos, so stock up. Although a tad expensive, this amazing product reaps nutritional and health benefits that are priceless. I use Coconut Secret brand. See Resources for more information.

Green Curry Paste – An indispensible addition to my Green Curry Portobellos (page 152), this paste contains lemongrass, Thai ginger, green chilis, and zesty, fragrant spices. Luckily for us, there is a company or two out there who offer dairy-free, vegan, gluten-free curry paste, and I tell you all about them in the Resources section.

Hot Sauce – Usually made from jalapeño peppers, vinegar, garlic, and salt, and variations thereof, hot sauce adds flavorful, strategically placed heat wherever you aim it. If you prefer to make your own rather than buy it, I provide a kick-keister, simple blueprint in my "Recipes within Recipes" chapter.

Liquid Smoke – This innocuous concoction of water and hickory smoke makes food taste like it was cured. Just a drop goes a long way, and the effects are dramatic. I highly recommend you keep a bottle in your fridge so you have it when it's called for.

Nutritional Yeast – I beg of you to stock up on this stuff. And if you don't have room in your pantry, give it its own parking space in your garage if you have to. I use it liberally in my recipes when I need cheese-like flavor. Nutritional yeast is deactivated yeast that's been grown on molasses. And true to its name, it is naturally nutritious and fortified with vitamin B$_{12}$. And if you're nice to it and provide it a good home, nutritional yeast allows you to call it "nooch."

Prepared Horseradish – This refers to the addition of vinegar to the root vegetable: horseradish. It is a potent spice that I love to use on Kasha Knishes (page 192), Krab Kakes (page 164), and even my Falafel Bowl (page 138). If you care to make your own, I have a recipe for you in the "Recipes within Recipes" chapter.

Spicy Mustard – This is my mustard of choice, which means it is made with the more potent brown mustard seeds rather than yellow or white. Mustard seed has the potential to cause allergic reactions, though this is not a common occurrence.

Sriracha Sauce – This is a type of hot or chili sauce that is slightly sweet. My only regret about Sriracha is that I didn't discover it sooner. So now I'm making up for lost time and I use it wherever I can. If you don't want to use store-bought, I provide a simple, out-of-this-world recipe in the "Recipes within Recipes" chapter.

Wasabi Powder – With this miraculous mix of horseradish, spirulina, and turmeric, all you have to do to get wasabi is add water. It makes an appearance in the Ultimate Boodle (Buddha Noodle) Bowl (page 156), so if you're interested, just keep this powder on deck. I use Hime brand. See Resources for more information.

Worcestershire Sauce – The conventional way to make this sauce is with barley malt vinegar, molasses, sugar, anchovies, and salt. Thankfully, there are vegan, gluten-free versions available that I tell you about in the Resources section. I use the Wizard's brand.

Seeds

Chia Seeds – These are related to the mint family and provide maximum nutrition in minimal square footage. These tiny black or sometimes white seeds come in very handy for nutritional purposes but also function as a binder in gluten-free baking and cooking.

If you are allergic to mustard or sesame seeds, you may also be allergic to chia seeds.

Hemp Seeds – If you don't believe in miracles, these teeny-weeny little seeds will change your mind. They contain the most powerful nutrition out of any seed in the world. I use them generously throughout the book, so you should always have them on hand.

Pumpkin Seeds – Also known as pepitas, pumpkin seeds are nutrient dense, hypoallergenic, and supremely tasty. I put shelled pumpkin seeds to good use in my Parmezan mix (page 24) and other strategic places in my recipes.

Sunflower Seeds – Since nuts are usually forbidden in an allergy-free kitchen, we turn to shelled sunflower seeds to save the day. I think I should mention that sunflower seeds are not really seeds. They are technically a fruit. When roasted and pureed, sunflower seeds imitate peanut butter to a T. They serve as a base for my Parmezan mix (page 24) as well as my Cheezy Marinara Sauce (page 112). They make an appearance in many other recipes in this book, so keep them in stock and you will be all set. In my "Recipes within Recipes" chapter, you will see how easy it is to make your own sunflower seed butter without any added oils.

Grains, Flours, and Powders

Amaranth Flour – An earthy, nutty seed, amaranth is a perfect protein unto itself and an indispensable addition to gluten-free baking. Stock this flour in your cupboard to make some of the bread and baked goods recipes in this cookbook.

Brown Rice Paper Wraps – I use these wrappers for Pad Thai Spring Rolls (page 114) and Egg Rolls (page 128). I prefer the Star Anise Foods brand. See Resources for more information.

Buckwheat – Buckwheat is related to rhubarb and is neither a grain nor made of wheat. It is a gluten-free seed that is really a fruit. For the purposes of this book, you will need to get buckwheat groats, which is the raw, unhulled, unroasted version of buckwheat, unless a recipe calls for kasha, in which case you'll get the roasted buckwheat groats. Where necessary you can easily grind the raw, unroasted groats into flour using a coffee grinder when a recipe calls for it.

Cacao Powder – I always have non-alkali, organic cacao powder in my pantry for chocolate baking cravings. Ever get those?

Chickpea Flour – This flour, made from ground, dried chickpeas, takes on an egg-like flavor when added to vegan omelets and French toast.

Guar Gum – This powder made from ground guar beans is used in gluten-free baking as a binder.

Kasha – This is the same as buckwheat groats, but toasted. It comes in three sizes: fine, medium, and whole. So depending on how big you like your groat, I give you creative freedom in choosing which to use in these recipes.

Millet Flour – This is a very mild and very easily digestible gluten-free grain. It is considered hypoallergenic and contains serotonin, so you can meditate while you bake.

Psyllium Husk Powder – I have a confession to make. I avoided using psyllium in my bread recipes for the longest time because I was afraid of it. Afraid of what, I don't know, but something came over me when writing "The Bread Basket" chapter in this book that nudged me in the direction of this safe and beneficial fiber from the *Plantago ovata* plant. Once I started incorporating it into the recipes, I couldn't believe how much better the breads tasted. And not only that, but the texture became that of regular bread.

So I can't emphasize enough how important this ingredient is when making gluten-free breads. Be brave and just have it in stock. I use Frontier brand. See Resources for more information.

Quinoa Flour and Flakes – A complete protein and really a seed, not a grain, quinoa contains the full amino acid spectrum and is used frequently in this book in its many incarnations. I use the flour version in my gluten-free flour mix, and I use the flakes to make matzo balls and spinach dumplings. Quinoa itself is used throughout. I prefer Ancient Grains Hot Cereal Quinoa Flakes. See Resources for more information.

Ramen Noodles – I use the gluten-free ramen noodles made by Lotus Foods. See Resources for more information.

Rice Bran – If you don't use wheat bran due to the gluten, rice bran provides that bran-like flavor and fiber you need and crave when baking certain muffins and scones. It comes in handy in my Raisin Bran Scones (page 37).

Rolled Oats – Oats are naturally gluten-free, but because they are usually grown in fields with wheat, a lot of cross-contamination occurs if the wind blows a little too hard. So to be safe, buy oats that say "gluten-free" on the packaging if you have a gluten sensitivity or celiac disease.

Sorghum Flour – This gluten-free flour imitates wheat flour on point and is used extensively in this book as well as in my gluten-free flour mix in the "Recipes within Recipes" chapter.

Sweet White Rice Flour – This starchy flour, made from sticky rice, is a great component of dumpling doughs and certain breads. It has a binding power that most gluten-free flours do not have.

Tapioca Flour – This is the starch you will use in several bread recipes as well as in my gluten-free flour mix. I also use it as a thickener in some of the sauces.

Teff Flour – This gluten-free grain comes in many colors, and I highly suggest you use the ivory hue due to its mild flavor and smooth texture. You can easily get this online and I let you know where in the Resources section.

Sweeteners

Coconut Nectar – This is my go-to sweetener for just about everything sweet in this book. Coconut nectar is derived from the sap of the coconut tree and is low glycemic and mineral dense. I use Coconut Secret brand. See Resources for more information.

Coconut Sugar – This is a low-glycemic sweetener derived from the coconut palm. I use it in some of my desserts and "Morning Munchies" recipes.

Erythritol – A natural, low-glycemic sugar substitute that is derived from fruits and vegetables, erythritol contains almost zero calories. I only use the powdered erythritol for my frostings. My favorite brand is Swerve. See Resources for more information.

Maple Syrup – This sweetener is used sparsely in this book, but when it is called for, I highly suggest you use Grade B if you can find it. It is higher in minerals than Grade A and has a more distinct, delicious maple flavor.

Medjool Dates – This chewy, decadent dried fruit from the date palm tree is reminiscent of a caramel and profoundly nutritious. I chop them into baked goods and also grind them into a date paste for bulk and sweetness.

Stevia Powder – In certain recipes I heighten the sweetness just a tad with stevia powder, which is a natural sweetener from the stevia plant and has zero calories. Some people say they don't like its aftertaste, but I use it in such small quantities that this is not an issue.

Canned and Packaged Goods

Cannellini Beans – These medium-size Italian beans, also known as white kidney beans, have a silky smooth texture that works like a charm for purees. I even make mayonnaise with them. If you have an allergy to legumes, such as peanuts or peas, you may be allergic to cannellini beans.

Chickpeas – Also known as garbanzo beans, chickpeas are used as the base for my Roasted

Root Vegetable Hummus (page 171) and Falafel Bowl (page 138) recipes. Chickpeas are legumes, so if you have an allergy to peanuts, peas, or other beans, you might also react to chickpeas.

Chocolate Chips – It's good to have these around in cases when you just have to bake a batch of cookies. I use Lily's brand dairy-free, sugar-free chocolate chips. See Resources for more information.

Fire-Roasted Tomatoes – I use these for my enchilada sauce, so a 15-ounce can is always in my cupboard.

Pumpkin Puree – I rely heavily on pumpkin puree to provide moistness and bulk to many of my recipes. If you are allergic to zucchini, cucumber, or melon, you may also be allergic to pumpkin.

Seaweed Salad Mix – I use this to make my Sea Vegetable and Cabbage Slaw (page 195). I recommend the brand SeaVegi Seaweed Salad Mix. See Resources for more information.

Water Chestnuts – This is really not a nut or even close to it. Water chestnuts are aquatic vegetables used in Asian cuisine.

Whole Peeled Tomatoes – After making my own marinara sauce for the first time several years ago I was never able to go back to buying it in jars. Homemade is just too good and easy. So I always have a 28-ounce can of whole peeled tomatoes for whenever a craving for Margherita Pizza Wheels (page 112) comes over me.

Dairy and Soy Alternatives

Coconut Milk – I use the unsweetened variety that is found in cans and shelf-stable cardboard boxes. Once opened, it needs refrigeration. I prefer So Delicious Dairy Free Unsweetened Coconut Milk. See Resources for more information.

Coconut Milk Yogurt – A coconut milk–based yogurt has all the benefits of regular yogurt without the allergens. I use So Delicious Unsweetened Plain Coconut Milk Yogurt.

Full-Fat Coconut Milk – This is a full-fat version of coconut milk, found in cans and shelf-stable cardboard containers. When refrigerated, the cream that rises to the top of the can or box can be used as whipped cream. I give you more information on this in the Resources section. I prefer So Delicious Culinary Coconut Milk.

Hemp Tofu – This hemp substitute for soy tofu can be used in the same exact way as firm tofu. I use Tempt brand. See Resources for more information.

CHAPTER 2

Fully Equipped

It doesn't take a warehouse of appliances to make astoundingly delicious gourmet meals. It's sort of like the way I view clothing. I buy a few key pieces every year and then wear them for the rest of my life. It's the same thing with kitchen appliances. I get a few things that I really, really want, and then I wait a year to get the next must-have appliance. It's taken me years to acquire every little thing mentioned here, but no worries if you need to improvise. I would say the only things that need to be exactly as I mention are the sizes of the baking pans and a functional food processor and blender. Otherwise, feel free to use what you have right now, buy what you can afford, and make a wish list for the rest. I broke down what you'll need for the savory meals and what you'll need for the desserts, just so it's easier to keep track.

Tool Kit for Savory

5-Quart Pot – Unless you're feeding an army, this is a big enough pot to cook the soups, grains, and sauces in this book. I highly recommend stainless steel with an inner core of aluminum or copper for better heat distribution. I like stainless steel because it is nonreactive. Pots and pans that are reactive to alkaline or acidic ingredients make your food taste metallic.

6-Inch and 8-Inch Ramekins – You'll need six of each for the "Meals in Muffin Tins and Ramekins" chapter. Luckily, they are very inexpensive.

13 × 9-Inch Oven-Safe Casserole Dish – You will need this for some of the casseroles in the book, such as the Spaghetti Squash Chow Mein (page 147).

Chef's Knife – I'm not a chef, but I do wield a chef's knife. You'll use this for chopping vegetables, mushrooms, onions, and fruit.

Cutting Board – I have several of these, but you only need one. Since we're only cutting veggies (not meat and dairy), there's no need to segregate your beautiful blocks of maple wood.

Food Processor – You'll need a reliable, full-size food processor with an "S" blade to get through this book.

Garlic Press – You'll need this for mincing.

High-Speed Blender – I swear by my Vitamix because it does everything I tell it to do. How many things can you say that about? But if you have a blender that works well, it will be all you need for the purposes of this book.

Mandoline Slicer – I don't know what I did before I bought a mandoline to evenly slice my vegetables with ease and perfection. My chopping life was much more stressful, that's for sure. I highly recommend you put this one on your wish list.

Microplane Zester – I recently got one of these and I'm here to tell you that it outshines my box grater. Microplane zesters are grate! I mean great!

One Really Big Spoon – I'm not a fancy person, so I just use a big metal spoon to mix things together in a pan or stir in a pot.

Paring Knife – This is much smaller than a chef's knife, and I use a paring knife mostly for peeling when a peeler just won't do. Have a peeler on hand, as well.

Pizza Slicer – This lets you slice dough into perfect triangles, squares, and rectangles.

Pizza Stone – This helps create a crisp crust for pizza like nobody's business. The stone is usually made from ceramic and helps distribute heat evenly. It took me a while to get one of these and it totally changed my pizza's destiny.

Sauté Pan – There is a difference between a sauté pan and a skillet, and I didn't know what it was until recently. A skillet has slightly flared-out sides and a sauté pan has sides that go straight up. I highly suggest you buy a sauté pan or two, because it usually comes with a cover, and sometimes you need to cover the pan while simmering. This pan should be stainless steel for the reasons mentioned above, and if you have them in various sizes, that's great. If not, one 12-inch sauté pan will serve you well throughout this book.

Skillet – I use a skillet every so often if I need to sauté some veggies and onions without using a cover. If you have a skillet, fabulous. If not, a sauté pan will get you through this book just fine.

Slotted Spoon – When you're fishing out dough balls from water, this is a good thing to have on hand.

Variety of Bowls – I mostly use glass because unlike plastic it doesn't leak toxins. I use these for mixing ingredients by hand.

Tool Kit for Sweet

2-Inch Ice Cream Scoop – This is for carving out perfectly round macaroons and perfectly proportioned cupcake and muffin batter.

8-Inch Square Aluminum Baking Pan – Aluminum is best, as it conducts heat evenly.

9-Inch Square Aluminum Baking Pan – I use this for baking crackers and focaccia.

9-Inch Round Springform Baking Pan – You'll need this for breads, cinnamon buns, and pancakes, believe it or not. I love the way the outside rim pops away from the circular bottom so it's easy to remove whatever's inside.

9 × 5 × 2-Inch Loaf Pan – You'll want this on hand to make Cinnamon Raisin Bread (page 222) and Banana Java Date Bread (page 208), among other sweet loaves.

15 × 10 × 1-Inch Aluminum Jelly-Roll Pan or Rimmed Baking Sheet – This pan has a little border around it.

15 × 13-Inch Aluminum Cookie or Baking Sheet – This doesn't have a border on the long sides, so you can easily transfer cookies from it.

Biscuit Cutter – This is a 3-inch circular cutter that makes your life a whole lot neater when cutting out mini tortillas and dough circles.

Coffee Grinder – I use this to grind seeds and grains when necessary.

Measuring Cups – I prefer stainless steel measuring cups in 1-, ½-, ⅓-, and ¼-cup increments.

Measuring Spoons – I prefer stainless steel measuring spoons and I always like to have a ⅛ teaspoon, which a lot of sets don't include. Make sure yours has it because you'll need it in several recipes.

Parchment Paper – This lines your baking sheets so that nothing sticks, making cleanup easier after baking.

Rolling Pin – You'll need this to roll out the dough for fun stuff like pizza wheels, cinnamon buns, and a whole lot more. Your kids will love to do this task for you. I promise.

Slotted Spatula – I prefer stainless steel and use it for lifting things like cookies and brownies out of their cozy baking sheet homes.

Standard 6-Well Doughnut Pan – I know you're going to want to make doughnuts, so keep this in your cupboard.

Standard 12-Cup Muffin Tin – You'll use this for muffins and cupcakes.

Standard Paper Baking Cups – These line the standard muffin tins.

CHAPTER 3

Recipes within Recipes
(Homemade Staples)

I use a bunch of staples throughout this book. I want to give you the opportunity to make these from scratch rather than depend on store-bought, although I think it's fine if you buy these ready made. I just want you to see how easy it is to make your favorite sauces and seed butters so that you can save money, be safe, and create the most sublime versions of your favorite condiments and spreads.

All-Purpose Gluten-Free Flour Mix

MAKES 3 CUPS

This is the all-purpose, gluten-free flour mix we use at my bakery and what I use at home. I always recommend doubling or tripling the recipe, storing it in an airtight container, and placing it in the freezer. Storing it this way prevents spoilage. You never know when the baking mood will strike, and the last thing you want to do is start hauling out separate bags of flour and mixing it in the right proportions. It just might ruin that mood.

Must Have

1 cup tapioca flour
¾ cup sorghum flour
¾ cup millet flour
¼ cup ivory teff flour
¼ cup quinoa flour

Must Do

1. Whisk together the tapioca flour, sorghum flour, millet flour, ivory teff flour, and quinoa flour in a large bowl.

2. Pour the flour mix into a large zip-top bag or freezer-safe airtight container. The mix will stay fresh for up to 1 year in the freezer.

SERVING SIZE: 2 TABLESPOONS
Calories 50; Total Fat 0.3g; Protein 1.0g; Cholesterol 0.0g; Sodium 0.4mg; Fiber 0.8g; Sugars 0.0g; Total Carbohydrate 9.0g

Sunflower Seed Butter

MAKES ABOUT 1¼ CUPS

This is the easiest recipe you'll ever make and it'll save you a ton of money if you've been buying your seed butters at the grocery store.

Must Have

2 cups raw, unsalted sunflower seeds

Must Do

1. Add the sunflower seeds to a large skillet over low heat, stirring occasionally, until the sunflower seeds turn a light golden brown, about 8 minutes.

2. After they cool, place the sunflower seeds in a food processor. Blend the seeds until they start to come together. Scrape down the flyaway seeds and keep processing until a smooth paste starts to form. This may take up to 25 minutes. The heat from the food processor brings out the natural oils from the sunflower seeds, so there is no need to add any oil. I suggest giving your food processor a break about halfway through so it doesn't burn out.

3. Transfer the sunflower seed butter to a glass jar and store in the refrigerator. It will keep for about 2 months.

SERVING SIZE: 2 TABLESPOONS
Calories 60; Total Fat 4.2g; Protein 2.6g; Cholesterol 0.0g; Sodium 0.4mg; Fiber 1.9g; Sugars 0.3g; Total Carbohydrate 3.1g

Hot Sauce

MAKES ABOUT 2 CUPS

There's something very empowering about being able to control the heat and ingredients in your hot sauce. I believe hot sauce is a very personal condiment, and it should be customized as such. I love the way the kitchen smells when the peppers are simmering. After you've tried this hot sauce once, you'll never go back to bottled. I guarantee it. Please use disposable plastic gloves when handling the hot peppers.

Must Have

12 red jalapeño or Fresno chili peppers, seeded and chopped (leave seeds in if you want extra heat)
1 shallot, sliced
2 tablespoons coconut aminos
2 cloves garlic, minced
1 cup water
½ cup apple cider vinegar
1 tablespoon coconut nectar

Must Do

1. Add the peppers and shallot to a medium sauté pan over medium heat and cook until fragrant, about 1 minute.

2. Add the coconut aminos and garlic, and cook, stirring occasionally, until the shallots are translucent and the garlic is fragrant, about 1 minute.

3. Add the water, apple cider vinegar, and coconut nectar, and bring to a boil.

4. Lower the heat, cover the pan, and simmer until the peppers become tender and some of the liquid is absorbed, about 10 minutes.

5. Turn off the heat and let cool.

6. Pour the mixture into a high-speed blender and process until smooth.

7. Pour into a jar, seal it, and store in the fridge. It will keep for about 4 weeks.

SERVING SIZE: 2 TABLESPOONS
Calories 8; Total Fat 0.1g; Protein 0.2g; Cholesterol 0.0g; Sodium 33mg; Fiber 0.3g; Sugars 1.1g; Total Carbohydrate 1.5g

Sriracha

MAKES ABOUT 2 CUPS

Sriracha coming to our shores from Thailand in the 1950s was nothing short of a culinary phenomenon akin to the cultural hysteria of the Beatles performing at the Hollywood Bowl in 1964. People went crazy when this radical, spicy sauce was introduced, and for good reason. It adds a *je ne sais quoi* that elevates food lucky enough to receive its anointing to a whole new level. Please use disposable plastic gloves when handling the hot peppers.

Must Have

- 6 habanero, Fresno, or red jalapeño peppers, seeded and chopped (leave seeds in if you want more heat)
- 3 small red bell peppers, seeded and chopped
- 2 small heirloom tomatoes, chopped
- 4 cloves garlic, minced
- 2 tablespoons coconut aminos
- ¼ cup apple cider vinegar
- 3 tablespoons coconut nectar
- 1 teaspoon red pepper flakes
- ¼ teaspoon cayenne pepper

Must Do

1. Add the jalapeño peppers, bell peppers, tomatoes, garlic, and coconut aminos to a medium sauté pan over medium heat and cook, stirring occasionally, until the peppers and garlic become fragrant, about 1 minute.

2. Add the apple cider vinegar, coconut nectar, red pepper flakes, and cayenne, and stir to incorporate. Simmer until the peppers break down and soften, about 5 minutes.

3. Turn off the heat and let cool.

4. Pour the mixture into a high-speed blender and process until smooth. You can also use an immersion blender.

5. Pour into a jar, seal it, and store in the fridge. It will keep for about 3 weeks.

SERVING SIZE: 2 TABLESPOONS
Calories 12.3; Total Fat 0.2g; Protein 0.4g; Cholesterol 0.0g; Sodium 33mg; Fiber 0.3g; Sugars 2.1g; Total Carbohydrate 2.8g

SRIRACHA HEMP NOODLES
(SEE RECIPE ON PAGE 123)

Horseradish

MAKES ABOUT 1 CUP

Horseradish is a very polarizing tuber root. You either love it or hate it. I love it and dab it on almost everything. If you're a fan, I especially recommend using it on my Kasha Knishes (page 192). Please open windows or use fans when grinding up the horseradish because it becomes more potent as enzymes break down during processing.

Must Have

6-inch-long horseradish root, peeled and chopped
¼ cup apple cider vinegar
¼ cup freshly squeezed lemon juice

Must Do

1. Add the horseradish and vinegar to a food processor. Process until the horseradish is broken down and smooth. Add the lemon juice, and pulse to combine.

2. Transfer the horseradish to a jar, seal it, and store in the fridge. It will keep for about 4 weeks.

SERVING SIZE: 2 TABLESPOONS
Calories 7.3; Total Fat 0.1g; Protein 0.2g; Cholesterol 0.0g; Sodium 30mg; Fiber 0.4g; Sugars 1.1g; Total Carbohydrate 1.6g

Inside Scoop: Turn your face away when taking off the cover of the food processor to transfer the horseradish, so your eyes don't start to sting.

Parmezan

MAKES ABOUT 2 CUPS

If there is one thing I might possibly miss about not eating dairy any more, it is Parmesan cheese. I used to love dousing pasta and vegetables and everything else I could think of with it. So it was at the top of my can't-live-without-it list when developing my plant-based, allergy-free swaps. And now this topping tastes even better than the classic I thought I'd die without. Go figure.

Must Have

1 cup sunflower seeds, ground (I use a coffee grinder)
½ cup pumpkin seeds, ground (I use a coffee grinder)
¼ cup nutritional yeast
3 tablespoons hemp seeds
1 teaspoon dried oregano
1 teaspoon garlic powder
½ teaspoon red pepper flakes

Must Do

1. Mix together the sunflower seeds, pumpkin seeds, nutritional yeast, hemp seeds, oregano, garlic powder, and red pepper flakes in a small bowl.

2. Use as instructed in the recipes and store lots of extra in a jar in the fridge. It will keep for 3 months.

SERVING SIZE: 2 TABLESPOONS
Calories 70; Total Fat 5.3g; Protein 3.3g; Cholesterol 0.0g; Sodium 1.2mg; Fiber 1.5g; Sugars 0.3g; Total Carbohydrate 4.4g

No-Sodium Vegetable Broth

I depend on vegetable broth for all my soup recipes as well as some others in this book and insist on using my own. You can also use it, instead of oil, for sautés. The boxed versions, even though they might be low sodium or oil free, aren't anywhere in the stratosphere as good as this. I encourage you to try this simple recipe and then freeze it into ice cubes so that you can defrost it on demand. Whenever I make this broth, I love the way my house smells as it sits on my stove simmering. There is nothing quite like it. And if I want a warm drink other than tea or coffee, this broth is so soothing, aromatic, and flavorful, it's like therapy in a cup.

Must Have

2 yellow onions, sliced
3 cloves garlic, minced
6 carrots, peeled and sliced
4 celery stalks, sliced
5 sprigs dill
4 sprigs parsley
4 chives
10 cups water

Must Do

1. Add the onions to a large pot over medium heat and stir until fragrant, about 1 minute. Add the garlic, carrots, celery, dill, parsley, and chives and cook, stirring occasionally, until the herbs become fragrant, about 1 minute.

2. Add the water and bring to a boil. Lower the heat, cover the pot, and let simmer for about 45 minutes.

3. Turn off the heat and let the broth cool down for about 15 minutes.

4. Strain the broth through a sieve and freeze the broth in ice cube trays, or if using right away, pour into glass jars. It will keep for about 1 week.

SERVING SIZE: 1 CUP
Calories 20; Total Fat 0.1g; Protein 0.6g; Cholesterol 0.0g;
Sodium 0.0mg; Fiber 1.3g; Sugars 0.7g; Total Carbohydrate 4.4g

FAKIIN BACON CRESENT ROLLS
(SEE RECIPE ON PAGE 48)

CHAPTER 4

Morning Munchies

I believe breakfast is definitely the most fun and action-packed meal of the day. After sleeping for eight hours without eating a morsel, I wake up eager and ready to prepare or reheat something hearty, to be properly escorted by my morning coffee through my digestive system. I sometimes crave something sweet to enable my coffee addiction, hence the need for Pumpkin Swirl Cinnamon Buns (page 42), Raisin Bran Scones (page 37), and Sunflower Butter & Jelly Doughnuts (page 50). There are times, though, that a pastry just won't cut it, so I whip up a Chipotle Mexican Omelet Tostada (page 44) or Quinoa & Kale Breakfast Burritos (page 52), and I'm good to go. Whether savory or sweet, these recipes are perfect during the week or on the weekends, as they are easy to make, freeze, and warm up on demand.

Blueberry Buckwheat Waffles

MAKES 10 WAFFLES

Several years ago, I had what some might call a midlife crisis. I questioned my purpose, my value in the world, the chaos around me, and who I was. But instead of seeking therapy, I bought a waffle iron. This seemingly frivolous purchase actually saved my life. It ignited a passion for making food from scratch that I never thought possible. I was used to eating frozen waffles and never knew any different. Discovering how easy it was to create my own honeycomb-shaped, crispy breakfast treats was just the catharsis I needed. Maybe I'm not so complicated after all.

This recipe is one of my favorite waffle creations. The blueberry is betrothed to the waffle in gooey wedded bliss, and the sunflower seed butter adds a good dose of plant-based protein as well as a satisfying nuttiness. These also make great freezer fare, so you can prepare them ahead of time and then pop them in the toaster oven on demand.

Must Have

WAFFLES

1 cup unsweetened coconut milk

1 teaspoon apple cider vinegar

¾ cup All-Purpose Gluten-Free Flour Mix (page 20)

¼ cup buckwheat groats, ground (I use a coffee grinder)

¼ cup amaranth flour

1 teaspoon sodium-free baking powder

¼ cup pumpkin puree

2 tablespoons Sunflower Seed Butter (page 20)

2 tablespoons coconut nectar

⅔ cup organic blueberries (fresh or frozen)

TOPPINGS

Grade B maple syrup

Sunflower Seed Butter (page 20)

Fresh blueberries

Banana slices

Coconut cream

Must Do

1. Preheat a nonstick waffle iron to the desired level of heat.

2. To make the waffles: Mix together the coconut milk and apple cider vinegar in a small bowl and let it sit for a few minutes to become "buttermilk."

3. Whisk together the all-purpose flour, ground buckwheat groats, amaranth flour, and baking powder in a large bowl. Make a well in the middle.

4. Add the pumpkin puree, sunflower butter, coconut nectar, and "buttermilk" mixture and stir to combine. Fold in the blueberries and stir to incorporate.

5. Once the waffle iron is ready, pour about ⅓ cup of batter onto each waffle grid, close the lid, and cook the waffles until they are golden brown, about 4 minutes. Repeat with the remaining batter.

6. Add the toppings of your choice.

7. Store leftover waffles in a freezer-safe bag and reheat in the toaster for best results. These will keep in the freezer for up to 3 months.

SERVING SIZE: 1 WAFFLE

Calories 95; Total Fat 2.8g; Protein 2.9g; Cholesterol 0.0g; Sodium 14.0mg; Fiber 2.5g; Sugars 2.3g; Total Carbohydrate 16.3g

Inside Scoop: You do not need to grease the waffle iron. Just wait until the waffles are cooked enough to easily lift without sticking.

Inside Scoop: To make more than one strawberry shortcake stack, double the recipe and use two 9-inch round springform baking pans. To bake, place one pan on the bottom rack and one pan on the top rack, and halfway through baking, switch the pans so the one that's on top is on the bottom and vice versa.

Strawberry Shortcake Pancakes

SERVES 4

The truth is, I have something sweet for breakfast almost every other day. It goes well with coffee, and that's all the reason I need. So I decided to transform one of my all-time favorite desserts, strawberry shortcake, into wholesome pancakes, a more acceptable thing to eat in the morning. The buckwheat groats and chia seeds add calcium, protein, vitamins, fiber, and antioxidants, and the strawberries add a shot of vitamin C. I make this in a round cake tin to guarantee a perfect circular hotcake every time. No flipping, no oil—what could be better? And it's such a sight to behold when you start stacking and spreading the coconut cream that people actually gasp on the presentation alone.

Must Have

PANCAKE

1½ cups All-Purpose Gluten-Free Flour Mix (page 20)

½ cup raw buckwheat groats, ground (I use a coffee grinder)

2 teaspoons sodium-free baking powder

1 teaspoon chia seeds, ground (I use a coffee grinder)

1 teaspoon ground ginger

½ teaspoon ground cinnamon

¼ teaspoon fine sea salt

1¼ cups coconut milk

3 tablespoons applesauce

2 tablespoons coconut nectar

¼ cup fresh organic strawberries, cut into ¼-inch pieces

TOPPINGS

Coconut cream

Sliced strawberries

Grade B maple syrup

Must Do

1. Preheat the oven to 350°F. Line a 9-inch round springform baking pan with parchment paper. Make sure the parchment goes up about an inch along the sides of the pan so the batter doesn't stick.

2. **To make the pancake:** Whisk together the all-purpose flour, ground buckwheat groats, baking powder, chia seeds, ginger, cinnamon, and salt in a large bowl. Make a well in the middle.

3. Add the coconut milk, applesauce, and coconut nectar, and stir to combine.

4. Fold in the strawberries and stir to incorporate.

5. Pour the batter evenly into the prepared baking pan. Bake until the pancake bounces back slightly to the touch, about 20 minutes.

6. Transfer the pan from the oven to a wire rack and let sit for 5 minutes before removing the springform circle and transferring the pancake to a plate.

7. Cut into quarters with a pizza slicer and layer the quartered pancakes on top of one another with cream and strawberries between each layer. Top with more strawberries, coconut cream, and maple syrup.

SERVING SIZE: ¼ PANCAKE

Calories 190; Total Fat 2.5g; Protein 6.2g; Cholesterol 0.0g; Sodium 143mg; Fiber 6.1g; Sugars 4.4g; Total Carbohydrate 41.0g

Raspberry Hemp Pancakes

SERVES 4

I'm a hard-core advocate for pancakes with borders. Free-form, irregular fried flapjacks are just not my thing. I like boundaries. That's why I bake pancakes in the secure circumference of a cake pan. You don't have to worry about curious batter leaking into the territory of its neighbors, and you don't have to panic about flipping a premature pancake. You just have to mix, pour, and wait. It's foolproof. Just the way I like it. The hemp seeds add a nutty, tender crunch as well as numerous life-enhancing nutritional benefits. The date paste is a fun way to add awesome sweetness, and the high-fiber, antioxidant-rich ground chia seeds hold everything together. This pancake's got it all.

Must Have

DATE PASTE
½ cup water
4 Medjool dates, pitted

PANCAKES
1 cup All-Purpose Gluten-Free
   Flour Mix (page 20)
½ cup buckwheat groats, ground
   (I use a coffee grinder)
¼ cup hemp seeds
2 teaspoons coconut sugar
2 teaspoons sodium-free baking
   powder
1 teaspoon chia seeds, ground (I
   use a coffee grinder)
¼ teaspoon sea salt
1 cup coconut milk
¼ cup pumpkin puree
½ cup fresh organic raspberries

TOPPINGS
Grade B maple syrup
Hemp seeds
Fresh raspberries
Coconut cream

Must Do

1. Preheat the oven to 350°F. Line a 9-inch round springform baking pan with parchment paper. Make sure the parchment goes up about an inch along the sides of the pan so the batter doesn't stick.

2. **To make the date paste:** Place the water and dates in a small bowl. Let them soak for about 20 minutes. Pour the dates and soaking water into a high-speed blender or food processor and blend until the mixture is smooth.

3. **To make the pancakes:** Whisk together the all-purpose flour, ground buckwheat groats, hemp seeds, coconut sugar, baking powder, ground chia seeds, and salt in a large bowl. Make a well in the middle.

4. Add the coconut milk, pumpkin puree, and date paste, and stir to combine.

5. Fold in the raspberries and stir to incorporate.

6. Pour the batter evenly into the prepared baking pan. Bake until the pancake turns a light golden brown and bounces back slightly to the touch, about 25 minutes.

7. Transfer the pan from the oven to a wire rack, and let it sit for 5 minutes before removing the springform circle and transferring the pancake to a plate.

8. Cut into quarters with a pizza slicer and serve with desired toppings.

SERVING SIZE: ¼ PANCAKE
Calories 140; Total Fat 4.5g; Protein 3.7g; Cholesterol 0.0g; Sodium 143mg; Fiber 3.5g; Sugars 4.0g; Total Carbohydrate 23.0g

Inside Scoop: To make more than one pancake, double the recipe and use two 9-inch springform baking pans. To bake, place one pan on the bottom rack and one pan on the top rack, and halfway through baking, switch the pans so the one that's on top is on the bottom and vice versa.

Orange Rosemary Scones

MAKES 12 SCONES

I have some friends who are real teahouse groupies. The minute they hear that a new, adorable tea cottage is opening up within a thirty-mile radius, they make a reservation. I usually go, too, since I like hanging out with them and learning about clotted cream. And as I sip cup after cup of tea poured from teapots dressed up in quaint, custom-made quilts, I admire all the pastries that are delivered on triple-decker silver trays on top of doilies. I especially drool over the scones. So here, I share with you my absolute favorite, one that meshes the earthiness of rosemary with the sweet tang of citrus and orange zest. It is one of the best scones I've ever tasted and is the perfect accompaniment to coffee. I'm such a traitor.

Must Have

SCONES

2 cups All-Purpose Gluten-Free Flour Mix (page 20)

1 tablespoon finely chopped fresh rosemary

2½ teaspoons sodium-free baking powder

1 teaspoon grated orange zest

¼ teaspoon guar gum

¼ teaspoon fine sea salt

⅓ cup pumpkin puree

¼ cup coconut milk

⅓ cup coconut nectar

2 tablespoons applesauce

2 teaspoons orange extract

1 teaspoon gluten-free vanilla extract

⅛ teaspoon stevia powder

GLAZE

1 cup powdered erythritol (I use confectioner's Swerve brand; see Resources)

2 tablespoons orange juice

1 teaspoon grated orange zest

Must Do

1. Preheat the oven to 325°F. Line a 15 × 13-inch baking sheet with parchment paper.

2. To make the scones: Whisk together the all-purpose flour, rosemary, baking powder, orange zest, guar gum, and salt in a large bowl. Make a well in the middle.

3. Add the pumpkin puree, ccoconut milk, coconut nectar, applesauce, orange and vanilla extracts, and stevia, and mix together until the liquid is absorbed and a dough is formed. Divide the dough evenly into 2 balls. Cut each ball in half with a chef's knife, and then cut the halves into thirds so that you have 6 pieces from each ball. Press down gently on each piece of dough and form a triangle about ½ inch thick. Place the 12 triangles on the prepared baking sheet.

4. Bake the scones until the edges are a light golden brown, about 13 minutes. Rotate the cookie sheet from front to back after 10 minutes of baking.

5. Transfer the baking sheet to a wire rack and let sit for about 10 minutes. Use a spatula to slide each scone off the baking sheet onto the wire rack to cool completely.

6. To make the glaze: Combine the erythritol and orange juice in a small bowl and mix until combined.

7. Brush the glaze on the scones when they are completely cool. Sprinkle the orange zest on top of the glaze.

8. Store the scones in an airtight container for up to 3 days, or wrap and freeze for up to 3 months.

SERVING SIZE: 1 SCONE
Calories 90; Total Fat 1.0g; Protein 2.0g; Cholesterol 0.0g; Sodium 50mg; Fiber 1.5g; Sugars 3.0g; Total Carbohydrate 20.0g

Raisin Bran Scones with Pomegranate Icing

MAKES 12 SCONES

I put pomegranate, raisins, sunflower butter, and bran into these scones because I like my food to multitask. I worked hard to create an utterly irresistible exotic dessert that delivers on vitamins, minerals, iron, and fiber so that it could easily qualify as breakfast. And if it qualifies as breakfast, then I can have it with my coffee. Which in the end is really all that matters.

Must Have

SCONES

1 cup rice bran
1 cup All-Purpose Gluten-Free Flour Mix (page 20)
2½ teaspoons sodium-free baking powder
¼ teaspoon guar gum
¼ teaspoon fine sea salt
⅓ cup applesauce
⅓ cup coconut nectar
¼ cup Sunflower Seed Butter (page 20)
2 teaspoons gluten-free vanilla extract
1 teaspoon pomegranate concentrate (I use Dynamic Health Laboratories; see Resources)
⅛ teaspoon stevia powder
¼ cup raisins
¼ cup coconut milk

ICING

1 cup powdered erythritol (I use confectioner's Swerve brand; see Resources)
3 tablespoons pomegranate concentrate
1 tablespoon coconut milk

Must Do

1. Preheat the oven to 325°F. Line a 15 × 13-inch baking sheet with parchment paper.

2. To make the scones: Whisk together the rice bran, all-purpose flour, baking powder, guar gum, and salt in a large bowl. Make a well in the middle.

3. Add the applesauce, coconut nectar, sunflower seed butter, vanilla, pomegranate concentrate, and stevia, and stir to combine. Fold in the raisins and stir to incorporate. Add the coconut milk and stir until the liquid is absorbed and a dough forms.

4. Divide the dough evenly into 2 balls. Cut each ball in half with a chef's knife, and then cut the halves into thirds so that you have 6 pieces from each ball. Press down gently on each piece of dough and form a triangle about ½ inch thick. Place the 12 triangles on the prepared baking sheet.

5. Bake the scones for about 12 minutes, or until the edges are golden brown. Rotate the baking sheet from front to back halfway through baking. Transfer the baking sheet to a wire rack and let sit for about 10 minutes.

6. To make the icing: Combine the powdered erythritol, pomegranate concentrate, and coconut milk in a small bowl and mix until combined.

7. Frost the scones when they have completely cooled.

8. Store the scones in an airtight container for up to 3 days, or wrap and freeze for up to 3 months.

SERVING SIZE: 1 SCONE
Calories 110; Total Fat 5.0g; Protein 3.5g; Cholesterol 0.0g; Sodium 50mg; Fiber 3.5g; Sugars 3.0g; Total Carbohydrate 17.0g

Lemon Streusel Basil Blackberry Muffins

MAKES 12 STANDARD-SIZE MUFFINS

Sometimes all you need is a little streusel to make your day. For the longest time I made these muffins without adding a topping. And though they were moist, sweet, and delicious, and as you can see from the pic, photogenic, I thought it would be fun to add a little more oomph. The oomph turned out to be a simple streusel. The exquisite conglomeration of citrus, spice, herbs, berries, and crumbly coating is a revelation.

Must Have

DATE PASTE
1 cup water
10 Medjool dates, pitted

MUFFINS
2 cups All-Purpose Gluten-Free Flour Mix (page 20)
2 teaspoons minced, dried basil
2 teaspoons sodium-free baking powder
1 teaspoon baking soda
2 teaspoons grated lemon zest
½ teaspoon guar gum
¼ teaspoon fine sea salt
⅛ teaspoon ground cardamom
¼ cup applesauce
¼ cup coconut nectar
3 tablespoons freshly squeezed lemon juice
½ teaspoon lemon extract
¼ teaspoon stevia powder
⅓ cup vegan, soy-free vanilla yogurt
¾ cup coconut milk
¾ cup organic blackberries, cut in half, divided

LEMON STREUSEL
½ cup coconut sugar
¼ cup date paste (see above)
2 tablespoons gluten-free oats, ground (I use a coffee grinder)
1 teaspoon grated lemon zest

Must Do

1. Preheat the oven to 350°F. Line a standard 12-cup muffin tin with paper baking cups.

2. To make the date paste: Place the water and dates in a small bowl. Let them soak for about 20 minutes. Drain the dates and keep the water they soaked in. Add the dates to a food processor. Puree the dates until combined. While the machine is still running, add the reserved water, 1 tablespoon at a time, until the dates are combined and the mixture is somewhat smooth. You should only need 2–3 tablespoons of the reserved soaking water. Set aside the date paste.

3. To make the muffins: Whisk together the all-purpose flour, basil, baking powder, baking soda, lemon zest, guar gum, salt, and cardamom in a large bowl. Make a well in the middle.

4. Add the applesauce, coconut nectar, lemon juice, lemon extract, and stevia, and stir to combine. Add the yogurt and coconut milk, and stir until the liquid is absorbed and the batter is smooth.

5. Fold in ½ cup of the blackberries, and stir to incorporate.

6. Spoon the batter into the prepared muffin tin, dividing it evenly. Each cup should be about three-quarters full.

7. To make the streusel: Whisk together the coconut sugar, date paste, oats, and lemon zest in a small bowl. Top each muffin with the streusel, dividing it evenly, and then top with the remaining ¼ cup blackberries.

8. Bake the muffins until they are a light golden brown and bounce back slightly to the touch, about 18 minutes. Rotate the muffin tin from front to back halfway through baking.

9. Transfer the muffin tin to a wire rack, and let it sit for 10 minutes before removing the muffins to cool completely.

10. Keep the muffins in an airtight container for up to 3 days, or wrap and freeze for up to 3 months.

SERVING SIZE: 1 MUFFIN
Calories 70; Total Fat 4.0g; Protein 1.0g; Cholesterol 0.0g; Sodium 50mg; Fiber 2.0g; Sugars 4.0g; Total Carbohydrate 20.0g

Tropical Pineapple Ginger Muffins

MAKES 12 STANDARD-SIZE MUFFINS

Whenever I talk about any pineapple recipe I'm developing, my friends are always adamant I should make them upside down. I'm all about yogi inversions to get a new perspective on life, but for my pineapples, I prefer them not to have vertigo. But despite being upright, these pineapple muffins have the power to transport you to a tropical island where coconuts abound and ginger is the spice of life. The streusel helps caramelize the pineapple so that you get all that gooey goodness without making the pineapple stand on its head.

Must Have

MUFFINS

2 cups All-Purpose Gluten-Free Flour Mix (page 20)
2 teaspoons sodium-free baking powder
1 tablespoon ground ginger
1 teaspoon baking soda
½ teaspoon guar gum
¼ teaspoon ground turmeric
¼ teaspoon fine sea salt
¼ cup applesauce
¼ cup coconut nectar
¼ teaspoon stevia powder
½ cup pureed pineapple
1 cup coconut milk
½ cup fresh or frozen (thawed) pineapple, cut into ¼-inch chunks, divided

STREUSEL

⅓ cup gluten-free oats, ground (I use a coffee grinder)
¼ cup shredded unsweetened coconut
¼ cup coconut sugar

Must Do

1. Preheat the oven to 350°F. Line a standard 12-cup muffin tin with paper baking cups.

2. To make the muffins: Whisk together the all-purpose flour, baking powder, ginger, baking soda, guar gum, turmeric, and salt in a large bowl. Make a well in the middle.

3. Add the applesauce, coconut nectar, and stevia, and stir to combine. Add the pureed pineapple and coconut milk, and stir until the liquid is absorbed and the batter is smooth. Fold in ¼ cup of the pineapple chunks.

4. Spoon the batter into the prepared muffin tin, dividing it evenly. Each cup should be about three-quarters full.

5. To make the streusel: Whisk together the oats, coconut, and coconut sugar in a small bowl. Top each muffin with the streusel, dividing it evenly. Top the muffins with the remaining ¼ cup pineapple chunks.

6. Bake the muffins until they are a light golden brown and bounce back slightly to the touch, about 18 minutes. Rotate the muffin tin from front to back halfway through baking.

7. Transfer the muffin tin from the oven to a wire rack and let sit for 15 minutes before removing the muffins to cool completely.

8. Keep the muffins in an airtight container for up to 3 days, or wrap and freeze for up to 3 months.

SERVING SIZE: 1 MUFFIN
Calories 107; Total Fat 2.0g; Protein 2.5g; Cholesterol 0.0g; Sodium 50mg; Fiber 2.5g; Sugars 2.0g; Total Carbohydrate 23.0g

Pumpkin Swirl Cinnamon Buns

MAKES 8 BUNS

There's only one thing better than cinnamon buns and that's pumpkin swirl cinnamon buns. I mean, really, I can't think of four words that get me salivating any faster, except for maybe someone saying, "You won the lottery."

In addition to the allure of the cinnamon- and nutmeg-spiced, pumpkin-infused dough, lush pumpkin icing, and sweet coconut sugar filling, you get the satisfying knowledge that you're eating all this gooey goodness with no butter or refined sugar. And, on top of that, you're getting a quick infusion of vitamin A from the pumpkin and fiber from the psyllium. And trust me when I say that you sacrifice nothing in terms of taste and texture. So if you didn't believe in miracles before, you may after taking a bite of these buns.

Must Have

BUNS

1¼ cups warm coconut milk, about 108°F (I microwave it for 30 seconds)

1 (2¼-teaspoon) packet active dry yeast

2 tablespoons coconut nectar

2¼ cups All-Purpose Gluten-Free Flour Mix (page 20)

1 cup sweet white rice flour

1 tablespoon psyllium husk powder

2 teaspoons ground cinnamon

¼ teaspoon ground nutmeg

¼ teaspoon fine sea salt

¼ cup pumpkin puree

FILLING

1 cup coconut sugar

1½ teaspoons ground cinnamon

PUMPKIN ICING

1 cup powdered erythritol (I use confectioner's Swerve brand; see Resources)

½ teaspoon ground cinnamon

3 tablespoons pumpkin puree

¼ cup water

Must Do

1. Preheat the oven to 200°F and then turn it off. Line an 8 × 8-inch baking pan with parchment paper.

2. **To make the buns:** Stir together the coconut milk and yeast in a small bowl. Stir in the coconut nectar and let it sit for about 8 minutes, or until frothy.

3. Whisk together the all-purpose flour, sweet white rice flour, psyllium husk powder, cinnamon, nutmeg, and salt in a large bowl. Make a well in the middle.

4. Add the pumpkin puree to the yeast mixture, stir to combine, and then pour into the flour mixture. Mix together until a dough forms.

5. Roll out the dough on a lightly floured piece of parchment paper with another piece of parchment paper on top of the dough and make a 12 × 9-inch rectangle. Make sure the longer side of the rectangle is facing you. Remove the top piece of parchment.

6. **To make the filling:** Mix together the coconut sugar and cinnamon in a small bowl. Spread the filling evenly over the dough, leaving a 1-inch border around the perimeter.

7. Roll the dough tightly, from bottom to top, away from you, using the parchment paper for guidance and to prevent the dough from tearing. Trim the edges on both ends and then press the ends together to seal.

8. Cut the rolled dough into 8 even pieces with a serrated knife by cutting the log in half, then cutting the halves in half, and then cutting those pieces in half.

9. Place the cinnamon buns in the prepared pan, cut side down. Cover with a clean dishtowel and put them in the oven for 1 hour of rising time.

10. After the dough has risen, take the pan out of the oven, and preheat the oven to 375°F.

11. Remove the dishtowel and bake the buns until they are a light golden brown and the dough is firm on the sides, about 18 minutes.

12. Transfer the pan from the oven to a wire rack, and let it sit for 10 minutes before removing the buns for a complete cooldown.

13. To make the icing: Mix together the powdered erythritol, cinnamon, pumpkin puree, and water in a small bowl until smooth.

14. Frost the completely cooled cinnamon buns.

15. Keep in an airtight container for up to 3 days, or wrap and freeze for up to 3 months.

SERVING SIZE: 1 BUN
Calories 200; Total Fat 2.5g; Protein 4.3g; Cholesterol 0.0g; Sodium 70mg; Fiber 4.5g; Sugars 5.0g; Total Carbohydrate 43.0g

Chipotle Mexican Omelet Tostada

SERVES 2

When I went to Indianapolis for the first time, I didn't expect much in terms of restaurants that had options for plant-based eaters who were gluten-free and sugar-free and loved fair trade, organic coffee roasted in small batches. Lo and behold, much to my pleasant surprise, Indianapolis was brewing with restaurants and coffeehouses that fit the bill. The meal that I remember most was a fully loaded Mexican vegan omelet. It was such a culinary inspiration that I vowed to try to reproduce it once I got home. After many tweaks, turns, and about-faces, I reproduced what I ate in the Circle City and gave it my own signature twist.

Must Have

OMELET

1 cup chickpea flour
2 tablespoons nutritional yeast flakes
1 tablespoon chia seeds, ground (I use a coffee grinder)
¼ teaspoon baking soda
⅛ teaspoon sodium-free baking powder
⅛ teaspoon sea salt
½ teaspoon ground cumin
¼ teaspoon ground turmeric
¼ teaspoon chipotle chili powder
3 tablespoons vegan, soy-free plain yogurt
1 serrano pepper, diced
½ cup fresh cilantro, roughly chopped
1 cup water
1 gluten-free tortilla

TOPPINGS

Chopped heirloom tomatoes
Chopped avocado
Black beans
Chopped fresh cilantro
Hot Sauce (page 21)
Corn

Must Do

1. Preheat the oven to 350°F. Line a 9-inch round springform baking pan with parchment paper. Make sure the parchment goes up about an inch along the sides of the baking pan so the batter doesn't stick.

2. To make the omelet: Whisk together the chickpea flour, nutritional yeast, ground chia seeds, baking soda, baking powder, salt, cumin, turmeric, and chipotle powder in a large bowl. Make a well in the middle.

3. Add the yogurt, serrano pepper, cilantro, and water, and stir to combine.

4. Pour the batter evenly into the prepared cake pan.

5. Bake until the omelet turns a light golden brown and bounces back slightly to the touch, about 25 minutes. Transfer the pan from the oven to a wire rack, and let it sit for 5 minutes before removing the springform circle.

6. Heat the tortilla in a medium sauté pan over low heat until the tortilla gets crisp, about 1 minute on each side.

7. To assemble the tostada, place the tortilla on a large plate and top it with the omelet.

8. Cut the tostada into quarters with a pizza slicer and serve with desired toppings.

SERVING SIZE: ½ TOSTADA
Calories 100; Total Fat 2.5g; Protein 4.5g; Cholesterol 0.0g; Sodium 140mg; Fiber 2.7g; Sugars 3.3g; Total Carbohydrate 15.0g

Inside Scoop: An easy way to transfer the omelet onto the plated tortilla is to place your hand under the parchment-lined omelet, flip it onto the tortilla, and peel the parchment paper off.

Trail Mix Granola

MAKES ABOUT 4 CUPS

The first time I made granola, I told my son that it was a new cereal he could eat in the morning. He looked dubiously at the bowl of toasted, caramelized oats, seeds, and dried fruit and said, "Where's the cereal?" I realized then that he was so used to getting his breakfast from a box that anything else was suspect. That was the day I got an F on my mommy report card! After that, I was determined to make sure my son ate mostly unprocessed foods and more of the "real" stuff. The transition was not as hard as I thought it would be, and now this granola is his favorite thing to eat, any time of the day. The crunchy texture, the "popped" quinoa, which is a revelation in and of itself, and the natural sweetness of it all is a slam-dunk in deliciousness.

Must Have

½ cup yellow quinoa
3 cups gluten-free rolled oats
½ cup pumpkin seeds
½ cup sunflower seeds
¼ cup hemp seeds
¼ cup chia seeds
¼ teaspoon sea salt
½ cup orange juice
½ cup coconut nectar
1 teaspoon gluten-free vanilla extract
⅓ cup dried cranberries, dried blueberries, or raisins (you can use any dried fruit you desire)

Must Do

1. Preheat the oven to 300°F. Line a 15 × 10-inch jelly-roll pan with parchment paper.

2. Add the quinoa to a medium skillet over medium heat and give the pan a few shakes until you hear the quinoa popping, about 5 minutes. Turn off the heat and let it cool in the pan for a few minutes.

3. Mix together the oats, pumpkin seeds, sunflower seeds, hemp seeds, chia seeds, and salt in a large bowl. Add the popped quinoa and make a well in the middle.

4. Add the orange juice, coconut nectar, and vanilla extract, and stir to combine.

5. Spoon the mixture onto the prepared baking sheet and spread it around evenly.

6. Bake until the oats are golden brown and toasted, about 25 minutes. Stir the mixture halfway through baking. Transfer the sheet from the oven to a wire rack, and let it sit for about 10 minutes. Mix in the dried fruit.

7. Serve over yogurt, ice cream, or oatmeal with nondairy milk, or just eat it on its own. I also use it in my Trail Mix Macaroons (page 256).

SERVING SIZE: ½ CUP

Calories 175; Total Fat 7.0g; Protein 6.5g; Cholesterol 0.0g; Sodium 20mg; Fiber 4.5g; Sugars 10.0g; Total Carbohydrate 33.0g

Fakiin Bacon Crescent Rolls

MAKES 12 CRESCENT ROLLS **(SEE PHOTO ON PAGE 26)**

If you feel a void in your life because your paleo friends are talking about eating bacon every other five minutes, fear not, because I have something here that's not only better tasting than bacon, but better *for* you—fakiin bacon, or shiitake mushrooms that are marinated, roasted, and shrunk to within an inch of their lives. They impersonate a strip of smoked pork to a T, and, when strategically inserted into these crescent rolls, provide irresistible down-home comfort. In addition to eating them in the morning, I have them with salads and soups and sometimes all by themselves as a snack.

Must Have

FAKIIN BACON

1½ cups sliced shiitake mushrooms (¼ inch thick)

3 tablespoons coconut aminos

½ teaspoon liquid smoke

¼ teaspoon sea salt

DOUGH

1 cup warm coconut milk, about 108°F (I microwave it for 30 seconds)

2¼ teaspoons rapid-rise yeast

1 tablespoon coconut nectar

2 cups sorghum flour

½ cup tapioca flour

½ cup sweet white rice flour

1 tablespoon psyllium husk powder

½ teaspoon fine sea salt

3 tablespoons pumpkin puree

GLAZE

1 tablespoon coconut aminos

1 tablespoon coconut milk

Must Do

1. Preheat the oven to 350°F. Line a 15 × 10-inch jelly-roll pan with parchment paper.

2. To make the fakiin bacon: Spread the shiitake mushrooms on the prepared pan. Drizzle the coconut aminos and liquid smoke on the mushrooms, toss them gently with your hands to coat, and sprinkle with the salt. Bake for 40 minutes, or until the mushrooms are crisp. Set the pan aside to cool a bit while you make the dough. Be sure to turn the oven off at this point so you can put the crescent rolls in the oven to rise.

3. To make the dough: Combine the warm coconut milk and yeast in a small bowl. Add the coconut nectar and stir to combine. Let the yeast mixture sit for about 8 minutes, or until foamy.

4. Whisk together the sorghum flour, tapioca flour, sweet white rice flour, psyllium husk powder, and salt in a large bowl. Make a well in the middle.

5. Add the pumpkin puree to the yeast mixture, stir to combine, and then pour into the flour mixture. Add the fakiin bacon and stir to combine until a dough forms.

6. Roll out the dough on a lightly floured piece of parchment paper with another piece of parchment on top of the dough and make a 10 × 9-inch rectangle. Remove the top piece of parchment.

7. Divide the rectangle in half by slicing down the middle of the 10-inch side with a pizza cutter. Then cut six triangles from each of the resulting two rectangles by zigzagging back and forth along the width of each rectangle strip with the pizza cutter.

8. Roll each triangle into a crescent roll, starting from the longest side and rolling down to the point of the triangle.

9. Place the crescents on the prepared pan that you used for the mushrooms, cover with a clean dishtowel, and place in the oven for 30 minutes of rising time.

10. **To make the glaze:** Whisk together the coconut aminos and coconut milk in a small bowl.

11. After the dough has risen, take the pan out of the oven, and preheat the oven to 375°F.

12. Remove the dishtowel, brush the crescent rolls with the glaze, and bake for about 30 minutes, or until they are golden brown.

13. Transfer the pan from the oven to a wire rack, and let it sit for 10 minutes before removing the rolls for a complete cooldown.

14. Eat right away or keep in an airtight container for up to 3 days, or wrap and freeze for up to 3 months.

SERVING SIZE: 1 CRESCENT ROLL
Calories 125; Total Fat 1.3g; Protein 3.3g; Cholesterol 0.0g; Sodium 143mg; Fiber 2.5g; Sugars 0.5g; Total Carbohydrate 26.0g

Inside Scoop: To get the coconut milk heated to just the right temperature without killing the yeast, I put room-temperature coconut milk in the microwave for 30 seconds.

Sunflower Butter & Jelly Doughnuts

MAKES 6 DOUGHNUTS

I believe if a food item has sufficient nutritional value and you'd really like it to escort your morning coffee to your nervous system, then it qualifies as breakfast. And with that logic, I introduce to you my Sunflower Butter & Jelly Doughnuts. They are far more nutrient dense than your typical garden variety jelly-filled fried dough, and you can really drive that nutritional nail home with the suggested toppings below. Sunflower seed butter replicates the taste of peanut butter so well that the whole experience is also quite nostalgic.

Must Have

DOUGHNUTS

1 cup All-Purpose Gluten-Free Flour Mix (page 20)
½ cup sweet white rice flour
¼ cup amaranth flour
¼ cup cacao powder
1½ teaspoons sodium-free baking powder
½ teaspoon baking soda
¼ teaspoon guar gum
¼ teaspoon sea salt
¾ cup Sunflower Seed Butter (page 20), divided
¾ cup jelly (I use grape), divided
½ cup coconut milk
¼ cup applesauce
¼ cup coconut nectar
⅜ teaspoon stevia powder

FUDGE FROSTING

½ cup coconut nectar
2 tablespoons mashed avocado
1 cup powdered erythritol (I use confectioner's Swerve brand; see Resources)
½ cup cacao powder
1 tablespoon warm water
⅛ teaspoon stevia powder
⅛ teaspoon sea salt

TOPPINGS

Trail Mix Granola (page 47)
Roasted sunflower or pumpkin seeds, chopped
Shredded coconut
Chopped mango

Must Do

1. Preheat the oven to 325°F.

2. To make the doughnuts: Whisk together the all-purpose flour, sweet white rice flour, amaranth flour, cacao powder, baking powder, baking soda, guar gum, and salt in a large bowl. Make a well in the middle.

3. Add ¼ cup of the sunflower seed butter, ¼ cup of the jelly, the coconut milk, applesauce, coconut nectar, and stevia, and stir to combine.

4. Fill the wells of a 6-hole doughnut pan halfway with the batter. Spread the remaining ½ cup sunflower seed butter around the top of the batter, dividing it evenly. Do the same with the remaining ½ cup jelly and spread it on top of the sunflower seed butter.

5. Pour the remaining batter on top of the jelly, dividing it evenly. Each of the doughnut wells should be full.

6. Bake the doughnuts until they spring back lightly to the touch, about 17 minutes. Rotate the doughnut pan halfway through baking.

7. Transfer the doughnut pan from the oven to a wire rack, and let it sit for 10 minutes before removing the doughnuts to cool completely.

8. To make the fudge frosting: Add the coconut nectar and avocado to a medium bowl and stir to combine. Add the powdered erythritol, cacao powder, water, stevia, and salt, and stir until smooth.

9. Frost the completely cooled doughnuts. Dip into your favorite toppings.

SERVING SIZE: 1 DOUGHNUT
Calories 275; Total Fat 13.0g; Protein 8.1g; Cholesterol 0.0g; Sodium 95mg; Fiber 4.5g; Sugars 10.0g; Total Carbohydrate 57.0g

Inside Scoop: Be sure to thoroughly combine the mashed avocado into the frosting. Otherwise, you'll have green flecks sticking out and it might scare people.

Quinoa & Kale Breakfast Burritos

MAKES 6 BURRITOS

When I was pregnant with my son, I craved breakfast burritos morning, noon, and night. If I happened to be shopping in a grocery store, I would go to the prepared hot foods area, pick one up, and eat it while walking up and down the aisles shopping. Then I would have to confess to the cashier. There was no telling when the mood would strike, and until I could devour a cheesy, eggy, fried potato–ridden tortilla, I was nauseous beyond comprehension. Makes sense, right? So now that my hormone levels have stabilized, and my way of eating has taken a right turn, so to speak, I still have hankerings for breakfast burritos, but of a different kind. And this recipe is a new and improved incarnation. The crispy quinoa and kale cake is the perfect yin to the sweet yang of the hash brown yams. It is a more evolved comfort food, but just as satiating and satisfying.

Must Have

QUINOA & KALE PATTIES
1 cup uncooked quinoa
2 cups water
½ yellow onion, diced
2 tablespoons coconut aminos
1 teaspoon ground cumin
1 teaspoon fresh rosemary
½ teaspoon dried thyme
½ teaspoon sea salt
½ teaspoon freshly ground black pepper
3 kale leaves, stemmed and roughly chopped

1 tablespoon tapioca flour
1 tablespoon chia seeds, ground (I use a coffee grinder)

YAM HASH BROWNS
1 medium yam, peeled and shredded
½ yellow onion, diced
½ teaspoon sea salt
½ teaspoon freshly ground black pepper
1 tablespoon water

ULTIMATE GUACAMOLE
1 medium ripe avocado, peeled, pitted, and diced
6 cherry tomatoes, seeded and diced
1 clove garlic, minced
1 small jalapeño, minced
1 tablespoon freshly squeezed lime juice
¼ cup fresh cilantro, finely chopped
½ teaspoon ground cumin

6 gluten-free tortillas

Must Do

1. Preheat the oven to 425°F. Line a 15 × 13-inch baking sheet with parchment paper.

2. To make the quinoa & kale patties: Add the quinoa to a small pot over high heat. Toast the quinoa until it is fragrant, about 1 minute. Add the water and bring to a boil.

3. Lower the heat, cover the pot, and let simmer until the water is absorbed, about 15 minutes.

4. Heat the onion in a medium skillet over medium heat and stir until fragrant, about 1 minute.

5. Add the coconut aminos, cumin, rosemary, thyme, salt, black pepper, and kale to the skillet and cook, stirring occasionally, until the kale is tender and bright green and the spices are fragrant, about 2 minutes.

6. Add the mixture from the skillet to a food processor, along with the cooked quinoa, tapioca flour, and chia seeds, and pulse until the mixture comes together but still has texture.

7. Form small patties, about 2 tablespoons each, with your hands and flatten them a little more as you place them on the prepared baking sheet.

8. Bake the patties until they are a light golden brown and the outside is crisp, about 20 minutes. Flip the patties halfway through baking.

9. To make the yam hash browns: Heat the shredded yam in a medium sauté pan over medium heat, along with the onion, salt, and black pepper. Add the water and stir to combine. Cook and stir occasionally until the yams are tender, about 10 minutes.

10. To make the ultimate guacamole: Add the avocado, tomatoes, garlic, jalapeño, lime juice, cilantro, and cumin to a medium bowl and stir to combine.

11. To assemble the burritos, warm a tortilla in a medium skillet over medium heat on both sides for about 30 seconds. Fill the tortilla with 2 or 3 quinoa & kale patties, some hash browns, and a spoonful of guacamole in the lower middle of the tortilla. Then tuck in the right and left sides, and roll the tortilla away from you to make your burrito. Cut in half and serve. Repeat with the remaining tortillas.

SERVING SIZE: 1 BURRITO
Calories 120; Total Fat 5.5g; Protein 3.0g; Cholesterol 0.0g; Sodium 300mg; Fiber 4.3g; Sugars 1.0g; Total Carbohydrate 18.0g

Inside Scoop: If fresh figs aren't in season, you can use any fruit you like. If you can't find hemp tofu and can tolerate soy, firm tofu is a good substitute.

Fig & Ricotta Challah French Toast

SERVES 4

I think challah was invented by Jewish people so that we could make something French with it. After all, French bread is the best, am I right? And so it is with this recipe. French toast is SO much better when made with a thick bread like challah. And you can make the challah yourself with the recipe on page 214. Then wait a day or two, and make this luxurious breakfast with the added bonus of fresh figs, if they're in season. I know that sometimes food allergies, celiac problems, and a host of other issues may make it feel like your diet has to be extremely limited, but my mission is to figure out what may seem like a culinary impossibility and bring you the blueprint. So here is the manual for the perfect weekend brunch. *Bon appétit!*

Must Have

CHALLAH FRENCH TOAST
¼ cup chickpea flour
¼ cup nutritional yeast
2 tablespoons coconut nectar
1½ cups coconut milk
1 teaspoon ground cinnamon
¼ teaspoon ground nutmeg
⅛ teaspoon sea salt
4 thick slices Challah (page 214)

SWEET RICOTTA
1 (8-ounce) package hemp tofu, crumbled
3 tablespoons coconut nectar
2 tablespoons nutritional yeast
1 teaspoon chickpea miso paste
1 teaspoon Sunflower Seed Butter (page 20)
8 fresh figs, sliced

TOPPINGS
Grade B maple syrup
Coconut nectar
Hemp seeds
Blackberries

Must Do

1. **To make the French toast:** Whisk together the chickpea flour, nutritional yeast, coconut nectar, coconut milk, cinnamon, nutmeg, and salt in a medium bowl.

2. Pour this mixture into a 13 × 9-inch casserole dish and place the challah slices in the dish to soak up the liquid, about 40 minutes. Turn over the challah slices halfway through soaking.

3. **To make the sweet ricotta:** Mix together the tofu, coconut nectar, nutritional yeast, miso, and sunflower seed butter in a small bowl until thoroughly combined.

4. Add the ricotta to a medium sauté pan over medium heat and cook, stirring occasionally, until the mixture is heated through, about 2 minutes.

5. Remove the tofu mixture from the pan and set aside in a bowl. Clean the sauté pan.

6. Place two of the challah slices in the sauté pan over medium heat and cook until the bottom is golden brown and crisp, about 8 minutes. Flip the challah over and cook for another 8 minutes. Repeat with the remaining slices.

7. Top each challah slice with the ricotta mixture and then top with the fig slices.

8. Serve immediately with any or all of the suggested toppings.

SERVING SIZE: 1 SLICE FRENCH TOAST
Calories 270; Total Fat 5.5g; Protein 10.5g; Cholesterol 0.0g; Sodium 115mg; Fiber 5.2g; Sugars 13.0g; Total Carbohydrate 53.0g

CHAPTER 5

Soup Is Good Food

I have to say that soup is probably one of the most satisfying meals you can put together with relative ease. It offers lots of room for creativity, can be infused with enormous flavor, and promises at least another day's worth of leftovers . . . maybe. It's also a good excuse to eat a hunk of bread. That's one of the reasons why I included "The Bread Basket" chapter, where you have over a dozen incarnations of dough to help you soak up some soupy goodness. I find soup to be the perfect meal for those cold and rainy days when nothing else will do. Soup just makes you feel good.

Matzo Ball Soup

SERVES 4

You would think I found the Holy Grail the way people react when I tell them I figured out how to make matzo balls without eggs. Well, it's true, and they are just as light, fluffy, and flavorful as their conventional counterparts. Even though matzo ball soup is usually reserved for holidays, I also make it when someone in my family feels a cold coming on, because even without the chicken, this soup is divine Jewish "penicillin."

Must Have

MATZO BALLS
1½ cups quinoa flakes
1½ cups All-Purpose Gluten-Free Flour Mix (page 20)
2 teaspoons onion powder
1 teaspoon garlic powder
¼ teaspoon sea salt
2 cups boiling water
6 tablespoons pumpkin puree

SOUP
1 medium yellow onion, chopped
¼ cup coconut aminos
½ teaspoon freshly ground black pepper
5 medium carrots, peeled and sliced
3 celery stalks, diced
2 parsnips, peeled and sliced
1 cup fresh parsley, chopped
8 cups No-Sodium Vegetable Broth (page 25)

TOPPING
3 tablespoons finely chopped fresh dill

Must Do

1. Preheat the oven to 300°F. Line a 15 × 13-inch baking sheet with parchment paper.

2. To make the matzo balls: Whisk the quinoa flakes, flour, onion powder, garlic powder, and salt together in a medium bowl. Add the boiling water and pumpkin and stir to combine.

3. Take about 1 tablespoon of the mixture and shape it into a ball. Place the ball on the prepared baking sheet. Repeat until you have used up all the mixture. You should have about 30 balls.

4. Bake the matzo balls until they are a light golden brown, about 20 minutes. Turn the balls over halfway through.

5. Transfer the baking sheet from the oven to a wire rack, and let it sit for 10 minutes.

6. To make the soup: Heat the onion in a large pot over medium heat and stir until fragrant, about 1 minute.

7. Add the coconut aminos, black pepper, carrots, celery, parsnips, and parsley and cook, stirring occasionally, until the vegetables become fragrant and slightly tender, about 2 minutes. Add the broth and bring to a boil.

8. Lower the heat, cover the pot, and let simmer for about 35 minutes.

9. Serve immediately and place several matzo balls in each soup bowl. Sprinkle in the dill.

10. This soup tastes even better the next day, and even better two days after that.

SERVING SIZE: 2 CUPS
Calories 200; Total Fat 2.5g; Protein 6.9g; Cholesterol 0.0g; Sodium 280mg; Fiber 6.9g; Sugars 4.9g; Total Carbohydrate 45.0g

Creamy Celery Root Soup

SERVES 4

I like to find the inner beauty in people as well as in vegetables. And it is extremely important to keep that credo in mind when buying celery roots. They are UGLY! But besides looking gnarly and dangerous, these celeriacs, as they are formally called, are the kindest, most gentle root vegetables you'd ever want to meet (and eat). They also have the good sense to contain a lot of essential vitamins, especially B, C, and K, and are a stunning choice for this creamy soup.

Must Have

SOUP

1 small leek (about 6 ounces), pale green and white parts only, finely sliced
¼ cup coconut aminos
2 cloves garlic, minced
¼ teaspoon ground nutmeg
2 medium celery roots (about 2 pounds total), peeled and diced
2 medium Yukon gold potatoes (about 10 ounces total), peeled and diced
1 medium sweet potato (about 5 ounces), peeled and diced
2 cups No-Sodium Vegetable Broth (page 25)
1 cup coconut milk
3 tablespoons nutritional yeast
1 tablespoon coconut nectar

TOPPING
Freshly ground black pepper

Must Do

1. **To make the soup:** Heat the leeks in a large pot over medium heat and cook, stirring, until fragrant, about 1 minute.

2. Add the coconut aminos, garlic, and nutmeg and cook, stirring occasionally, until the spices become fragrant, about 1 minute.

3. Add the celery root, Yukon potatoes, and sweet potatoes, and stir to incorporate.

4. Add the broth, coconut milk, nutritional yeast, and coconut nectar, and bring to a boil.

5. Lower the heat, cover the pot, and let simmer until the vegetables are tender, about 20 minutes.

6. Transfer the soup in batches to a high-speed blender and puree until smooth. You can also use an immersion blender.

7. Serve immediately with a grind of black pepper.

SERVING SIZE: 2 CUPS
Calories 125; Total Fat 1.7g; Protein 4.8g; Cholesterol 0.0g; Sodium 200mg; Fiber 5.1g; Sugars 0.9g; Total Carbohydrate 25.0g

Sweet Corn Soup

SERVES 4

My husband is crazy about corn. He even peddled it on Highway 1 in New Jersey after harvesting it off his aunt's farm when he was a little boy. I'm surprised there was any inventory left to sell, since he ate it raw in the fields while picking it. I always make sure to buy organic corn at the farmers' market or grocery store. It's one of those crops that tends to be genetically modified, so you have to be careful. This soup brings out the best of the corn's savory and sweet essence and is a cinch to make. My husband says it brings him right back to the farm.

Must Have

SOUP
1 large ear corn
1 small yellow onion, chopped
½ cup coconut aminos
1 clove garlic, minced
2 celery stalks, diced
1 small parsnip, peeled and sliced
3 tablespoons nutritional yeast
2 cups coconut milk

TOPPINGS
Reserved kernels from soup
2 tablespoons chopped scallion
Freshly ground black pepper

Must Do

1. **To make the soup:** Scrape the kernels from the corncob, set aside about 3 tablespoons, and add the rest to a large pot over medium heat. Add the onion and stir until fragrant, about 1 minute.

2. Add the coconut aminos, garlic, celery, parsnip, and nutritional yeast and cook, stirring occasionally, until the garlic is fragrant and the vegetables are slightly tender, about 2 minutes.

3. Add the coconut milk and bring to a boil.

4. Lower the heat, cover the pot, and let the soup simmer until the vegetables are fork tender, about 20 minutes.

5. Transfer the soup in batches to a high-speed blender and puree until smooth. You can also use an immersion blender.

6. **To make the topping:** Toast the reserved corn kernels in a skillet over medium heat for about 2 minutes.

7. Serve the soup immediately, topped with the toasted corn kernels, scallion, and a grind of black pepper.

SERVING SIZE: 2 CUPS
Calories 150; Total Fat 5.3g; Protein 6.3g; Cholesterol 0.0g; Sodium 280mg; Fiber 6.9g; Sugars 2.0g; Total Carbohydrate 24.0g

Creamy Minestrone

SERVES 4

When my son was born, we slowly but surely started to burst out of our small apartment due to all the stuff we were quickly accumulating. It's incredible how one small baby can require so much gear. So we started to look for a house. But it took forever to find something, because my husband insisted that the backyard have enough room for a garden. This may not seem like a big deal to people in the Midwest, but in Los Angeles, a big backyard is hard to come by, even if it's just a little extra land to plant some rutabagas. So we looked and looked. One year passed and then two. I thought our real estate agent was going to enroll in a witness protection program so that we would never be able to find her again. But she stuck with us, and after two and a half years we found our dream house with a small garden in the back. I tell you this not to comment on the state of the housing market in Southern California, but to make a point about that small garden. It has become my lifeline. I grow practically all my vegetables in it, and my son absolutely loves to hoe and harvest. And I always use our homegrown vegetables to make this hearty, life-affirming, thick and creamy minestrone that you don't even realize is devoid of pasta or rice. The best part is that you can use this recipe as a template and add your own favorite homegrown or store-bought vegetables, because I promise it will be just as nourishing and delicious.

Must Have

SOUP

1 medium yellow onion, diced
¼ cup coconut aminos
2 cloves garlic, minced
1 tablespoon dried oregano
2 teaspoons dried thyme
1 tablespoon coconut nectar
1 cup sliced cherry tomatoes
1 cup peeled and diced carrots
1 cup diced celery
1 cup chopped green beans
1 cup cooked kidney beans (from a can is fine)
4 cups No-Sodium Vegetable Broth (page 25)
2 cups coconut milk
6 tablespoons nutritional yeast
¼ cup tomato paste
1 medium sweet potato, peeled and diced
¼ cup fresh basil leaves, thinly sliced

TOPPING

Freshly ground black pepper

Must Do

1. **To make the soup:** Heat the onion in a large pot over medium heat and stir until fragrant, about 1 minute.

2. Add the coconut aminos, garlic, oregano, thyme, and coconut nectar and cook, stirring occasionally, until the spices become fragrant, about 2 minutes.

3. Add the tomatoes, carrot, celery, green beans, and kidney beans, and stir to incorporate.

4. Add the broth, coconut milk, nutritional yeast, tomato paste, sweet potato, and basil leaves, and bring to a boil.

5. Lower the heat, cover the pot, and let simmer until the sweet potato is tender, about 20 minutes.

6. Serve immediately and top with a grind of black pepper over each serving.

SERVING SIZE: 2 CUPS

Calories 103; Total Fat 1.5g; Protein 6.9g; Cholesterol 0.0g; Sodium 200mg; Fiber 6.2g; Sugars 2.6g; Total Carbohydrate 18.8g

Sweet Miso Forbidden Rice Ramen Noodle Bowl

SERVES 4

Ramen may remind you of your college days when insta-noodles and a packet of MSG-fortified broth in a Styrofoam cup provided insta-gratification and was called dinner. This is not that. This soup is an amalgam of Asian cuisines that creates an ambrosia of flavors and tangy spices, all rolled into a creamy broth and oh-so-satisfying chewy noodles. If you can't find the forbidden rice variety, fear not, this soup is just as enchanting with any type of ramen noodle. Your college days are over!

Must Have

SOUP
1 small yellow onion, diced
¼ cup coconut aminos
3 cloves garlic, minced
3 teaspoons grated fresh ginger
1 tablespoon ground turmeric
2 strips kombu
2 medium sweet potatoes, peeled and sliced
¼ cup chickpea miso paste
2 tablespoons coconut nectar
4 cups green tea or water

NOODLES
1 (10-ounce) package forbidden rice ramen (I use Lotus Foods; see Resources)

TOPPING
2 scallions, chopped

Must Do

1. **To make the soup:** Heat the onion in a large pot over medium heat and stir until fragrant, about 1 minute.

2. Add the coconut aminos, garlic, ginger, turmeric, kombu, sweet potatoes, miso, and coconut nectar and cook, stirring occasionally, until the herbs and spices become fragrant, about 2 minutes.

3. Add the green tea and bring to a boil.

4. Lower the heat, cover the pot, and simmer until the sweet potatoes are tender, about 20 minutes.

5. Transfer the soup in batches to a high-speed blender and puree until smooth. You can also use an immersion blender.

6. **To make the noodles:** Cook the noodles according to the package instructions. Drain the noodles in a colander and rinse with cold water.

7. Divide the soup evenly among 4 soup bowls, add the ramen noodles, and top with the scallions. If you prefer, you can remove the kombu from the soup prior to blending, cut it into 1-inch strips, and divide them evenly among the soup bowls. I just blend it with the rest of the soup.

SERVING SIZE: 2 CUPS
Calories 155; Total Fat 2.0g; Protein 2.8g; Cholesterol 0.0g; Sodium 225mg; Fiber 3.2g; Sugars 3.0g; Total Carbohydrate 31.3g

Inside Scoop: Kombu is an edible dried sea vegetable that contains many valuable nutrients and minerals, such as calcium, potassium, iron, and iodine. When you cook beans, adding some kombu to the pot will make the beans more digestible.

Cauliflower Chowder

SERVES 4

I saw the most vibrant orange cauliflower at the farmers' market one Sunday and was inspired. Orange cauliflowers are certainly not the norm, so if you can only find the white kind, this recipe doesn't discriminate. All colors and creeds of cauliflower provide vitamins B_1, B_6, C, and K, folate, fiber, and lots of health protection through antioxidants. As far as flavor and texture, this soup comes out creamy and smooth, smoky, and slightly sweet—the perfect combination for equal-opportunity cauliflower chowder.

Must Have

SOUP
1 small yellow onion, chopped
¼ cup coconut aminos
3 cloves garlic, minced
1 teaspoon ground cumin
1 teaspoon ground turmeric
½ teaspoon smoked paprika
½ teaspoon freshly ground black pepper
1 tablespoon coconut nectar
1 large orange cauliflower (about 3 pounds), cut into florets (white cauliflower is okay)
1 sweet potato, peeled and diced
1 medium parsnip, peeled and sliced
5 cups No-Sodium Vegetable Broth (page 25)
1 cup coconut milk
3 tablespoons nutritional yeast

TOPPINGS
Chopped fresh chives
Chopped fresh dill

Must Do

1. **To make the soup:** Heat the onion in a large pot over medium heat and stir until fragrant, about 1 minute.

2. Add the coconut aminos, garlic, cumin, turmeric, smoked paprika, black pepper, and coconut nectar and cook, stirring occasionally, until the spices become fragrant, about 2 minutes.

3. Add the cauliflower, sweet potato, and parsnip, and stir to incorporate.

4. Add the broth, coconut milk, and nutritional yeast, and bring to a boil.

5. Lower the heat, cover the pot, and let simmer until the vegetables are tender, about 20 minutes.

6. Transfer the soup in batches to a high-speed blender and puree until smooth. You can also use an immersion blender.

7. Serve immediately with the toppings.

SERVING SIZE: 2 CUPS
Calories 160; Total Fat 1.5g; Protein 8.0g; Cholesterol 0.0g; Sodium 200mg; Fiber 8.2g; Sugars 7.0g; Total Carbohydrate 31.0g

Split Pea Soup

SERVES 4

I don't think you can have a more hearty and comforting soup than split pea. The trick is to cook it long enough so that the split peas surrender and become mush. That's when you know the soup is done. The hour or so it takes is so worth the wait. I like this soup thick, but if you want to make it looser you can add some coconut milk to thin it out a bit; that will also make it creamier.

Must Have

SOUP
1 small yellow onion, diced
¼ cup coconut aminos
2 cloves garlic, minced
1 teaspoon dried thyme
½ teaspoon dried oregano
¼ teaspoon smoked paprika
2 tablespoons coconut nectar
1 medium parsnip, peeled and sliced
8 cups No-Sodium Vegetable Broth (page 25)
2 cups split peas, rinsed
2 tablespoons nutritional yeast
1 teaspoon liquid smoke

TOPPING
Freshly ground black pepper

Must Do

1. To make the soup: Heat the onion in a large pot over medium heat and stir until fragrant, about 1 minute.

2. Add the coconut aminos, garlic, thyme, oregano, smoked paprika, and coconut nectar and cook, stirring occasionally, until the spices become fragrant, about 2 minutes.

3. Add the parsnip and stir to incorporate. Add the broth, split peas, nutritional yeast, and liquid smoke, and bring to a boil.

4. Lower the heat, cover the pot, and simmer for about 60 minutes, or until the peas are completely soft and mushy.

5. Transfer the soup in batches to a high-speed blender and puree until smooth. You can also use an immersion blender.

6. Serve immediately with a grind of black pepper.

SERVING SIZE: 2 CUPS
Calories 250; Total Fat 2.3g; Protein 7.3g; Cholesterol 0.0g; Sodium 200mg; Fiber 7.5g; Sugars 2.0g; Total Carbohydrate 21.0g

Curried Pumpkin Soup

SERVES 4

The best advice I can give you: please do not try to make this recipe with pumpkin puree. The first time I made this soup, I wanted to save myself the time of cutting and roasting a whole pumpkin by using the canned stuff, and it was a complete and utter failure. On the other hand, when I did take the time to carve and bake, the results were spectacular. The roasting brings out the pumpkin's true flavor, and then by combining it with the curry spices, it becomes irresistible. And just like its fellow orange warriors—sweet potato, butternut squash, and carrot—pumpkin protects you from free radical invaders with its potent supply of beta-carotene and other antioxidants.

Must Have

1 cup water
1 medium pumpkin (about 7 pounds)
1 medium onion, chopped
¼ cup coconut aminos
2 cloves garlic, minced
1 tablespoon grated fresh ginger
1 teaspoon smoked paprika
1 teaspoon ground cumin
1 teaspoon curry powder
2 tablespoons coconut nectar
2 tablespoons nutritional yeast
2½ cups green tea or water
1½ cups coconut milk

Must Do

1. Preheat the oven to 375°F. Add the water to a 13 × 9-inch glass casserole dish.

2. Cut the top off the pumpkin and then cut it in half. Scrape out the seeds. Place the pumpkin halves, skin side down, in the prepared casserole dish. Bake until it is tender, about 60 minutes.

3. Transfer the casserole dish from the oven to a wire rack, and let it sit for about 15 minutes before removing the pumpkin skin. Cut the pumpkin into ½-inch cubes.

4. Heat the onion in a large pot over medium heat and stir until fragrant, about 1 minute.

5. Add the coconut aminos, garlic, ginger, smoked paprika, cumin, and curry powder and cook, stirring occasionally, until the spices become fragrant, about 2 minutes.

6. Add the pumpkin cubes, coconut nectar, and nutritional yeast, and stir to incorporate.

7. Add the green tea and coconut milk and bring to a boil.

8. Lower the heat, cover the pot, and let simmer until the pumpkin is tender, about 20 minutes.

9. Transfer the soup in batches to a high-speed blender and puree until smooth. You can also use an immersion blender.

10. Serve immediately.

SERVING SIZE: 2 CUPS
Calories 105; Total Fat 1.5g; Protein 3.4g; Cholesterol 0.0g; Sodium 200mg; Fiber 4.4g; Sugars 6.9g; Total Carbohydrate 23.0

Super Greens Soup

SERVES 4

This soup is immensely mellow and regenerative and will nourish your body and soothe your soul. As a matter of fact, when I first started to make this soup several years ago, it came out so good that I served it for a full week straight for dinner. No one could get enough of it. If you need to improvise with the "greens," by all means, do so. I hate to categorize this as a "detox" soup because it's so rich and delicious, but if you have splurged a little more than you'd like over a holiday or weekend, this soup is a great way to get back on course.

Must Have

SOUP
1 medium yellow onion, chopped
¼ cup coconut aminos
1 serrano pepper, chopped
3 cloves garlic, minced
½ teaspoon freshly ground black pepper
½ cup uncooked brown rice
2 tablespoons coconut nectar
1 medium parsnip, peeled and sliced
1 medium carrot, peeled and sliced
6 cups No-Sodium Vegetable Broth (page 25)
3 tablespoons nutritional yeast
2 cups baby spinach
2 cups stemmed and chopped kale
4 sprigs dill
4 chives

TOPPING
4 lemon wedges

Must Do

1. **To make the soup:** Heat the onion in a large pot over medium heat and stir until fragrant, about 1 minute.

2. Add the coconut aminos, serrano pepper, garlic, black pepper, brown rice, and coconut nectar and cook, stirring occasionally, until the spices become fragrant, about 2 minutes.

3. Add the parsnip and carrot, and stir to incorporate. Add the broth and nutritional yeast, and bring to a boil.

4. Lower the heat, cover the pot, and let the soup simmer until the vegetables are tender and the rice is cooked, about 20 minutes.

5. Add the spinach, kale, dill, and chives, and simmer for another 5 minutes.

6. Transfer the soup in batches to a high-speed blender and puree until smooth. You can also use an immersion blender.

7. Serve immediately and drizzle each serving with a squeeze of lemon.

SERVING SIZE: 2 CUPS
Calories 100; Total Fat 0.5g; Protein 4.0g; Cholesterol 0.0g; Sodium 200mg; Fiber 3.4g; Sugars 2.0g; Total Carbohydrate 15.0g

Carrot Bisque

SERVES 4

What do you do when you get a little over-zealous at the farmers' market or grocery store and buy a five-pound bag of organic carrots? You become a carrot ninja and blitz every dish with a hit of orange ammo. And that is how this dish came about, with all the relish and zeal of an enthu-siastic cook with extra root vegetables. I remember that my favorite soup used to be lobster bisque and was reminiscing to myself about all that wicked goodness, when I decided to sub in the carrots. And boy was that a revelation! One slurp of this bisque and I forgot all about that crusta-cean debauchery.

Must Have

SOUP

1 small yellow onion, chopped
¼ cup coconut aminos
2 cloves garlic, minced
2 teaspoons ground turmeric
1 teaspoon ground cumin
1 teaspoon curry powder
2 celery stalks, chopped
1 parsnip, peeled and sliced
10 medium carrots, peeled and sliced
¼ cup nutritional yeast
4 cups coconut milk

TOPPING

Freshly ground black pepper
Pumpkin seeds

Must Do

1. **To make the soup:** Heat the onion in a large pot over medium heat and stir until fragrant, about 1 minute.

2. Add the coconut aminos, garlic, turmeric, cumin, and curry powder and cook, stirring occasionally, until the spices become fragrant, about 2 minutes.

3. Add the celery, parsnip, carrots, and nutritional yeast, and stir to incorporate. Add the coconut milk and bring to a boil.

4. Lower the heat, cover the pot, and simmer the soup until the vegetables are tender, about 20 minutes.

5. Transfer the soup in batches to a high-speed blender and puree until smooth. You can also use an immersion blender.

6. Serve immediately with a grind of pepper.

SERVING SIZE: 2 CUPS
Calories 105; Total Fat 3.5g; Protein 4.3g;
Cholesterol 0.0g; Sodium 200mg; Fiber 5.4g;
Sugars 7.0g; Total Carbohydrate 17.0g

Spicy Tortilla Soup

SERVES 4

One day, out of the blue, my husband asked me to make him tortilla soup. I had never made it before, but as with all things related to food, I felt summoned to the task. And what I learned rather quickly about this soup is that you can destroy an entire house with an open can's worth of chopped tomatoes in their own natural juices. I won't go into the details of how I forgot to put the lid on the Vitamix, but having to paint my kitchen red afterward was a small price to pay after tasting this soul-satisfying, earthy, down-home fusion of flavors and spice.

Must Have

SOUP

1 jalapeño pepper, seeded and diced

1 small yellow onion, chopped

¼ cup coconut aminos

2 cloves garlic, minced

½ teaspoon chipotle chili powder

½ teaspoon ground cumin

½ teaspoon smoked paprika

¼ teaspoon freshly ground black pepper

2 tablespoons coconut nectar

1 small sweet potato, peeled and sliced

1 (28-ounce) can chopped tomatoes

1 cup No-Sodium Vegetable Broth (page 25)

1 cup coconut milk

½ cup chopped fresh cilantro

½ cup chopped baby bok choy

2 tablespoons freshly squeezed lime juice

TOPPINGS

Avocado cubes

Nutritional yeast

Lime wedges

Corn tortilla strips

Must Do

1. To make the soup: Heat the pepper and onion in a large pot over medium heat and stir until fragrant, about 1 minute.

2. Add the coconut aminos, garlic, chili powder, cumin, smoked paprika, black pepper, and coconut nectar and cook, stirring occasionally, until the spices become fragrant, about 2 minutes.

3. Add the sweet potato and stir to incorporate. Add the chopped tomatoes with their juice, the broth, and coconut milk, and bring to a boil.

4. Lower the heat, cover the pot, and simmer until the sweet potato is tender, about 20 minutes.

5. Transfer the soup in batches to a high-speed blender and puree until smooth. You can also use an immersion blender.

6. Pour the soup back into the pot and add the cilantro, bok choy, and lime juice. Stir to incorporate.

7. Serve immediately with the toppings of your choice.

SERVING SIZE: 2 CUPS

Calories 100; Total Fat 1.3g; Protein 1.2g; Cholesterol 0.0g; Sodium 200mg; Fiber 2.6g; Sugars 4.0g; Total Carbohydrate 15.0g

CREAMED KALE
(SEE RECIPE ON PAGE 92)

CHAPTER 6

Meals in Muffin Tins & Ramekins

There is something very comforting and cozy about mac cuddling up with cheeze in a round, pleated ramekin, and spinach and kale quiches being baked within the confines of a smooth 3-inch muffin tin. As a baker, I'm fond of doing this kind of thing, and preparing mini meals in this type of delivery system is very exciting for me. Of course, you can use these dishes as a side to a larger meal as well.

Eggplant Parmezan Florentine

SERVES 6

Before I was married, I used to make eggplant Parmesan for any boyfriend I wanted to bowl over with my virtuosic cooking skills. It worked. They loved my eggplant Parmesan because it was truly remarkable. And so was my mom's. Actually, she was the one who always made it. I was an imposter. Eventually I felt guilty for the deception, so I stopped serving it and started baking huge chocolate chip cookies with my boyfriends' names written in the middle with M&M's. When I moved west and had to start cooking for myself, I remembered my mom's eggplant Parmesan and re-created it with a vegan twist. I tested it out on a boyfriend back in 1999 and he eventually became my husband. I guess I got the recipe right.

Must Have

DIP
¾ cup coconut milk
¼ cup coconut aminos
1 recipe Parmezan (page 24), divided

EGGPLANT FLORENTINE
1 long, medium eggplant (about 1½ pounds), peeled and very thinly sliced

MARINARA SAUCE
1 small yellow onion, diced
½ cup coconut aminos
3 cloves garlic, minced
2 medium carrots, peeled and sliced
6 cremini mushrooms, sliced
2 teaspoons minced fresh parsley
1 teaspoon dried oregano
1 (28-ounce) can whole peeled tomatoes
½ teaspoon freshly ground black pepper
1 cup chopped baby spinach

Must Do

1. Preheat the oven to 325°F. Line two 15 × 13-inch baking sheets with parchment paper. Place six 8-ounce ramekins on a 15 × 10-inch baking sheet.

2. To make the dip: Whisk together the coconut milk and coconut aminos in a medium shallow dish.

3. Set aside ½ cup of the parmezan for the filling and topping. Place the rest in a shallow dish for the dredge.

4. To make the eggplant Florentine: Dunk each slice of eggplant into the dip and then dredge it in the parmezan. Place the eggplant slices in a single layer on the prepared baking sheets.

5. Bake the eggplant until very tender and a light golden brown, about 25 minutes.

6. Increase the oven temperature to 375°F.

7. To make the sauce: Heat the onion in a medium sauté pan over medium heat and stir until fragrant, about 1 minute.

8. Add the coconut aminos, garlic, carrots, mushrooms, parsley, and oregano and cook, stirring occasionally, until the spices and vegetables become fragrant, about 2 minutes.

Inside Scoop: I highly recommend using a mandoline to slice the eggplant as thinly and evenly as possible.

9. Add the tomatoes with their juice and the black pepper and bring to a boil. Lower the heat, cover the sauté pan, and simmer until the carrots are soft, about 15 minutes.

10. Transfer the sauce in batches to a high-speed blender and puree until smooth. You can also use an immersion blender.

11. Ladle about 2 tablespoons of the marinara in the bottom of each of the ramekins.

12. Add 2 or 3 slices of eggplant, a sprinkle of spinach, 2 more tablespoons of marinara, and 1 teaspoon of the reserved parmezan in each. Continue to layer until the

ramekins are filled to the top. Top each ramekin with the remaining parmezan, dividing it evenly.

13. Bake the eggplant until the edges and the parmezan turn a light golden brown, about 20 minutes.

14. Transfer the baking sheet from the oven to a wire rack and let sit for 10 minutes before serving.

SERVING SIZE: 1 RAMEKIN
Calories 65; Total Fat 0.8g; Protein 2.1g; Cholesterol 0.0g; Sodium 280mg; Fiber 2.6g; Sugars 3.9g; Total Carbohydrate 8.8g

Green Mac & Cheeze

SERVES 6

It doesn't have to be Saint Patrick's Day for you to make this festive green manna from nirvana. Spinach and basil add ridiculous amounts of nutrients, protective phytochemicals, and exquisite color, while the trifecta of sunflower seeds, hemp seeds, and nutritional yeast does an outstanding job impersonating cheese. The whole smoky, creamy, cheezy combination makes this one helluva healthy comfort food that is sure to please even the pickiest of eaters.

Must Have

MAC
8 ounces gluten-free spiral or elbow pasta

GREEN SAUCE
1 yellow onion, diced

¼ cup coconut aminos

2 cups baby spinach

½ cup fresh basil leaves

1 cup sunflower seeds, soaked in water for 2 hours at room temperature or overnight in the fridge and drained

¾ cup hemp seeds

¼ cup nutritional yeast

3 cloves garlic, minced

2 serrano peppers, seeded and diced

¼ cup freshly squeezed lemon juice

1 tablespoon coconut nectar

2 teaspoons liquid smoke

2 teaspoons smoked paprika

1 teaspoon spicy mustard

1 teaspoon ground turmeric

¼ teaspoon ground nutmeg

¼ teaspoon freshly ground black pepper

½ cup warm coconut milk

TOPPINGS
½ cup Parmezan (page 24)

Smoked paprika

Must Do

1. Preheat the oven to 350°F. Place six 8-ounce ramekins on a 15 × 10-inch baking sheet.

2. To make the macaroni: Cook the pasta according to the instructions on the package. Drain in a colander, rinse under cold water, and transfer to a large bowl.

3. To make the sauce: Heat the onion in a medium sauté pan over medium heat and stir until fragrant, about 1 minute. Add the coconut aminos and cook, stirring occasionally, until the onions are translucent, about 2 minutes. Turn off the heat.

4. Add the spinach, basil, sunflower seeds, hemp seeds, nutritional yeast, garlic, serrano peppers, lemon juice, coconut nectar, liquid smoke, smoked paprika, mustard, turmeric, nutmeg, and black pepper to a food processor and blend to combine. While the machine is still running, add the coconut milk, 1 tablespoon at a time, until the mixture is smooth and not too thick.

5. Add the green sauce to the cooked pasta and stir until thoroughly combined.

6. Add the sautéed onions and stir to incorporate.

7. Divide the mixture evenly among the ramekins. They should be full. Top each generously with the parmezan, dividing it evenly, and sprinkle with the smoked paprika.

8. Bake the mac & cheeze until the parmezan turns a light golden brown, about 15 minutes.

9. Transfer the baking sheet from the oven to a wire rack and let sit for 5 minutes before serving.

SERVING SIZE: 1 RAMEKIN

Calories 250; Total Fat 10.4g; Protein 13.6g; Cholesterol 0.0g; Sodium 180mg; Fiber 7.0g; Sugars 2.7g; Total Carbohydrate 38.2g

Inside Scoop: It's very important to soak the sunflower seeds for the time suggested, or the sauce will not be as smooth as it should be.

Veggie Lentil Enchilada Rounds

SERVES 6

It wasn't until my aunt visited from Chicago a few short years ago and suggested we make enchiladas that I realized I'd been living in the mecca of Mexican food for twenty years without eating one enchilada. Once I did, I was hooked. I eventually learned how to make enchiladas from scratch, and I decided it was safer to make them in individual servings lest I eat the entire casserole dish.

Must Have

CHEEZE SAUCE
¾ cup coconut milk
1 tablespoon tapioca flour
1 tablespoon cold water
½ cup nutritional yeast
¼ cup ground hemp seeds
1 teaspoon ground turmeric
¼ teaspoon smoked paprika

ENCHILADA SAUCE
1 shallot, diced
2 tablespoons coconut aminos
2 cloves garlic, minced
1 teaspoon chipotle chili powder
1 teaspoon cacao powder
½ teaspoon ground cumin
¼ teaspoon freshly ground black
    pepper
1 tablespoon coconut nectar
1 (15-ounce) can diced fire-
    roasted tomatoes
½ cup coconut milk

FILLING
4 cups water
1 cup red lentils
½ yellow onion, diced
¼ cup coconut aminos
1 teaspoon ground cumin
1 teaspoon garlic powder
1 teaspoon onion powder
¼ teaspoon chipotle chili powder
2 celery stalks, thinly sliced
1 cup dinosaur kale, stemmed
    and chopped
1 cup thinly sliced cremini
    mushrooms
6 gluten-free tortillas

Must Do

1. Preheat the oven to 350°F. Place six 8-ounce ramekins on a 15 × 10-inch baking sheet.

2. To make the cheeze sauce: Heat the coconut milk in a small pot over medium heat. Combine the tapioca flour and cold water in a small bowl, and stir until a paste forms. Whisk this mixture into the pot. Doing it this way helps prevent lumps. Keep stirring every few minutes until the sauce thickens and bubbles.

3. Add the nutritional yeast, hemp seeds, turmeric, and smoked paprika, and stir until smooth, adding more coconut milk if the sauce is too thick.

4. To make the enchilada sauce: Heat the shallot in a medium pot over medium heat and stir until fragrant, about 1 minute.

5. Add the coconut aminos, garlic, chipotle chili powder, cacao, cumin, and black pepper and cook, stirring occasionally, until the spices become fragrant, about 2 minutes.

6. Add the coconut nectar, tomatoes with their juice, and coconut milk, and bring to a boil. Lower the heat, cover the pot, and simmer until the sauce thickens, about 15 minutes.

7. Transfer the sauce in batches to a high-speed blender and puree until smooth. You can also use an immersion blender.

8. To make the filling: Add the water and lentils to a medium pot over high heat and bring to a boil. Lower the heat and let simmer until all the water is absorbed and the lentils are mushy, about 15 minutes.

9. Add the onion to a medium sauté pan over medium heat and stir until fragrant, about 1 minute.

10. Add the coconut aminos, cumin, garlic powder, onion powder, and chipotle chili powder to the onion and cook, stirring occasionally, until the spices become fragrant, about 2 minutes.

11. Add the celery, kale, and mushrooms, and cook until the vegetables are slightly tender, about 2 minutes. Add the cooked lentils to the sauté pan and stir to incorporate.

12. Take each tortilla and cut out 3 rounds from each, using a biscuit cutter, so that you have 18 mini tortillas.

13. Ladle about 2 tablespoons of the enchilada sauce in the bottom of each of the ramekins and then add a tortilla round. Add about ¼ cup of the filling to each ramekin and then about 2 tablespoons each of the enchilada sauce and cheeze sauce.

14. Continue to layer until you have 2 layers of filling and sauce and 3 mini tortillas in each ramekin. Top each filled ramekin with more enchilada sauce and then top with the cheeze sauce.

15. Bake the enchilada rounds until the edges turn a light golden brown, about 20 minutes.

16. Transfer the baking sheet from the oven to a wire rack, and let it sit for 5 minutes before serving.

SERVING SIZE: 1 RAMEKIN
Calories 135; Total Fat 4.5g; Protein 9.9g; Cholesterol 0.0g; Sodium 250mg; Fiber 6.4g; Sugars 2.3g; Total Carbohydrate 17.2g

Pot Pie Primavera

SERVES 6

Any recipe with the words *pot* and *pie* is analogous to a culinary security blanket. That's how I feel about this pot pie primavera. It oozes all the warmth and coziness you crave from home cooking, and it is chock-full of spice, flavor, and sustentative deliciousness. I know some people are intimidated by making their own doughs or crusts, but this one is a breeze to put together in the food processor. And once you throw in the filling and bake it all up, these are easy to freeze and reheat, so you have a quick and satisfying meal all set and waiting when you need it.

Must Have

CRUST

1 (15-ounce) can cannellini beans, rinsed and drained
1 cup sorghum flour
1 cup tapioca flour
¼ teaspoon sea salt
6 tablespoons coconut milk

FILLING

1 small sweet onion, diced
¼ cup coconut aminos
1 small (2-pound) butternut squash, peeled, seeded, and chopped into ½-inch pieces
1 clove garlic, minced
4 celery stalks, diced
2 medium carrots, peeled and diced
Corn kernels freshly cut from 1 cob
12 cremini mushrooms, chopped
2 teaspoons smoked paprika
1½ cups No-Sodium Vegetable Broth (page 25)
2 tablespoons tapioca flour
2 tablespoons cold water
½ cup coconut milk
7 kale leaves, stemmed and chopped
½ teaspoon freshly ground black pepper

GLAZE

¼ cup Grade B maple syrup
1 tablespoon nutritional yeast

Must Do

1. Preheat the oven to 375°F. Place six 8-ounce ramekins on a 15 × 10-inch baking sheet.

2. **To make the crust:** Add the beans to a food processor and blend until smooth. Add the sorghum flour, tapioca flour, and salt, and pulse until the dough starts to look crumbled. Add the coconut milk, 1 tablespoon at a time, and pulse until the dough comes together.

3. Take the dough out of the food processor, form it into a disk, wrap it in plastic, and place it in the refrigerator for 30 minutes.

4. **To make the filling:** Heat the onion in a medium sauté pan over medium heat and stir until fragrant, about 1 minute.

5. Add the coconut aminos, butternut squash, garlic, celery, carrots, corn, mushrooms, and smoked paprika and cook, stirring occasionally, until the spices become fragrant, about 2 minutes. Add the vegetable broth and stir to combine.

6. Combine the tapioca flour and cold water in a bowl and stir until a paste forms. Whisk this mixture into the sauté pan. This helps prevent lumps. Add the coconut milk and simmer for 5 minutes, stirring occasionally.

7. Add the kale and pepper, and cook until the kale softens and turns bright green, about 2 minutes.

8. Take the dough out of the refrigerator, place it on a lightly floured piece of parchment paper, and place another piece of parchment on top of the dough. Roll out the dough until it is a little less than ¼ inch thick. Remove the top piece of parchment.

9. Place each ramekin upside down on top of the dough and cut around it, adding about a ½ inch for the overhang. Reuse any scraps of dough by rolling them out again and cutting out more circles until you have 6 all together.

10. Add the filling to each of the ramekins almost to the top, dividing it evenly.

11. Place the circles of dough over each ramekin and pinch around the perimeter to seal. Crimp the edges with a fork and make 4 little slits on top with a paring knife.

12. To make the glaze: Whisk together the maple syrup and the nutritional yeast in a small bowl. Brush the tops of each pie.

13. Bake the pot pies until the crusts turn a light golden brown, about 25 minutes.

14. Transfer the baking sheet from the oven to a wire rack, and let it sit for 10 minutes before serving.

SERVING SIZE: 1 RAMEKIN
Calories 400; Total Fat 10.5g; Protein 11.9g; Cholesterol 0.0g; Sodium 280mg; Fiber 13.4g; Sugars 4.4g; Total Carbohydrate 48.2g

Creamy Pumpkin & Mushroom Stuffing Rounds

SERVES 6

My favorite part of Thanksgiving dinner is, hands down, the stuffing. I don't think I'm alone on this. But the thing is, if someone passes me the stuffing, I'm bound to unload the entire contents of the casserole dish onto my plate. No joke. I have no self-control. See my banana bread story (page 208). That's why I created these individualized jumbo stuffing mounds—so I can have a mountain of stuffing all to myself. And to tell you the truth, if that's all I have for Thanksgiving, that's okay, because I've managed to cram every imaginable element of the Thanksgiving table into them, from the mushrooms to the pumpkin puree and the spices to go along with it. So, even if there's nothing else for you to eat at the T-table, I've got you covered.

Must Have

6 cups gluten-free bread cubes
1 shallot, minced
½ cup coconut aminos
4 cups sliced cremini mushrooms (about 1 pound)
2 cups diced celery
3 cloves garlic, minced
1 teaspoon grated fresh ginger
2 teaspoons dried thyme
1 teaspoon smoked paprika
1 teaspoon ground cumin
½ teaspoon ground cinnamon
½ teaspoon ground nutmeg
¾ cup pumpkin puree
1 tablespoon coconut nectar
2 cups coconut milk

SERVING SIZE: 1 RAMEKIN
Calories 120; Total Fat 2.7g; Protein 3.2g; Cholesterol 0.0g; Sodium 180mg; Fiber 3.3g; Sugars 3.8g; Total Carbohydrate 20.2g

Must Do

1. Preheat the oven to 400°F. Line a 15 × 13-inch baking sheet with parchment paper. Place six 8-ounce ramekins on a 15 × 10-inch baking sheet.

2. Spread the bread cubes evenly across the prepared 15 × 13-inch baking sheet and bake until the cubes are toasted, about 15 minutes.

3. Lower the oven temperature to 350°F.

4. Heat the shallot in a medium sauté pan over medium heat and stir until fragrant, about 1 minute.

5. Add the coconut aminos, mushrooms, celery, garlic, ginger, thyme, smoked paprika, cumin, cinnamon, and nutmeg and cook, stirring occasionally, until the spices are fragrant and the vegetables are tender, about 3 minutes.

6. Add the pumpkin puree, coconut nectar, and toasted bread cubes and stir to combine. Add 1 cup of the coconut milk, wait for it to be absorbed, about 3 minutes, and then add the second cup and stir. Cook until most of the liquid is absorbed.

7. Divide the stuffing evenly among the 6 ramekins. Each cup should be completely full. Bake the stuffing mounds until they are crispy on top, about 20 minutes.

8. Transfer the baking sheet from the oven to a wire rack and let sit for 10 minutes before serving.

Inside Scoop: I use my Challah (page 214) or Kalamata Rosemary Rustic Boule (page 216) for the bread cubes, but any thick, gluten-free bread will do.

Asian Fusion Noodle Kugel

SERVES 6

It's written in ancient texts that Jews originally from New York have to dine on Asian cuisine at least once a week, and it should be Sunday. At least this was the custom at my house. So I thought how fun it would be to add Asian accents to a traditional Jewish comfort food that my mother used to serve, called noodle kugel, also known as noodle pudding. It turns out that the addition of ginger, miso, and bok choy takes this carbed-out kugel to a whole new level. It's a match made in gastronomic heaven. And now my mom won't make it any other way. Only on Sundays, of course.

Must Have

KUGEL

1 (13-ounce) package bow tie or any shape gluten-free noodles
1 shallot, finely chopped
2 tablespoons coconut aminos
1 cup finely chopped baby bok choy, green parts only
1 cup chopped cremini mushrooms

SAUCE

¼ cup chickpea miso paste
¼ cup canned cannellini beans
¼ cup coconut aminos
¼ cup pumpkin puree
3 tablespoons chia seeds, ground (I use a coffee grinder)
2 tablespoons Grade B maple syrup
2 teaspoons grated fresh ginger
¼ cup water

Must Do

1. Preheat the oven to 350°F. Place six 8-ounce ramekins on a 15 × 10-inch baking sheet.

2. To make the kugel: Cook the noodles according to the package directions. Drain the noodles in a colander and rinse under cold water.

3. Heat the shallot in a medium sauté pan over medium heat and stir until fragrant, about 1 minute.

4. Add the coconut aminos, bok choy, and cremini mushrooms and cook, stirring occasionally, until the vegetables are slightly tender, about 2 minutes.

5. To make the sauce: Add the miso, cannellini beans, coconut aminos, pumpkin, chia seeds, maple syrup, and ginger to a food processor. Pulse just until the mixture comes together. While the machine is running, slowly add the water, 1 tablespoon at a time, until the sauce is fluid and smooth.

6. Pour the sauce into the sauté pan and add the cooked noodles. Stir to incorporate.

7. Spoon the mixture into the ramekins, dividing it evenly. They should be completely full.

8. Bake the kugels until the edges are a light golden brown, about 20 minutes.

9. Transfer the baking sheet from the oven to a wire rack, and let it sit for 10 minutes before serving.

SERVING SIZE: 1 RAMEKIN
Calories 280; Total Fat 2.5g; Protein 10.1g; Cholesterol 0.0g; Sodium 180mg; Fiber 3.7g; Sugars 3.6g; Total Carbohydrate 54.3g

Spaghetti Piccata Twirls

MAKES 12 PICCATA TWIRLS

I would take a bet that chicken piccata is one of the most beloved items on an Italian restaurant menu. And from what I remember, it is usually served with spaghetti. Since I nixed chicken from my diet many years ago, I thought it would be fun to just keep the piccata spaghetti. You get all the lemony, buttery, and caper-y goodness of this exquisite dish without sacrifice. Yes, I did say buttery, and somehow this is. Don't ask me how or why. *Mangia!*

Must Have

SPAGHETTI PICCATA
8 ounces gluten-free spaghetti
1 small yellow onion, finely
    chopped
2 tablespoons coconut aminos
½ cup chopped cremini
    mushrooms
½ cup chopped cherry tomatoes,
    seeds squeezed out
3 tablespoons freshly squeezed
    lemon juice
2 tablespoons capers
2 tablespoons chopped fresh
    parsley
2 tablespoons nutritional yeast
1 tablespoon coconut nectar
1 cup No-Sodium Vegetable
    Broth (page 25)

TOPPING
¼ cup chopped fresh parsley

Must Do

1. Preheat the oven to 375°F. Line a standard 12-cup muffin tin with paper baking cups.

2. To make the spaghetti piccata: Cook the spaghetti according to the package instructions. Drain the spaghetti in a colander and rinse under cold water.

3. Heat the onion in a medium sauté pan over medium heat and stir until fragrant, about 1 minute.

4. Add the coconut aminos, mushrooms, tomatoes, lemon juice, capers, parsley, and nutritional yeast and cook, stirring occasionally, until the vegetables are fragrant, about 2 minutes.

5. Add the coconut nectar and broth, and bring to a boil.

6. Lower the heat, cover the sauté pan, and let simmer until the liquid cooks down, about 5 minutes.

7. Add the cooked spaghetti and stir to incorporate.

8. Transfer the spaghetti with a fork, so you can twirl it into the muffin tins, dividing it evenly. Each well should be completely full.

9. Bake until the top layer of spaghetti is crispy and a light golden brown, about 15 minutes.

10. Transfer the muffin tin from the oven to a wire rack, and let it sit for 15 minutes, until the spaghetti cools. This helps get the spaghetti out of the liners cleanly.

11. Peel off the paper liners, top with the parsley, and serve.

SERVING SIZE: 1 SPAGHETTI TWIRL
Calories 90; Total Fat 0.5g; Protein 3.1g; Cholesterol 0.0g;
Sodium 70mg; Fiber 1.7g; Sugars 3.3g; Total Carbohydrate 18.5g

Inside Scoop: If you can't find hemp tofu and can tolerate soy, firm tofu is a good substitute.

Spicy Spinach & Kale Quiche

MAKES 12 QUICHES

No one will miss the crust on this exquisite, easy-to-make quiche. All you need to do is take one bite to experience the fullness of flavors and the pudding-like consistency. I couldn't decide whether to make it spinach or kale, so I went with both and really love the combo. It's like supersized micronutrients in a happier meal. This is so good that I think you'll be able to convert the real men in your life into quiche eaters.

Must Have

1 small yellow onion, diced
¼ cup coconut aminos
1 clove garlic, minced
1 jalapeño pepper, seeded and chopped
1 teaspoon freshly ground black pepper
½ teaspoon ground nutmeg
2 tablespoons Grade B maple syrup
1 (8-ounce) package hemp tofu
¼ cup nutritional yeast
¼ cup roughly chopped fresh parsley
¼ cup roughly chopped fresh dill
3 tablespoons chia seeds, ground (I use a coffee grinder)
3 tablespoons chickpea miso paste
6 cups fresh baby spinach
8 ounces kale, stemmed and chopped
3 tablespoons freshly squeezed lemon juice
¼ cup coconut milk

Must Do

1. Preheat the oven to 350°F. Line a standard 12-cup muffin tin with paper baking cups.

2. Heat the onion in a medium sauté pan over medium heat and stir until fragrant, about 1 minute.

3. Add the coconut aminos, garlic, jalapeño pepper, black pepper, and nutmeg and cook, stirring occasionally, until the onion is translucent and the spices become fragrant, about 2 minutes.

4. Add the maple syrup, hemp tofu, nutritional yeast, parsley, dill, chia seeds, miso, spinach, and kale and cook, stirring, until the vegetables turn bright green, about 1 minute.

5. Add the vegetable mixture and lemon juice to a food processor and pulse until combined.

6. While the machine is still running, add the coconut milk, 1 tablespoon at a time, until the vegetable mixture is combined but still has some texture. You might not need the full ¼ cup.

7. Spoon the vegetable mixture into the prepared muffin cups, dividing it evenly. Each cup should be filled to the top.

8. Bake the quiches until the edges are a light golden brown, about 25 minutes.

9. Transfer the muffin tin from the oven to a wire rack and let sit for 15 minutes before removing the quiches. Peel off the paper liners and serve warm or at room temperature.

SERVING SIZE: 1 QUICHE
Calories 55; Total Fat 1.1g; Protein 2.9g; Cholesterol 0.0g; Sodium 90mg; Fiber 1.7g; Sugars 2.1g; Total Carbohydrate 6.0g

Creamed Kale

SERVES 6

My favorite side dish of all time is creamed spinach. But because I have a habit of upsetting the status quo, I decided to use kale for this recipe. It's just as pleasing to the palate in every respect. The nutritional yeast adds the suggestion of cheesy ambience, while the dill heightens the aromatic complexity. It comes together so perfectly in one silky-smooth, green, creamy feast.

Must Have

CREAMED KALE

1 shallot, diced
2 tablespoons tapioca flour
2 tablespoons cold water
½ cup coconut aminos
2 cups coconut milk
1 tablespoon coconut nectar
¼ cup nutritional yeast
3 tablespoons finely chopped
  fresh dill
1 teaspoon garlic powder
½ teaspoon freshly ground black
  pepper
½ teaspoon ground nutmeg
1½ pounds kale, stemmed and
  finely chopped

TOPPING
⅓ cup Parmezan (page 24)

Must Do

1. Preheat the oven to 350°F. Place six 6-ounce ramekins on a 15 × 10-inch baking sheet.

2. To make the creamed kale: Heat the shallot in a medium sauté pan over medium heat and stir until fragrant, about 1 minute.

3. Add the tapioca flour to the cold water in a small bowl and stir until a paste forms.

4. Add the coconut aminos, tapioca flour mixture, and coconut milk to the sauté pan and stir until the tapioca flour completely dissolves, about 30 seconds.

5. Add the coconut nectar, nutritional yeast, dill, garlic powder, black pepper, and nutmeg and cook, stirring occasionally, until the spices become fragrant, about 2 minutes.

6. Keep stirring until the mixture begins to thicken, about 1 minute.

7. Add the kale and stir to incorporate.

8. Divide the mixture evenly among the ramekins, filling them to the top.

9. Sprinkle the parmezan evenly among the ramekins, completely covering the kale mixture.

10. Bake until the edges of the topping turn a light golden brown, about 15 minutes.

11. Transfer the baking sheet from the oven to a wire rack and let sit for a few minutes before serving.

SERVING SIZE: 1 RAMEKIN

Calories 75; Total Fat 2.2g; Protein 5.0g; Cholesterol 0.0g; Sodium 180mg; Fiber 3.5g; Sugars 4.1g; Total Carbohydrate 11.2g

Herb-Stuffed Grape Leaves Casserole with Mushroom Béchamel

SERVES 6

I might have just adulterated an innocent, well-meaning Middle Eastern dish, but I felt a different format and flavor were in order for this very popular stuffed vegetable. As you may know by now, I like making things in ramekins, and this one is no different. I add a dreamy, creamy béchamel to cuddle with the wild rice–stuffed dolma and the results are spectacular. I love the casserole aspect and the fact that I don't have to roll hundreds of grape leaves to get dinner on the table.

Must Have

GRAPE LEAVES
18 grape leaves

FILLING
1 cup millet
2 cups water
½ cup coconut aminos
¼ cup finely chopped fresh parsley
¼ cup finely chopped fresh dill
¼ cup finely chopped fresh mint
¼ cup freshly squeezed lemon juice

MUSHROOM BÉCHAMEL
1 small yellow onion, diced
¼ cup coconut aminos
½ cup All-Purpose Gluten-Free Flour Mix (page 20)
4 cloves garlic, minced
4 cups chopped cremini mushrooms (about 1 pound)
2 cups coconut milk
1 teaspoon dried dill
1 teaspoon dried thyme
1 teaspoon dried oregano

TOPPING
½ teaspoon freshly ground black pepper
¼ cup roasted pumpkin seeds

Must Do

1. Preheat the oven to 350°F. Place six 8-ounce ramekins on a 15 × 10-inch baking sheet.

2. To prepare the grape leaves: Add the grape leaves to a medium pot of boiling water, cover the pot, lower the heat, and simmer until the grape leaves soften, about 2 minutes. Drain the grape leaves in a colander, rinse under cold water, and pat dry.

3. To make the filling: Toast the millet in a medium pot over high heat until fragrant, about 1 minute.

4. Add the water and bring to a boil. Lower the heat, cover the pot, and let simmer until all the water is absorbed, about 20 minutes.

5. After the millet is cooked, add the coconut aminos, parsley, dill, mint, and lemon juice, and stir to combine.

6. To make the béchamel: Add the onion to a medium sauté pan over medium heat and stir until fragrant, about 1 minute.

7. Add the coconut aminos and flour, and stir until a paste forms. Add the garlic, mushrooms, and coconut milk and cook, stirring occasionally, until the mushrooms are tender and the sauce thickens, about 3 minutes.

8. Add the dill, thyme, and oregano, and stir to incorporate. Turn off the heat.

9. Place a large grape leaf in the bottom of each of the prepared ramekins.

10. Add about ¼ cup of the millet mixture to each ramekin and fold over the excess portion of the grape leaf. Add 2 tablespoons of the béchamel. Repeat the layers one more time, using up the remaining filling. Top with a last grape leaf and the remaining béchamel.

11. Bake until the béchamel is a light golden brown, about 15 minutes.

12. Transfer the baking sheet from the oven to a wire rack, and let it sit for 10 minutes before serving.

13. Top each ramekin with a grind of freshly ground black pepper and the roasted pumpkin seeds.

SERVING SIZE: 1 RAMEKIN
Calories 100; Total Fat 1.5g; Protein 3.0g; Cholesterol 0.0g; Sodium 250mg; Fiber 2.5g; Sugars 0.9g; Total Carbohydrate 15.5g

Inside Scoop: An alternative to using the whole grape leaf to line the ramekins is to cut the leaves into strips with kitchen shears and layer them in the ramekins. This makes it easier to eat the casserole without using a knife.

Cannellini Cupcakes with Whipped Parsnip

MAKES 12 STANDARD-SIZE CUPCAKES

It's not often you can eat a cupcake for dinner and feel good about it. I got the idea to do a savory cupcake a few years back, but wasn't sure what kind to make. I decided to try a variety of different flavors ranging from lentil to mashed potato. As I do with my dinner parties (see introduction), I conducted a randomized, double-blind, placebo-controlled study, the "gold standard" in medical research. I would expect nothing less in a study of cupcakes. The participants were all healthy at the beginning of this trial. They were given a variety of the savory flavors I developed. The outcome of the study determined unequivocally that the favorite among them all was the Cannellini with Whipped Parsnip.

Must Have

CANNELLINI CUPCAKES

1 medium sweet potato (about 4 ounces)
1 small yellow onion, chopped
½ cup coconut aminos
½ teaspoon ground cumin
½ teaspoon ground turmeric
2 celery stalks, chopped
2 medium carrots, peeled and chopped
¾ cup gluten-free oats
1 cup water
1 (15-ounce) can cannellini beans, rinsed and drained
¼ cup Kalamata olives, pitted and chopped

WHIPPED PARSNIP

2 medium parsnips, peeled and sliced (about 8 ounces)
¼ cup coconut aminos
1 cup coconut milk
2 cloves garlic, minced
2 tablespoons onion powder
1 tablespoon nutritional yeast
1 teaspoon dried thyme

TOPPING

3 tablespoons finely chopped fresh parsley
1 teaspoon freshly ground black pepper

Must Do

1. Preheat the oven to 350°F. Line a standard 12-cup muffin tin with paper baking cups.

2. **To make the cannellini cupcakes:** Add the sweet potato to a small pot of boiling water, cover the pot, lower the heat, and cook until it is fork tender, about 10 minutes. Drain. Once the potato cools slightly, peel it and slice it into rounds.

3. Heat the onion in a medium sauté pan over medium heat and stir until fragrant, about 1 minute.

4. Add the coconut aminos, cumin, turmeric, sweet potato, celery, carrots, oats, and water and cook, stirring occasionally, until the vegetables are tender, the spices are fragrant, and the water is absorbed, about 10 minutes.

5. Transfer the vegetable mixture to a food processor and add the cannellini beans and olives. Pulse to combine until the mixture comes together but still has texture.

6. Spoon the mixture into the prepared muffin cups, dividing it evenly. Each cup should be almost full.

7. Bake the cupcakes until they are a light golden brown around the edges, about 15 minutes.

8. Transfer the muffin tin from the oven to a wire rack, and let it sit for 15 minutes before removing the baking cup liners.

9. To make the whipped parsnip: Add the parsnips, coconut aminos, coconut milk, garlic, onion powder, nutritional yeast, and thyme to a sauté pan over medium heat and bring to a boil. Lower the heat, cover with a lid, and let simmer until the parsnips are tender, about 8 minutes.

10. Transfer the parsnip mixture to a food processor and puree until smooth.

11. Frost the cannellini cupcakes with the whipped parsnip, and top with the parsley and pepper.

SERVING SIZE: 1 CANNELLINI CUPCAKE
Calories 70; Total Fat 2.1g; Protein 1.9g; Cholesterol 0.0g; Sodium 200mg; Fiber 2.1g; Sugars 1.0g; Total Carbohydrate 11.2g

Broccolini Tarts

SERVES 6

These easy-to-make tarts are the perfect crowd-pleasers for parties or brunch, or as quaint little snacks just for yourself. I've always been more of a pesto person than a marinara one, and these tarts bring out the best that pesto has to offer. Broccolini is just another term for baby broccoli, and it gives you all the nutritional benefits big mamma broccoli has to offer, including an alphabet's worth of vitamins, minerals, flavonoids, and antioxidants.

Must Have

PESTO SAUCE
¾ cup hemp seeds
2 cups fresh basil
¼ cup freshly squeezed lemon juice
1 clove garlic, minced
1 tablespoon Grade B maple syrup
½ teaspoon fine sea salt
¼ cup water
½ teaspoon red pepper flakes
¼ teaspoon freshly ground black pepper

CRUST
1¼ cups sorghum flour
¾ cup tapioca flour
¼ cup sunflower seeds, ground (I use a coffee grinder)
¼ cup mashed avocado
¾ cup water

RICOTTA CHEEZE
1 (8-ounce) package hemp tofu
¼ cup nutritional yeast
1 teaspoon freshly squeezed lemon juice
1 teaspoon garlic powder
1 teaspoon dried basil
½ teaspoon onion powder
½ teaspoon black pepper

FILLING
1 shallot, diced
¼ cup coconut aminos
5 cups chopped broccolini (about 2 pounds)

2 tablespoons coconut aminos

Must Do

1. Preheat the oven to 350°F. Place six 6-ounce ramekins on a 15 × 10-inch baking sheet.

2. To make the pesto: Place the hemp seeds, basil, lemon juice, garlic, maple syrup, and salt in a food processor and pulse until the mixture comes together.

3. With the motor running, add the water, 1 tablespoon at a time, until the pesto is smooth and not too thick.

4. Add the red pepper flakes and the black pepper, and pulse to combine.

5. To make the crust: Whisk together the sorghum flour, tapioca flour, and ground sunflower seeds in a large bowl. Make a well in the middle.

6. Add the mashed avocado and water, and stir to combine until a dough forms.

7. Roll out the dough on a lightly floured piece of parchment paper with another piece of parchment on top until it is about ¼ inch thick. Remove the top piece of parchment.

8. Place each ramekin upside down on top of the dough and cut around it, adding about a ½ inch for the overhang. Do this until you have 12 circles. Reuse any scraps of dough by rolling them out again and cutting out more circles.

9. Place 6 of the dough circles in the bottom of the ramekins and press in and around the sides as far up as you can go.

10. To make the ricotta: Place the tofu, nutritional yeast, lemon juice, garlic powder, basil, onion powder, and black pepper in a food processor and pulse until the mixture comes together.

11. To make the filling: Heat the shallot in a medium sauté pan over medium heat and stir until fragrant, about 1 minute.

12. Add the coconut aminos and broccolini and cook, stirring, until the broccolini turns bright green, about 2 minutes. Turn off the heat.

13. To assemble the tarts, mix together the pesto sauce, ricotta, and broccolini in a medium bowl. Add the mixture to the prepared ramekins, dividing it evenly.

14. Place the remaining circles of dough over each ramekin and pinch around the perimeter to seal. Crimp the edges with a fork and, with a paring knife, make 4 little slits on top.

15. Brush the tops of each tart with the the coconut aminos.

16. Bake the tarts until the dough turns a light golden brown, about 20 minutes.

17. Transfer the baking sheet from the oven to a wire rack, and let it sit for 5 minutes before serving.

SERVING SIZE: 1 RAMEKIN
Calories 290; Total Fat 10.0g; Protein 13.6g; Cholesterol 0.0g; Sodium 180mg; Fiber 7.4g; Sugars 2.7g; Total Carbohydrate 39.0g

Inside Scoop: If you can't find hemp tofu and can tolerate soy, firm tofu is a good substitute.

Sunflower Butter, Raisin & Chocolate Chip Oatmeal Cups

MAKES 12 OATMEAL CUPS

I always feel like the biggest mommy loser if I don't make my son a green smoothie in the morning followed by a bowl of hot oatmeal. All this mom guilt and desperation led me to create these adorable oatmeal cups. You just make them over the weekend, store them in the freezer in an airtight container, and then warm them up on demand. They are also portable, so you can even carry them in your purse, still frozen, and, once they defrost, give them to your kids as a snack at the park or on a road trip. They are so powerfully packed with wholesome nourishment, fiber, and natural sweetness that you can tell that mommy guilt trip to go take a hike.

Must Have

OATMEAL CUPS

3 cups gluten-free oats

3 tablespoons chia seeds, ground (I use a coffee grinder)

2 tablespoons All-Purpose Gluten-Free Flour Mix (page 20)

2 teaspoons sodium-free baking powder

2 teaspoons ground cinnamon

⅜ teaspoon stevia powder

¼ teaspoon sea salt

1 cup coconut milk

¼ cup applesauce

¼ cup coconut nectar

¼ cup Sunflower Seed Butter (page 20)

¼ cup pumpkin puree

2 teaspoons gluten-free vanilla extract

¼ cup raisins

TOPPINGS

¼ cup sugar-free, dairy-free chocolate chips (I use Lily's brand; see Resources)

Must Do

1. Preheat the oven to 350°F. Line a standard 12-cup muffin tin with paper baking cups.

2. To make the oatmeal cups: Whisk together the oats, chia seeds, flour, baking powder, cinnamon, stevia, and salt in a large bowl. Make a well in the middle.

3. Add the coconut milk, applesauce, coconut nectar, sunflower seed butter, pumpkin, and vanilla and stir to combine. Fold in the raisins.

4. Pour the batter into the prepared muffin cups, dividing it evenly. Each cup should be about two-thirds full. Top with the chocolate chips.

5. Bake the oatmeal cups until the oats are a light golden brown, about 20 minutes.

6. Transfer the muffin tin from the oven to a wire rack, and let sit for 10 minutes before removing the oatmeal cups.

7. You can store these in an airtight container in the freezer for up to 3 months.

SERVING SIZE: 1 OATMEAL CUP

Calories 150; Total Fat 5.0g; Protein 4.1g; Cholesterol 0.0g; Sodium 50mg; Fiber 3.4g; Sugars 6.3g; Total Carbohydrate 23.2g

MARGHERITA PIZZA WHEELS
(SEE RECIPE ON PAGE 112)

CHAPTER 7

Pizza, Pasta, Rice & Noodles

I can't think of any downside to linguini, Arborio rice, or ramen other than I become a weapon of massive consumption when these soft, chewy carbs are put on a plate in front of me. To counter the blow of this potentially dangerous caloric intake, I usually stuff a lot of vegetables, mushrooms, and seeds into these types of dishes. The meals not only have fewer calories this way, but they are also more filling and satisfying, with a variety of fiber, crunch, and texture.

The Ultimate Veggie Pad Thai

SERVES 8

My introduction to Thai food many years ago was pad thai. What better way to familiarize yourself with the edible vernacular of an ethnic cuisine than with their most popular noodle dish? Pad thai is so easy to add vegetables to, and it doesn't even matter which ones. It is accepting of produce from all walks of life. So go to town, have fun, and feel free to improvise when need be.

Must Have

NOODLES
1 (8-ounce) package brown rice pad thai noodles

SAUCE
¾ cup Sunflower Seed Butter (page 20)
½ cup coconut aminos
¼ cup mirin (Japanese rice cooking wine)
¼ cup rice vinegar
1 tablespoon grated fresh ginger
1 teaspoon red pepper flakes

VEGGIES
½ cup chopped scallions, divided
¼ cup coconut aminos
3 cloves garlic, minced
1 jalapeño, seeded and minced
1 teaspoon red pepper flakes
1 tablespoon coconut nectar
1 cup shredded baby bok choy
1 carrot, peeled and finely shredded
1 cup shredded red cabbage
1 cup chopped string beans
1 cup chopped fresh cilantro, divided
¼ cup freshly squeezed lime juice

Must Do

1. **To make the noodles:** Cook the pad thai noodles according to the package instructions. Drain the noodles in a colander and rinse under cold water.

2. **To make the sauce:** Mix together the sunflower seed butter, coconut aminos, mirin, rice vinegar, ginger, and red pepper flakes in a small bowl.

3. **To make the veggies:** Add ¼ cup of the chopped scallions to a medium sauté pan over medium heat and stir until fragrant, about 1 minute.

4. Add the coconut aminos, garlic, jalapeño, and red pepper flakes and cook, stirring occasionally, until the spices become fragrant, about 2 minutes.

5. Add the coconut nectar, baby bok choy, carrot, red cabbage, and string beans, and cook until the vegetables become tender, about 4 minutes. Add ½ cup of the cilantro and stir to incorporate.

6. Add the lime juice, sauce, and noodles, and stir to combine. Top with the remaining ¼ cup scallions and ½ cup cilantro and serve.

SERVING SIZE: 1 CUP

Calories 150; Total Fat 7.5g; Protein 4.1g; Cholesterol 0.0g; Sodium 200mg; Fiber 1.7g; Sugars 1.3g; Total Carbohydrate 15.5g

It's All Greek to Me Pizza

SERVES 6

What I love most when coming up with recipes is combining ethnic foods in new and surprising ways. And so it is with this one. I gathered all foods Grecian, marched them front and center into Italian territory, and came out victorious with a Big Fat Greek Pizza. And the best part is everyone gets along so well. The olives, onions, spinach, feta, and cherry tomatoes get all aromatic and spicy with the oregano and red pepper flakes. And they sit together so comfortable and cozy in the chewy and crisp crust. It was meant to be all along.

Must Have

CRUST
1 cup warm water, about 108°F
  (I microwave for 30 seconds)
1 (2¼-teaspoon) packet active
  dry yeast
1 tablespoon coconut nectar
1½ cups sorghum flour
¾ cup tapioca flour
½ cup amaranth flour
½ teaspoon xanthan gum
⅛ teaspoon sea salt
1 tablespoon applesauce

FETA CHEEZE
4 ounces hemp tofu, cubed
¼ cup apple cider vinegar
¼ cup freshly squeezed lemon
  juice
1 tablespoon dried oregano
1 tablespoon dried thyme

OTHER GREEK TOPPINGS
1 small red onion, thinly sliced
  into rings
2 cups sliced cherry tomatoes
1 cup chopped spinach
½ cup pitted and chopped
  Kalamata olives
2 tablespoons nutritional yeast
1 tablespoon dried oregano
2 teaspoons red pepper flakes

GLAZE
2 tablespoons molasses
1 tablespoon water
1 tablespoon nutritional yeast

Must Do

1. Preheat the oven to 200°F and then turn it off. Place a pizza stone in the oven while it is preheating.

2. **To make the crust:** Combine the warm water and yeast in a small bowl. Add the coconut nectar and stir to combine. Let the yeast mixture sit for about 8 minutes, or until foamy.

3. Whisk together the sorghum flour, tapioca flour, amaranth flour, xanthan gum, and salt in a large bowl. Make a well in the middle.

4. Add the applesauce to the yeast mixture, stir to combine, and pour into the flour mixture.

5. Mix the dough together and form it into a ball.

6. Place the dough in a bowl. Cover the bowl with a clean dishtowel, place it in the oven, and allow the dough to rise for 1 hour.

7. **To make the feta cheeze:** Combine the tofu, apple cider vinegar, lemon juice, oregano, and thyme in a small bowl. Let this mixture marinate in the refrigerator for at least 1 hour.

8. After the dough has risen, remove the dishtowel and place the dough on a lightly floured piece of parchment paper with another piece of parchment on top of the dough. Roll it out into a circle about 11 inches in diameter. Remove the top piece of parchment.

Inside Scoop: If you don't have a pizza stone, you can place the pizza dough on a 15 × 13-inch baking sheet.

9. Place the pizza dough with just the bottom parchment paper on the heated pizza stone.

10. Preheat the oven to 500°F.

11. Bake the pizza crust for 10 minutes.

12. Take the cheeze out of the refrigerator and drain the liquid.

13. To use the other Greek toppings: Take the pizza dough out of the oven, top with the onions, tomatoes, spinach, olives, nutritional yeast, oregano, red pepper flakes, and feta cheeze.

14. To make the glaze: Mix together the molasses, water, and nutritional yeast in a small bowl. Brush the perimeter of the pizza dough with the glaze.

15. Place the pizza back in the oven until the crust is a light golden brown, about 10 minutes.

16. Transfer the pizza stone from the oven to a wire rack, and let sit for 15 minutes before cutting the pizza into 6 slices. This allows the dough to come together without getting gummy.

SERVING SIZE: 1 SLICE
Calories 205; Total Fat 2.2g; Protein 6.6g; Cholesterol 0.0g; Sodium 150mg; Fiber 3.8g; Sugars 6.0g; Total Carbohydrate 40.5g

Inside Scoop: If you can't find hemp tofu and can tolerate soy, firm tofu is a good substitute.

Inside Scoop: If you can't find hemp tofu and can tolerate soy, firm tofu is a good substitute.

Hot 'n Spicy Yakisoba

SERVES 8

Whenever I have a bad day, yakisoba makes it all okay. I call it noodle therapy. The snuggly warmth of the soba noodles mating with the spicy sauce and earthy vegetables is soothing and restorative. Everything that seemed so dire a few minutes prior melts away with each bite. I swear that this dish and a few minutes of meditation every day could lead to world peace.

Must Have

- 1 (8-ounce) package buckwheat soba noodles
- ¾ cup coconut aminos
- 3 tablespoons mirin (Japanese rice cooking wine)
- 1 tablespoon vegan Worcestershire sauce
- 1 tablespoon Hot Sauce (page 21)
- 1 (8-ounce) package hemp tofu, cubed
- 1 small yellow onion, diced
- 1 clove garlic, minced
- 1 tablespoon grated fresh ginger
- 2 cups shredded savoy or Napa cabbage
- 1 cup sliced shiitake mushrooms
- 3 medium carrots, peeled and grated
- 1 cup baby spinach
- 2 scallions, chopped

Must Do

1. Cook the soba noodles according to the package instructions. Drain the noodles in a colander and rinse under cold water.

2. Add the coconut aminos, mirin, Worcestershire, and hot sauce to a medium sauté pan over medium heat and whisk to combine. Add the tofu and cook until it browns a little bit, about 5 minutes. Be sure to turn it over to coat all sides with the sauce.

3. Escort the tofu to one side of the pan and add the onion, garlic, ginger, cabbage, mushrooms, and carrots, and sauté, stirring occasionally, until the vegetables are slightly tender, about 5 minutes.

4. Add the baby spinach and cooked noodles, and toss with tongs to incorporate. Simmer until the spinach turns bright green.

5. Serve immediately and top with the scallions.

SERVING SIZE: 1 CUP

Calories 100; Total Fat 1.6g; Protein 4.6g; Cholesterol 0.0g; Sodium 280mg; Fiber 2.9g; Sugars 6.3g; Total Carbohydrate 18.5g

Cajun Wild Mushroom Risotto

SERVES 6

I'm not being figurative here when I say that this risotto is a labor of love. It takes hard work and elbow grease to get this dish on the table. To get the right consistency, the rice has to be stirred for eternity plus 5 minutes to get it right. This is a small price to pay, though, for the immeasurable pleasure you will undoubtedly experience once this rice passes your lips. And it's not just any rice. It's risotto rice. For risotto, you should use Arborio, which has a talent for soaking up whatever spices and liquids it happens to be swimming in at the time. Not only that, but Arborio also has a habit of leaking amylopectin, a starch, when it's cooked, so the sauce gets even creamier the longer it wades. It works out really well in the end that way.

Must Have

1 shallot, finely diced
¼ cup coconut aminos
1 teaspoon ground cumin
1 teaspoon smoked paprika
1 teaspoon dried oregano
1 teaspoon red pepper flakes
½ teaspoon dried thyme
¼ teaspoon ground coriander
¼ teaspoon freshly ground black pepper
1 tablespoon Grade B maple syrup
3 cups sliced wild mushrooms (chanterelles, porcini, cremini, shiitake, oyster)
1½ cups Arborio rice
5 cups No-Sodium Vegetable Broth (page 25)
2 tablespoons nutritional yeast
¼ cup finely chopped fresh parsley
2 tablespoons finely chopped fresh chives

Must Do

1. Heat the shallot in a medium sauté pan over medium heat and stir until fragrant, about 1 minute.

2. Add the coconut aminos, cumin, paprika, oregano, red pepper flakes, thyme, coriander, and black pepper and cook, stirring occasionally, until the spices become fragrant, about 2 minutes.

3. Add the maple syrup, mushrooms, and rice, and stir to incorporate.

4. Add the broth, about ½ cup at a time, stirring constantly, and wait until it is absorbed before adding the next ½ cup. Continue until all broth is added.

5. Stir the rice until it is soft and creamy, about 25 minutes. Add the nutritional yeast and parsley, and stir to combine.

6. Serve immediately and top each serving with the chives.

SERVING SIZE: 1 CUP
Calories 130; Total Fat 0.3g; Protein 4.3g; Cholesterol 0.0g; Sodium 180mg; Fiber 1.0g; Sugars 4.3g; Total Carbohydrate 32.5g

Margherita Pizza Wheels

MAKES 10 PIZZA WHEELS **(SEE PHOTO ON PAGE 102)**

These pizza wheels are such a treat, and I have to give credit for this to the sauce. I combine my vegan cheeze recipe with my go-to marinara, which is good enough to eat on its own. I sometimes hide the extra sauce in a refrigerated cubbyhole and eat it when no one is home to interrupt me. But if you have more magnanimous tendencies toward the people you live with, then you can also use the extra cheezy marinara sauce as a dip for the wheels, which is really its true calling.

Must Have

DOUGH
1½ cups warm water, about 108°F (I microwave for 30 seconds)
1 (2¼-teaspoon) packet active dry yeast
1 tablespoon coconut nectar
2 cups sorghum flour
1 cup tapioca flour
½ cup sweet white rice flour
2 teaspoons finely chopped fresh oregano
2 teaspoons finely chopped fresh rosemary
¾ teaspoon xanthan gum
¼ teaspoon sea salt
2 tablespoons pumpkin puree

CHEEZY MARINARA SAUCE
1 small yellow onion, diced
3 tablespoons coconut aminos
3 cloves garlic, minced
1 (28-ounce) can whole peeled tomatoes
¼ cup nutritional yeast
¼ cup uncooked millet
¼ cup sunflower seeds
½ teaspoon smoked paprika
½ teaspoon freshly ground black pepper
¼ cup finely sliced fresh basil

GLAZE
2 tablespoons molasses
1 tablespoon water
1 tablespoon nutritional yeast

Must Do

1. Preheat the oven to 200°F and then turn it off. Line a 15 × 10-inch baking sheet with parchment paper.

2. **To make the dough:** Combine the warm water and yeast in a small bowl. Add the coconut nectar and stir to combine. Let the yeast mixture sit for about 8 minutes, or until foamy.

3. Whisk together the sorghum flour, tapioca flour, sweet white rice flour, oregano, rosemary, xanthan gum, and salt in a large bowl. Make a well in the middle.

4. Add the pumpkin puree to the yeast mixture, stir to incorporate, and then pour into the flour mixture. Stir until a dough forms.

5. Form the dough into a ball and place it in a bowl. Cover the bowl with a clean dishtowel and place it in the oven for 1 hour to allow the dough to rise.

6. **To make the sauce:** Heat the onion in a medium sauté pan over medium heat and stir until fragrant, about 1 minute.

7. Add the coconut aminos, garlic, tomatoes with their juice, nutritional yeast, millet, sunflower seeds, smoked paprika, and black pepper, stir to incorporate, and bring to a boil. Lower the heat, cover the pan, and let simmer until the millet is cooked, about 20 minutes.

> **Inside Scoop:** You can use the extra cheezy marinara sauce for any pasta dish you make later in the week. It keeps in the fridge in an airtight jar for up to 7 days.

8. Transfer the sauce in batches to a high-speed blender and puree until smooth. You can also use an immersion blender. Add the basil and stir to incorporate.

9. After the dough has risen, remove the dishtowel from the bowl and roll out the dough on a lightly floured piece of parchment paper with another piece of parchment paper over the dough. Form it into a 12 × 10-inch rectangle about ¼ inch thick. Remove the top piece of parchment.

10. Preheat the oven to 400°F.

11. Spread 1 cup of the cheezy marinara sauce evenly over the top of the dough, leaving a 1-inch border around the perimeter.

12. Starting from the longest side of the rectangle closest to you, roll the dough into a tight log, ending with the seam side down. Use the parchment paper for guidance and for insurance that the dough doesn't tear. If it does tear, just patch it up with some water and a pinch and that should do the trick.

13. Tuck in both ends and then cut the log into 10 wheels, each about 1½ inches thick, using a wet serrated knife. Place each wheel, cut side down, on the prepared baking sheet.

14. To make the glaze: Whisk together the molasses, water, and nutritional yeast in a small bowl.

15. Brush the outside and tops of the wheels with the glaze.

16. Bake the pizza wheels until they are golden brown, about 20 minutes.

17. Transfer the baking sheet from the oven to a wire rack, and let it sit for 10 minutes before removing the pizza wheels.

SERVING SIZE: 1 PIZZA WHEEL
Calories 200; Total Fat 5.3g; Protein 6.4g; Cholesterol 0.0g; Sodium 130mg; Fiber 4.3g; Sugars 0.3g; Total Carbohydrate 40.0g

Pad Thai Spring Rolls

MAKES 10 SPRING ROLLS

Spring rolls are like a party in a rice wrap. With all the shredded goodness tucked into a transparent wrapper that you can dunk into a sweet and sour dip, this is a shindig I don't want to miss. And the best part is that you can sub in any veggies, sprouts, or noodles you have on hand and it will come out just as fun and festive.

Must Have

SWEET & SOUR MISO DIP AND DRESSING

¼ cup chickpea miso paste

3 teaspoons grated fresh ginger

1 clove garlic, minced

¼ cup green tea or water, at room temperature

2 tablespoons coconut aminos

2 tablespoons Grade B maple syrup

2 tablespoons rice vinegar

2 tablespoons mirin (Japanese rice cooking wine)

1 teaspoon red pepper flakes

SPRING ROLLS

4 ounces gluten-free pad thai noodles

10 brown rice paper wraps

1 cup chopped mixed greens

1 cup chopped fresh cilantro

1 carrot, peeled and cut into matchsticks

1 seedless cucumber, cut into matchsticks

1 small red bell pepper, seeded and thinly sliced

1 avocado, pitted, peeled, and sliced into crescents

Must Do

1. **To make the dressing:** Combine the miso, ginger, garlic, tea, coconut aminos, maple syrup, vinegar, mirin, and red pepper flakes in a small bowl. Stir well.

2. **To make the spring rolls:** Cook the pad thai noodles according to the package instructions. Drain the noodles in a colander and rinse under cold water.

3. Pour warm water into a 9-inch cake pan. Place one brown rice paper wrap in the water and let it sit until it softens, about 1 minute.

4. Place the softened wrap on a plate and add some mixed greens, cilantro, carrot, cucumber, bell pepper, and avocado in the center. Add about 2 tablespoons of pad thai noodles and drizzle about 1 tablespoon of the miso dressing on top.

5. Fold in the right and left sides of the wrap and then roll it up, starting from the side nearest to you, until it's closed.

6. Continue to fill and roll the rest of the wrappers. The dressing can also be used as a dip.

SERVING SIZE: 1 SPRING ROLL

Calories 50; Total Fat 3.5g; Protein 3.1g; Cholesterol 0.0g; Sodium 180mg; Fiber 1.7g; Sugars 3.3g; Total Carbohydrate 18.5g

Paella

SERVES 6

Paella is a Spanish creation that begs to be tinkered with. There are so many variations that I feel justified in throwing tradition to the wind and cooking on a blank canvas. The one thing that doesn't stray is the saffron. If nothing else, saffron is the signature spice that gives paella the aromatic overtone that envelops whatever else you throw in the pan. So here's my template and I invite you to paint your pan your way.

Must Have

4 cups boiling water
1 teaspoon saffron threads
1 sweet onion, diced
1 clove garlic, minced
2 carrots, peeled and diced
1½ cups short-grain brown rice, rinsed
1 cup chopped green beans
1 cup cherry tomatoes, halved
½ cup pitted and sliced Kalamata olives
¼ cup finely chopped fresh parsley
1 large lemon, cut into wedges

Must Do

1. Add the water and saffron threads to a medium bowl and stir. Let the saffron steep for about 5 minutes.

2. Add ¼ cup of the saffron water to a large sauté pan over medium heat. Add the onion and stir until fragrant, about 1 minute.

3. Add the garlic, carrots, and brown rice, pour in the remaining 3¾ cups saffron water, and bring to a boil. Lower the heat, cover the pan, and simmer until the water is absorbed, about 40 minutes.

4. Turn off the heat and add the green beans, tomatoes, olives, and parsley. Let it sit for 7 minutes.

5. Stir to combine and serve in bowls. Squeeze some lemon juice on top of each serving.

SERVING SIZE: 1 CUP
Calories 160; Total Fat 0.1g; Protein 3.1g; Cholesterol 0.0g; Sodium 120mg; Fiber 2.9g; Sugars 1.4g; Total Carbohydrate 27.5g

Spinach, Cabbage & Yam Empanadas

MAKES 18 EMPANADAS

I have a confession to make. I've never tasted any empanadas other than these. Every time I was offered an empanada, it was of the meat variety, so that was the end of that. Not having a reference point, I asked other empanada-eating folks to taste these, and they were impressed. They said they love that there is yam puree folded right into the dough, which gives the empanada a golden-orange hue and sweetness that blends magically with the umami filling.

Must Have

DOUGH
1 medium yam (about 4 ounces)
1½ cups sweet white rice flour
½ cup tapioca flour
½ teaspoon sea salt
½ teaspoon xanthan gum
¼ teaspoon smoked paprika
¾ cup coconut milk

FILLING
1 shallot, finely diced
2 tablespoons coconut aminos
2 cloves garlic, minced
¼ teaspoon sea salt
¼ teaspoon ground nutmeg
½ cup chopped baby spinach
½ cup finely chopped Napa
   cabbage

GLAZE
2 tablespoons coconut aminos
1 tablespoon Grade B maple
   syrup
1 tablespoon nutritional yeast

Must Do

1. Preheat the oven to 350°F. Line a 15 × 13-inch baking sheet with parchment paper.

2. **To make the dough:** Add the yam to a medium pot of boiling water, lower the heat, cover the pot, and let simmer until fork tender, about 9 minutes.

3. Drain the yam in a colander. When the yam has cooled a bit, peel off the skin. Slice the yam, add it to a food processor, and pulse until smooth. You can also mash it well with a fork.

4. Whisk together the sweet white rice flour, tapioca flour, salt, xanthan gum, and smoked paprika in a large bowl. Make a well in the middle.

5. Add the coconut milk and 2 tablespoons of the yam puree, and stir to combine. Form the dough into a disk, wrap it in plastic, and place it in the refrigerator for 10 minutes.

6. **To make the filling:** Heat the shallot in a medium sauté pan over medium heat and stir until fragrant, about 1 minute.

7. Add the coconut aminos, garlic, salt, nutmeg, spinach, cabbage, and the remaining yam puree and cook, stirring occasionally, until the spices become fragrant and the vegetables are slightly tender, about 3 minutes.

8. Roll out the dough on a lightly floured piece of parchment paper, with another piece of parchment paper on top of the dough, until it is about ¼ inch thick. Remove the top piece of parchment.

9. Cut out 18 circles with a biscuit cutter, glass, or jar with a 3-inch rim. Reuse any scraps of dough by rolling them out again and cut out more circles.

10. Place about ½ tablespoon of the filling mixture in the middle of each dough circle. Fold the circle in half and press the seams together. Crimp the edges of the seam with fork prongs.

11. To make the glaze: Whisk together the coconut aminos, maple syrup, and nutritional yeast in a small bowl. Brush the tops of the empanadas with the glaze.

12. Place the empanadas on the prepared baking sheet and bake until the dough is a light golden brown, about 30 minutes.

13. Transfer the baking sheet from the oven to a wire rack, and let it sit for 10 minutes before removing the empanadas.

SERVING SIZE: 1 EMPANADA
Calories 90; Total Fat 1.4g; Protein 3.1g; Cholesterol 0.0g; Sodium 100mg; Fiber 0.8g; Sugars 0.4g; Total Carbohydrate 18.7g

Pumpkin Ravioli

MAKES 18 RAVIOLI

I love ravioli. No matter its shape or size, I am helplessly under its spell. So, similar to build-ing your picture-perfect house, I tailor-make my ravioli. I take everything I love about food and pack it into this billowy dough and filling. As I'm known to do, I let pumpkin mingle with the dough boys while the paraphernalia inside is padded with hearty mushrooms and sweet Vidalia. I hope your spouse is not the jealous type because when you bring these guys into your home, your sweetie will have some tough competition for your love.

Must Have

DOUGH
1 cup quinoa flour
1 cup chickpea flour
1 cup sweet white rice flour
1 cup tapioca flour
½ teaspoon sea salt
¼ teaspoon ground nutmeg
1 cup pumpkin puree
2 tablespoons applesauce
9–10 tablespoons green tea or water, at room temperature

FILLING
½ cup chopped Vidalia onion
2 tablespoons coconut aminos
¼ teaspoon sea salt
¼ teaspoon smoked paprika
1 cup chopped cremini mushrooms

GLAZE
3 tablespoons coconut milk

PEPITA PESTO SAUCE
2 cups fresh basil leaves
¼ cup roasted unsalted pepitas (pumpkin seeds)

3 tablespoons nutritional yeast
1 clove garlic, minced
¼ cup freshly squeezed lemon juice
½ teaspoon freshly ground black pepper
⅛ teaspoon stevia powder
¼ cup coconut milk

TOPPING
¼ cup roasted unsalted pepitas, roughly chopped

Must Do

1. Preheat the oven to 375°F. Line a 15 × 13-inch baking sheet with parchment paper.

2. To make the dough: Whisk together the quinoa flour, chickpea flour, sweet white rice flour, tapioca flour, salt, and nutmeg in a large bowl. Make a well in the middle.

3. Add the pumpkin puree and applesauce, and stir to combine. Add the green tea, 1 tablespoon at a time, until a dough forms but is not sticky. Shape the dough into a ball. Divide the dough into 4 equal pieces by cutting it in half, and then cut the halves in half. Press each piece into the shape of a disk.

4. Place each disk in plastic wrap and refrigerate for 10 minutes.

5. To make the filling: Heat the onion in a medium sauté pan over medium heat and stir until fragrant, about 1 minute.

6. Add the coconut aminos, salt, smoked paprika, and cremini mushrooms and cook, stirring occasionally, until the spices are fragrant and the mushrooms are tender, about 4 minutes.

CONTINUED ON NEXT PAGE

7. Take out the disks from the fridge. Place one disk on a lightly floured piece of parchment paper with another piece of parchment on top of the disk, and roll it out until it is a 9 × 9-inch square. Remove the top piece of parchment.

8. Place 1 tablespoon of the filling on the dough 3 times across, evenly spaced. Make 3 rows of filling, so that you have 9 little mounds sitting on the dough.

9. Roll another disk into another 9 × 9-inch square and place it on top of the dough with the filling mounds.

10. With a pizza cutter, cut the dough into 3 strips, 3 inches apart, and then do the same widthwise, to make 9 ravioli. It should look like a tic-tac-toe board. Press down the edges all around the perimeter of each ravioli with the prongs of a fork. Dip the fork in warm water as you do this so the dough sticks together and seals properly.

11. Repeat these steps with the other 2 disks of dough so that you wind up with 18 ravioli.

12. To cook the ravioli, fill a medium-size pot with water, place over medium heat, and bring to a boil. Add 3 ravioli at a time and remove with a slotted spoon when they float to the top, about 3 minutes.

13. To make the glaze: Place the ravioli on the prepared pan and brush the tops with the coconut milk.

14. Bake the ravioli until they turn a light golden brown, about 15 minutes.

15. Transfer the baking sheet from the oven to a wire rack, and let it sit for 5 minutes before removing the ravioli.

16. To make the sauce: Add the basil, pepitas, nutritional yeast, garlic, lemon juice, black pepper, and stevia to a food processor. Pulse to combine. While the machine is running, add the coconut milk, 1 tablespoon at a time, until the sauce is smooth and not too thick.

17. Serve the ravioli warm with the sauce and top with the roasted pepitas.

SERVING SIZE:
3 RAVIOLI, ¼ CUP PESTO SAUCE
Calories 300; Total Fat 6.1g; Protein 12.6g;
Cholesterol 0.0g; Sodium 190mg; Fiber 6.7g;
Sugars 1.2g; Total Carbohydrate 65.3g

Sriracha Hemp Noodles

SERVES 8 **(SEE PHOTO ON PAGE 23)**

Back in the days when I was working as an accountant on Wall Street, I ordered cold sesame noodles for lunch almost every day. It was THE THING to do at the time. It was a culture of greed and carbs and no one cared. But now that I have a more balanced approach to life, I have these noodles once in a while as a side dish. I don't use sesame seeds for the topping because my son is severely allergic to them, so I use hemp seeds instead. They make the perfect substitution, since they contain omega-3 fatty acids and protein, and are hypoallergenic to boot. So enjoy these noodles as a special treat, because they really are.

NOODLES
1 (16-ounce) package gluten-free spaghetti

SAUCE
3 tablespoons coconut aminos
3 cloves garlic, minced
2 teaspoons grated fresh ginger
½ cup Sunflower Seed Butter (page 20)
⅓ cup No-Sodium Vegetable Broth (page 25)
3 tablespoons rice vinegar
2 tablespoons Sriracha (page 22)
1 tablespoon coconut nectar

TOPPINGS
Hemp seeds
Chopped scallion
Red pepper flakes

Must Do

1. **To make the noodles:** Cook the spaghetti according to the package instructions. Drain in a colander and rinse under cold water.

2. **To make the sauce:** Add the coconut aminos, garlic, and ginger to a medium sauté pan over medium heat and cook, stirring occasionally, until the spices become fragrant, about 2 minutes.

3. Add the sunflower seed butter, broth, rice vinegar, Sriracha, and coconut nectar, and stir to combine. Lower the heat, cover the pan, and let simmer until the sauce thickens a little, about 5 minutes.

4. Add the noodles to a big bowl and toss with the sauce. Top with the hemp seeds, scallion, and red pepper flakes. Place in the refrigerator for at least 2 hours or overnight.

SERVING SIZE: 1 CUP
Calories 190; Total Fat 9.2g; Protein 6.4g; Cholesterol 0.0g; Sodium 100mg; Fiber 2.7g; Sugars 2.3g; Total Carbohydrate 21.0g

Sweet Onion & Potato Pierogi

MAKES 20 PIEROGI

Pierogi are the Slavic solution to Chinese dumplings. Both can be stuffed with savory or sweet fillings, and both are the ultimate comfort food. I'm a huge fan of them, but am partial to pierogi due to my Polish heritage. So here I show you how to serve up some sweet onion and potato pierogi that are miraculously savory AND sweet all in one dough crescent.

Must Have

FILLING
1 small sweet onion, diced
¼ cup coconut aminos
1 medium sweet potato (about 4 ounces), peeled and diced
¼ teaspoon sea salt
¼ teaspoon freshly ground black pepper
¼ teaspoon ground nutmeg
3 tablespoons coconut milk

DOUGH
1 cup sweet white rice flour
1½ cups sorghum flour
¼ cup tapioca flour
½ teaspoon sea salt
1 cup coconut milk
2 tablespoons pumpkin puree
2–3 tablespoons water

GLAZE
3 tablespoons coconut milk

Must Do

1. Preheat the oven to 400°F. Line a 15 × 13-inch baking sheet with parchment paper.

2. **To make the filling:** Heat the onion in a medium sauté pan over medium heat and stir until fragrant, about 1 minute.

3. Add the coconut aminos, sweet potato, salt, black pepper, and nutmeg and cook, stirring occasionally, until the spices are fragrant and the sweet potato is tender, about 7 minutes.

4. Transfer the sweet potato and onion mixture from the pan to a food processor and pulse until the mixture comes together. While the machine is running, add the coconut milk, 1 tablespoon at a time, until the mixture is smooth.

5. **To make the dough:** Whisk together the sweet white rice flour, sorghum flour, tapioca flour, and salt in a large bowl. Make a well in the middle.

6. Add the coconut milk and pumpkin puree, and stir to combine. Add the water, 1 tablespoon at a time, until a dough forms.

7. Roll out the dough on a lightly floured piece of parchment paper with another piece of parchment paper on top until it is about ¼ inch thick. Remove the top piece of parchment.

8. Cut out twenty 3-inch circles with a biscuit cutter, glass, or jar. Reuse any scraps of dough by rolling them out again and cutting out more circles.

9. Place ½ tablespoon of the filling in the middle of each circle and fold it in half. Close the seams with wet fingertips and seal by making prong marks along the edges with a fork.

10. To cook the pierogi, fill a medium-size pot with water, place over medium heat, and bring to a boil. Add the pierogi, 5 or 6 at a time, to the boiling water. Remove them when they float to the top, about 4 minutes.

11. Blot the pierogi with a paper towel and place them in an even layer on the prepared baking sheet.

12. **To make the glaze:** Brush the pierogi with the coconut milk and bake them until they turn golden brown, about 20 minutes. Turn them over halfway through baking.

13. Transfer the baking sheet from the oven to a wire rack, and let it sit for 10 minutes before removing the pierogi. Serve immediately.

SERVING SIZE: 2 PIEROGI
Calories 90; Total Fat 0.6g; Protein 2.1g; Cholesterol 0.0g; Sodium 150mg; Fiber 1.5g; Sugars 0.4g; Total Carbohydrate 19.0g

Stir-Fried Ramen with Garlic-Ginger Sauce

SERVES 8

This dish is so quick and easy to make that it's a staple in my weekly repertoire. As with any garden-variety stir-fry, I sometimes replace some of the vegetables depending on what's in the fridge. I usually make the sauce a day in advance, although that's not necessary. This is one the whole family is bound to love and request over and over again.

Must Have

NOODLES
1 (10-ounce) package gluten-free ramen noodles

GARLIC-GINGER SAUCE
½ cup coconut aminos

3 tablespoons mirin (Japanese rice cooking wine)

2 tablespoons coconut nectar

2 tablespoons chickpea miso paste

3 cloves garlic, minced

3 teaspoons grated fresh ginger

2 teaspoons red pepper flakes

STIR-FRY
1 small sweet onion, diced

¼ cup coconut aminos

1 small head red cabbage, shredded

2 medium carrots, peeled and diced

1 celery stalk, diced

1 red pepper, seeded and diced

1 cup chopped cremini mushrooms

1 cup finely sliced baby bok choy

1 (8-ounce) can sliced water chestnuts

TOPPING
¼ cup chopped scallion

Must Do

1. **To make the noodles:** Cook the ramen noodles according to the package directions. Drain in a colander and rinse with cold water.

2. **To make the sauce:** Whisk together the coconut aminos, mirin, coconut nectar, miso, garlic, ginger, and red pepper flakes in a small bowl.

3. **To make the stir-fry:** Heat the onion in a medium sauté pan over medium heat and stir until fragrant, about 1 minute.

4. Add the coconut aminos, cabbage, carrots, celery, and red pepper and cook, stirring occasionally, until the vegetables become fragrant, about 2 minutes.

5. Add the mushrooms, bok choy, water chestnuts, and cooked noodles, and stir to combine.

6. Add the ginger-garlic sauce, 1 tablespoon at a time, until you have added half the sauce, stirring constantly so that the noodles don't stick together.

7. Remove the pan from the heat and gradually add the remaining half of the sauce.

8. Top with the scallions and serve immediately.

SERVING SIZE: 1 CUP

Calories 100; Total Fat 0.2g; Protein 2.1g; Cholesterol 0.0g; Sodium 150mg; Fiber 1.6g; Sugars 3.3g; Total Carbohydrate 15.9g

Egg Rolls

MAKES 12 EGG ROLLS

I'm from New York City, where Chinese food was invented. So when I moved to Los Angeles, it was very hard to find egg rolls that were up to snuff. At first I started experimenting with making my own using homemade dough. They were really good, but when a friend suggested using spring roll wrappers instead, I forgot all about NYC takeout. These are easy to make and sublime as a side dish to an Asian-themed dinner party or as appetizers.

Must Have

FILLING
2 cloves garlic, minced
2 tablespoons coconut aminos
2 teaspoons grated fresh ginger
¼ teaspoon sea salt
1 cup finely shredded savoy or Napa cabbage
1 cup finely shredded baby bok choy
½ cup wood ear mushrooms
½ cup finely shredded carrot
¼ cup sliced water chestnuts, finely chopped

WRAPPERS
12 brown rice spring roll wrappers

GLAZE
¼ cup coconut aminos
1 tablespoon molasses

DUCK SAUCE
½ cup sugar-free apricot jam
6 tablespoons coconut aminos
2 tablespoons rice wine vinegar
2 tablespoons spicy mustard
1 tablespoon orange juice

Must Do

1. Preheat the oven to 400°F. Line a 15 × 13-inch baking sheet with parchment paper.

2. To make the filling: Heat the garlic and coconut aminos in a medium sauté pan over medium heat and stir until fragrant, about 1 minute.

3. Add the ginger, salt, cabbage, bok choy, mushrooms, carrot, and water chestnuts and cook, stirring occasionally, until the vegetables wilt a little and become slightly tender, about 5 minutes.

4. To prepare the wrappers, pour warm water into a 9-inch cake pan. Place one round brown rice wrapper in the water and let it sit until it turns soft, about 1 minute.

5. Place the softened wrapper on the prepared baking sheet and spread about 2 tablespoons of the filling across the bottom of the wrapper, widthwise. Fold the right and left sides in, and start rolling the wrapper from the side closest to you, upward. Keep tucking in the edges as you go along, and roll it tightly.

6. To make the glaze: Whisk together the coconut aminos and molasses in a small bowl. Brush the egg rolls on top and on the sides, and then bake them until they are crisp, about 25 minutes.

7. To make the duck sauce: Whisk together the jam, coconut aminos, vinegar, mustard, and orange juice in a small bowl.

8. Serve the egg rolls immediately with the duck sauce on the side.

SERVING SIZE: 1 EGG ROLL, 2 TABLESPOONS SAUCE
Calories 55; Total Fat 0.2g; Protein 0.7g; Cholesterol 0.0g; Sodium 170mg; Fiber 2.7g; Sugars 1.5g; Total Carbohydrate 12.5g

Inside Scoop: If you can't find wood ear mushrooms, you can use any mushrooms you like.

Yam Gnocchi with Sriracha Pesto

SERVES 7

Considering that most traditional gnocchi are made exclusively with wheat, eggs, and cheese, it's a wonder these petite doughy cylinders can be made without those ingredients and not suffer from an identity crisis. But this recipe defies all odds and it is *delizioso*. My favorite part is the heat from the Sriracha in the pesto. I invite you to make your own Sriracha, as it is super simple and really out of this world. I guarantee the stars will align and your universe will shift. And then there will undoubtedly be another person at your dinner table asking for more gnocchi.

Must Have

GNOCCHI

1 large yam
¼ cup unsalted, raw pumpkin
   seeds, finely ground (I use a
   coffee grinder)
¼ cup tapioca flour
½ teaspoon garlic powder
¼ teaspoon ground nutmeg
¼ teaspoon sea salt
¼ teaspoon freshly ground black
   pepper

SAUTÉ

¼ cup No-Sodium Vegetable
   Broth (page 25)

SRIRACHA PESTO

½ cup fresh basil leaves
⅓ cup hemp seeds
¼ cup freshly squeezed lemon
   juice
3 tablespoons Sriracha (page 22)
¼ teaspoon sea salt
¼ cup water

Must Do

1. **To make the gnocchi:** Add the yam to a medium pot of boiling water, lower the heat, cover the pot, and let simmer until fork tender, about 9 minutes.

2. Drain the yam in a colander. When the yam has cooled a bit, peel off the skin and grate the yam into a large bowl. Grating lets air into the yam, making for lighter gnocchi.

3. Whisk together the ground pumpkin seeds, tapioca flour, garlic powder, nutmeg, salt, and black pepper in a medium bowl. Add the grated yam to the flour mixture and stir to combine.

4. Divide the yam dough in half. Roll out one half of the dough into a 14-inch rope and then cut it into 1-inch pieces. Repeat with the remaining dough.

5. To cook the gnocchi, fill a medium-size pot with water, place over medium heat, and bring to a boil. Add half of the gnocchi to the water. Stir to prevent them from sticking to the bottom, and remove them with a slotted spoon after they float to the top, about 3 minutes. Repeat with the remaining gnocchi.

6. **To sauté:** Place the gnocchi immediately in a medium sauté pan over medium heat. Add the broth and simmer for about 1 minute.

7. Spoon the gnocchi into bowls.

8. **To make the pesto:** Add the basil, hemp seeds, lemon juice, Sriracha, and salt to a food processor, and pulse until the mixture comes together. With the machine still running, drizzle in the water, 1 tablespoon at a time, until the pesto is smooth.

9. To serve, heat the pesto and pour over the gnocchi.

SERVING SIZE: 4 GNOCCHI
Calories 140; Total Fat 4.5g; Protein 4.4g;
Cholesterol 0.0g; Sodium 180mg; Fiber 3.7g;
Sugars 0.4g; Total Carbohydrate 20.5g

Veggie Fried Rice with a Thai Twist

SERVES 8

People think if your fried rice doesn't taste like takeout, then you haven't done your job. So I decided to make the kind of fried rice that goes beyond your local Chinese fare and into a jurisdiction all its own. Thai accents are what this is all about. I'm talking mango. Mango hanging out with ginger and making out with lime. It's kind of *ménage à trois*-ish, and makes you feel like you've been missing out on something all your life. But when it comes to this fried rice, this is a good thing.

Must Have

FRIED RICE
5 cups water
2 cups brown rice, rinsed
1 small yellow onion, diced
¾ cup coconut aminos
3 cloves garlic, minced
1 tablespoon grated fresh ginger
2 teaspoons rice wine vinegar
2 carrots, peeled and diced
2 celery stalks, diced
1 cup chopped green beans
2 cups finely chopped dinosaur
  kale
½ cup diced mango

TOPPING
Lime wedges
1 scallion, chopped

Must Do

1. **To make the fried rice:** Add the water and rice to a medium pot over high heat and bring to a boil. Lower the heat, cover the pot, and simmer until all the water is absorbed, about 20 minutes.

2. Heat the onion in a medium sauté pan over medium heat and stir until fragrant, about 1 minute.

3. Add the coconut aminos, garlic, ginger, rice wine vinegar, carrots, celery, green beans, and kale and cook, stirring occasionally, until the vegetables become tender, about 5 minutes.

4. Add the mango and rice. Stir to incorporate.

5. Serve with a squeeze of lime on top of each bowl and a sprinkle of the scallion.

SERVING SIZE: 1 CUP
Calories 90; Total Fat 0.7g; Protein 2.6g; Cholesterol 0.0g; Sodium 190mg; Fiber 2.7g; Sugars 0.3g; Total Carbohydrate 19.1g

Lo Mein with Brown Sauce

SERVES 8

Many years ago, when I was still living with my parents in Queens, the big Sunday night fight was about what kind of sauce to get on the Chinese dishes we were ordering—white or brown. The brown sauce usually won out. But what was in it? No one knew. The Chinese restaurant wouldn't tell us because it was their family's secret. So, out of revenge, I decided to figure it out. No classified information from the Ming was going to keep me from making me some brown sauce. After many trials, tribulations, and gunk, I came out victorious, with a majestic brown sauce that I'm sure any Chinese restaurant would be proud to call its own.

Must Have

LO MEIN
1 (8-ounce) package gluten-free spaghetti
1 leek, light green and white parts only, finely sliced
2 tablespoons coconut aminos
2 cloves garlic, minced
1 cup sliced cremini mushrooms
2 celery stalks, sliced
1 carrot, peeled and sliced
1 red bell pepper, seeded and finely sliced
3 cups chopped baby spinach

BROWN SAUCE
1 tablespoon tapioca flour
1 tablespoon cold water
½ cup coconut aminos
1 teaspoon Sriracha (page 22)
1 teaspoon Grade B maple syrup
3 cloves garlic, minced
1 tablespoon grated fresh ginger
¾ cup No-Sodium Vegetable Broth (page 25)

TOPPING
¼ cup chopped scallion

Must Do

1. **To make the lo mein:** Cook the spaghetti according to the package instructions. Drain in a colander and rinse under cold water.

2. Heat the leek in a large sauté pan over medium heat and stir until fragrant, about 1 minute.

3. Add the coconut aminos, garlic, mushrooms, celery, carrot, bell pepper, and spinach and cook, stirring occasionally, until the spinach turns bright green and the vegetables are slightly tender, about 3 minutes.

4. **To make the sauce:** Combine the tapioca flour and cold water in a small bowl and stir until a paste forms. Doing it this way helps prevent lumps.

5. Add the tapioca mixture and coconut aminos to a medium sauté pan over low heat and cook, stirring constantly, until smooth, about 1 minute.

6. Add the Sriracha, maple syrup, garlic, ginger, and broth and cook, stirring occasionally, until the sauce thickens, about 2 minutes.

7. Add the noodles to the sauté pan containing the vegetables, stir to combine, and then add the sauce. Toss with tongs to incorporate. Top each serving with the scallions and serve immediately.

SERVING SIZE: 1 CUP

Calories 115; Total Fat 0.5g; Protein 4.3g; Cholesterol 0.0g; Sodium 180mg; Fiber 3.0g; Sugars 2.1g; Total Carbohydrate 24.5g

FALAFEL BOWL WITH
HORSERADISH DILL CREAM SAUCE
(SEE RECIPE ON PAGE 138)

CHAPTER 8

The Main Attraction

"What's for dinner?" is the resounding choral piece that is sung throughout the world every evening at around 6 p.m. in the respective time zones of 196 countries. Just as the "Hallelujah Chorus" culminates after the section of Handel's *Messiah* Part II, titled "God's Triumph," I think it can be said, without exaggeration, that a good, down-home meal that your family eats and enjoys should be considered *"Mom's* Triumph"! Let us all say "Amen!"

Falafel Bowl with Horseradish Dill Cream Sauce

SERVES 6 **(SEE PHOTO ON PAGE 136)**

My favorite Israeli fast food is falafel. When I went to Israel one summer, there were falafel stands on every corner similar to the hot dog stands in Manhattan. My goal when creating this recipe was to preserve the flavor and spice of the falafel I remember so well, and make it in the healthiest way possible. I also re-created the famous Israeli salad with a twist, which adds crunch and tang. Finally, the horseradish dill cream sauce pulls it all together in a most heavenly way.

Must Have

FALAFEL BALLS
1 medium sweet potato (about 4 ounces)
1 (15-ounce) can chickpeas, drained and rinsed
3 cloves garlic, minced
2 tablespoons chopped fresh parsley
2 teaspoons ground cumin
¼ teaspoon ground coriander
½ teaspoon sea salt
3 tablespoons water

HORSERADISH DILL CREAM SAUCE
1 medium avocado, peeled and pitted
¼ cup prepared Horseradish (page 24)
¼ cup fresh dill, chopped
3 tablespoons chopped fresh chives
2 tablespoons Hot Sauce (page 21)
¼ cup coconut milk

SALAD
1 head butter lettuce, hand torn
2 large tomatoes, halved, seeded, and chopped (I prefer heirloom or Roma)
2 large Persian cucumbers, chopped
½ cup diced red onion
4 dill pickles, chopped
3 tablespoons freshly squeezed lemon juice

Must Do

1. Preheat the oven to 375°F. Line a 15 × 10-inch baking sheet with parchment paper.

2. To make the falafel: Add the sweet potato to a small pot of boiling water, cover the pot, lower the heat, and cook until it is fork tender, about 10 minutes. Drain. Once it cools slightly, peel it and slice it into rounds.

3. Add the chickpeas, cooked sweet potato, garlic, parsley, cumin, coriander, salt, and water to a food processor. Pulse until the mixture comes together but still has some texture.

4. Make 18 falafel balls, using about 1 tablespoon per ball, and place them on the prepared baking sheet.

5. Place the baking sheet in the oven, and bake until the falafel balls turn a light golden brown, about 20 minutes. Turn the falafel balls over halfway through baking.

6. To make the horseradish sauce: Add the avocado, horseradish, dill, chives, and hot sauce to a food processor and pulse until the mixture comes together. While the machine is still running, add the coconut milk, 1 tablespoon at a time, until the sauce is very smooth. Add a little water if the sauce is too thick.

7. **To make the salad:** Combine the lettuce, tomatoes, cucumbers, onion, and pickles in a large bowl. Drizzle the vegetables with the lemon juice.

8. Transfer the baking sheet from the oven to a wire rack, and let it sit for 10 minutes. Add the salad and several falafel balls to each bowl, and drizzle the horseradish cream sauce over them.

SERVING SIZE: 3 FALAFEL BALLS, ½ CUP SALAD, 2 TABLESPOONS SAUCE
Calories 125; Total Fat 5.5g; Protein 3.5g; Cholesterol 0.0g; Sodium 190.0mg; Fiber 5.2g; Sugars 3.5g; Total Carbohydrate 17.3g

Inside Scoop: For extra fiber and B vitamins, you should leave the skin on the sweet potato.

Spanakopita Enchiladas

SERVES 6

Spanakopita is one of those recipes that can be reincarnated any which way and still be mind-blowing. As you may already know, I like to fuse different ethnic foods into one dish to come up with something uncommonly good. I think this one qualifies. The fact that you have spinach and dill and feta nestled in between layers of tortillas is one thing. The second thing is that they are lathered in a creamy roasted red pepper sauce that really brings it home. The third thing is: you may have noticed that I said layers of tortillas. I don't like rolling my tortillas to make enchiladas because either they tear or the filling falls out. Instead, I make it lasagna style. It's all in the name of fusion.

Must Have

ROASTED RED PEPPER CREAM SAUCE

3 medium red bell peppers

1½ cups sunflower seeds, soaked in water for 30 minutes at room temperature or overnight in the refrigerator and drained

3 cloves garlic, minced

¼ cup freshly squeezed lemon juice

¼ teaspoon sea salt

1¼ cups water

FETA CHEEZE

1 (8-ounce) package hemp tofu, cubed

½ cup apple cider vinegar

¼ cup freshly squeezed lemon juice

2 teaspoons dried oregano

1 teaspoon dried thyme

¼ teaspoon sea salt

½ teaspoon freshly ground black pepper

FILLING

1 small yellow onion, diced

¼ cup coconut aminos

1 pound baby spinach

½ cup chopped fresh dill

¼ teaspoon ground nutmeg

4 gluten-free tortillas

TOPPING

3 teaspoons finely chopped fresh dill

Must Do

1. Preheat the oven to 500°F. Line a 15 × 10-inch baking sheet with parchment paper.

2. **To make the roasted red pepper cream sauce:** Cut the red bell peppers in half and remove the seeds. Place the peppers on the parchment paper, skin side down, and roast until the skin turns black, about 30 minutes.

3. Take the peppers out of the oven and let cool completely. Once the peppers are cool, peel the skins off.

4. Add the peeled peppers to a high-speed blender. Add the sunflower seeds, garlic, lemon juice, salt, and water. Blend until you have a smooth sauce.

5. **To make the feta cheese:** Add the tofu, apple cider vinegar, lemon juice, oregano, thyme, salt, and black pepper to a medium bowl and stir to combine. Let the mixture sit in the refrigerator for at least 30 minutes.

6. **To make the filling:** Heat the onion in a large sauté pan over medium heat until fragrant, about 1 minute.

7. Add the coconut aminos, spinach, dill, and nutmeg and cook, stirring occasionally, until the spinach turns bright green, about 2 minutes.

8. Take the feta cheeze out of the fridge, drain the liquid, add it to the spinach mixture in the pan, and stir to combine.

Inside Scoop: If you can't find hemp tofu and can tolerate soy, firm tofu is a good substitute.

9. Transfer the spinach mixture to a food processor. Pulse to combine until the mixture comes together but still has texture.

10. Lower the oven temperature to 350°F.

11. Spread about ½ cup of the roasted red pepper cream sauce on the bottom of a 13 × 9-inch casserole dish. Line the bottom of the dish with 2 tortillas. They should overlap a little bit in the middle.

12. Spread the spinach mixture evenly over the 2 tortillas. Pour on 1 cup of the roasted red pepper cream sauce, spreading it evenly on top of the filling.

13. Cover the filling and sauce with 2 more tortillas, which should also overlap in the middle. Spread the remaining roasted red pepper cream sauce evenly on top of the tortillas, covering the entire surface.

14. Cover the pan with aluminum foil and bake until the sauce is bubbly, about 20 minutes.

15. Transfer the casserole dish from the oven to a wire rack, and let it sit for about 10 minutes. Top evenly with the dill and serve.

SERVING SIZE: 1 (6-OUNCE) SLICE
Calories 160; Total Fat 10.1g; Protein 6.2g; Cholesterol 0.0g; Sodium 180mg; Fiber 3.8g; Sugars 0.9g; Total Carbohydrate 14.1g

Mushroom Herb Ragù

SERVES 4

If you adore mushrooms even half as much as I do, you'll absolutely relish this recipe. I cram every mushroom that I know and love into this easy-to-make ragù that evolves into a hearty and full-flavored meal unto itself or can be served as a side dish with any of the other main attractions in this chapter. I think you'll also be excited to learn that fungi are ridiculously low in calories, about 22 calories for 6 white button mushrooms, and they contain immense amounts of essential nutrients that help keep your body and immune system healthy and strong.

Must Have

- 1 medium yellow onion, chopped
- ½ cup coconut aminos
- 3 cloves garlic, minced
- 3 cups roughly chopped mixed mushrooms (cremini, white button, oyster, shiitake)
- 2 tablespoons chopped fresh rosemary
- 1 teaspoon freshly ground black pepper
- 2 tablespoons tapioca flour
- 1 tablespoon cold water
- 1½ cups No-Sodium Vegetable Broth (page 25)
- ¼ cup coconut milk
- 1 tablespoon Grade B maple syrup
- 8 fresh basil leaves, finely sliced

Must Do

1. Heat the onion in a medium sauté pan over medium heat and stir until fragrant, about 1 minute.

2. Add the coconut aminos, garlic, mushrooms, rosemary, and pepper, and cook, stirring occasionally, until the herbs are fragrant and the mushrooms slightly tender, about 3 minutes.

3. Combine the tapioca flour and cold water in a small bowl and stir until a paste forms. Whisk this mixture into the pan.

4. Add the broth to the pan and stir vigorously to combine. Add the coconut milk and maple syrup, and simmer until the sauce thickens, about 30 minutes.

5. Take the pan off the stove and add the basil leaves. Serve warm over rice, kasha, quinoa, or gluten-free noodles.

SERVING SIZE: 1 CUP

Calories 60; Total Fat 0.5g; Protein 2.9g; Cholesterol 0.0g; Sodium 180mg; Fiber 4.3g; Sugars 4.1g; Total Carbohydrate 13.8g

Sweet & Spicy Eggplant

SERVES 6

With patience, this Lebanese dish comes together extremely well texturally and flavorfully. The key is to simmer the eggplant long enough so that it practically melts. In conjunction with the firm chickpeas and the bite of the juicy tomatoes, it is something special to savor. And if you can bear to share it, it is a sure crowd-pleaser.

Must Have

1 yellow onion, diced
½ cup coconut aminos
3 cloves garlic, minced
1 tablespoon curry powder
½ teaspoon ground turmeric
½ teaspoon ground cumin
½ teaspoon freshly ground black pepper
1 tablespoon coconut nectar
3 large heirloom tomatoes, diced
2 medium eggplants (about 3 pounds total), diced into ½-inch pieces
1 (15-ounce) can chickpeas, rinsed and drained
¾ cup fresh basil, chopped
3 tablespoons finely chopped fresh parsley

Must Do

1. Heat the onion in a medium sauté pan over medium heat and stir until fragrant, about 1 minute.

2. Add the coconut aminos, garlic, curry powder, turmeric, cumin, and black pepper and cook, stirring occasionally, until the spices become fragrant, about 2 minutes.

3. Add the coconut nectar, tomatoes, eggplant, and chickpeas, and stir to incorporate.

4. Cover the sauté pan and simmer until the eggplant is very tender, about 35 minutes.

5. Remove from the heat and add the basil. Top each serving with the parsley and serve over brown rice, quinoa, or kasha.

SERVING SIZE: 1 CUP
Calories 60; Total Fat 0.6g; Protein 3.2g; Cholesterol 0.0g; Sodium 180mg; Fiber 2.7g; Sugars 2.0g; Total Carbohydrate 10.3g

Spaghetti Squash Chow Mein

SERVES 8

Chow mein on the West Coast is quite different from chow mein on the East Coast. Where I'm originally from in Queens, chow mein is all vegetables and bean sprouts. I know this may seem sacrilegious to those who have only experienced this dish with noodles, but it's true. I never had noodles in my chow mein until moving to Los Angeles. And when I was served my first chow mein with noodles, I thought they got my order wrong. Now that I make my own version, I compromise by preparing it with spaghetti squash noodles. It's still a vegetable but I'm pretending it's spaghetti. Everything in Hollywood is an illusion anyway, so why not take it one step further and fool everyone with your food in a good way?

Must Have

- 4 cups water, divided
- 1 medium spaghetti squash (about 3 pounds)
- 1 cup quinoa
- 1 shallot, minced
- ½ cup coconut aminos
- 3 cloves garlic, minced
- 1 tablespoon freshly grated ginger
- 3 celery stalks, sliced diagonally
- 2 cups shredded Napa cabbage
- 1 cup sliced cremini mushrooms
- 1 cup shredded carrot
- 2 scallions, sliced

Must Do

1. Preheat the oven to 400°F. Add 2 cups of the water to a 13 × 9-inch oven-safe casserole dish.

2. Cut the spaghetti squash in half lengthwise and scoop out the seeds. Place the squash halves skin side down in the prepared dish. Bake the squash until tender, about 25 minutes. When the squash cools, scoop out the flesh with a fork to make the "spaghetti."

3. Toast the quinoa in a medium pot over high heat for about 2 minutes. Add the remaining 2 cups water and bring to a boil. Lower the heat, cover the pot, and let simmer until the water is absorbed, about 15 minutes.

4. Heat the shallot in a medium sauté pan over medium heat until fragrant, about 1 minute.

5. Add the coconut aminos, garlic, ginger, celery, cabbage, mushrooms, and carrot and cook, stirring occasionally, until the vegetables are slightly tender, about 5 minutes.

6. Add the cooked quinoa and spaghetti squash, and stir until well combined.

7. Top with the scallions and serve immediately.

SERVING SIZE: 1 CUP
Calories 150; Total Fat 3.0g; Protein 6.9g; Cholesterol 0.0g; Sodium 210mg; Fiber 4.0g; Sugars 4.5g; Total Carbohydrate 35.1g

Maple-Glazed Groatloaf

SERVES 6

If there were ever an underdog in the history of American cuisine, it would have to be classic meatloaf. I've eaten it sans meat for the past twenty years, and I honestly believe that meatloaf built exclusively with vegetables, fungi, and legumes is the best type. The ingredients in this version get you the benefit of nine essential amino acids, iron, energy-boosting B vitamins, and plenty of protein and palate-pleasing punch. But you'll be the ultimate judge after you make it, serve it, and try it. I think you will be pleasantly surprised.

Must Have

GROATLOAF

1 medium yam (about 6 ounces), peeled and sliced
½ cup buckwheat groats
1 cup water
½ small yellow onion
¼ cup coconut aminos
1 celery stalk, finely chopped
2 small carrots, peeled and finely chopped
1 cup chopped cremini mushrooms
½ cup cooked chickpeas (from a can is okay)
2 tablespoons Sriracha (page 22)
1 teaspoon ground cumin
½ teaspoon smoked paprika
¼ teaspoon sea salt

GLAZE

¼ cup tomato paste
1 tablespoon coconut aminos
½ tablespoon Grade B maple syrup
1 teaspoon ground cumin
½ teaspoon Hot Sauce (page 21)

SERVING SIZE: 1 GROATLOAF

Calories 120; Total Fat 0.8g; Protein 4.9g; Cholesterol 0.0g; Sodium 190mg; Fiber 4.6g; Sugars 7.5g; Total Carbohydrate 28.1g

Must Do

1. Preheat the oven to 375°F. Line a 15 × 10-inch baking sheet with parchment paper.

2. **To make the groatloaf:** Add the yam to a small pot of boiling water and cook until fork tender, about 10 minutes. Drain.

3. Toast the buckwheat groats in a medium pot over high heat for about 2 minutes. Add the water and bring to a boil. Lower the heat, cover the pot, and let simmer until the water is absorbed, about 8 minutes.

4. Heat the onion in a medium sauté pan over medium heat and stir until fragrant, about 1 minute.

5. Add the coconut aminos, celery, carrots, and mushrooms and cook, stirring occasionally, until the vegetables are slightly tender, about 5 minutes.

6. Add the cooked yam, cooked buckwheat groats, cooked vegetable mixture, chickpeas, Sriracha, cumin, smoked paprika, and salt to a food processor. Pulse to combine until the mixture comes together but still has texture.

7. Scoop out about ¼ cup of the mixture and shape it into a loaf. Place the loaf on the prepared baking sheet. Repeat to make 5 more loaves.

8. **To make the glaze:** Mix together the tomato paste, coconut aminos, maple syrup, cumin, and hot sauce in a small bowl. Brush the groatloaves with the glaze.

9. Bake until the groatloaves get a little crispy on the outside and the glaze gets slightly absorbed, about 25 minutes.

10. Serve immediately with the Smokin' Hot Mashed Yams (page 178).

Inside Scoop: If you can't find hemp tofu and can tolerate soy, firm tofu is a good substitute.

Palak Paneer

SERVES 8

My favorite Indian dish of all time is palak paneer. When I used to go out for Indian food, that was always what I ordered. But since going to Taste of India isn't an option anymore, I figured out how to imitate this usually cheesy, creamy orgy of a dish using hemp tofu and nutritional yeast to stand in for the cheese, and coconut milk to re-create the creaminess. Garam masala and other spices typically used in curries pull it all together, in a palak paneer performance worthy of a standing ovation.

Must Have

PANEER

¼ cup nutritional yeast
1 teaspoon ground cumin
⅛ teaspoon sea salt
¼ cup freshly squeezed lemon juice
1 tablespoon coconut nectar
1 (8-ounce) package hemp tofu, cut into ½-inch blocks

CURRY

6 cups baby spinach
½ cup nutritional yeast
½ cup cherry tomatoes, chopped with seeds squeezed out
¼ cup coconut aminos
2 tablespoons coconut nectar
1 tablespoon freshly squeezed lemon juice
½ teaspoon garam masala
½ teaspoon sea salt
1 cup coconut milk
3 cloves garlic, minced
1 tablespoon grated ginger
1 tablespoon tapioca flour
1 tablespoon cold water
2 tablespoons coconut cream

Must Do

1. **To make the paneer:** Whisk together the nutritional yeast, cumin, and salt in a medium bowl. Add the lemon juice and coconut nectar, and stir to combine. Add the tofu and stir to coat all sides. Place in the refrigerator.

2. **To make the curry:** Add the spinach, nutritional yeast, tomatoes, coconut aminos, coconut nectar, lemon juice, garam masala, and salt to a food processor. Pulse until the mixture comes together. While the machine is still running, drizzle in the coconut milk until the mixture is smooth.

3. Heat the garlic and ginger in a medium sauté pan over medium heat, stirring occasionally, until the spices are fragrant, about 30 seconds. Add the curry mixture from the food processor.

4. Combine the tapioca flour and cold water in a small bowl, and stir until a paste forms. Whisk this mixture into the pan. Cook until the liquid reduces down a bit and the curry comes together, about 15 minutes.

5. Add the coconut cream and stir to combine.

6. Remove the paneer from the fridge, add it to the sauté pan, and stir to incorporate.

7. Serve immediately over rice and with Caramelized Onion Naan (page 210).

SERVING SIZE: 1 CUP
Calories 90; Total Fat 2.0g; Protein 4.7g; Cholesterol 0.0g; Sodium 180mg; Fiber 2.3g; Sugars 2.7g; Total Carbohydrate 8.1g

Green Curry Portobellos

SERVES 6

I have a thing for curry and mushrooms, so I decided to combine them into this hearty, fragrant, and filling meal. The ingredients in the curry have a wonderful anti-inflammatory effect on the body, and the mushrooms work like magic to keep you healthy. And let me not forget to mention that they are super low in calories. So add as many 'shrooms as you like to this dish. It takes just a few minutes to prepare and is extraordinarily satisfying. You can add a little more or less curry paste depending on your heat tolerance. Rice is the perfect partner for the sauce, as it absorbs it completely.

Must Have

1 small sweet onion, chopped
2 tablespoons coconut aminos
1 tablespoon grated fresh ginger
¼ cup green curry paste
2 tablespoons coconut nectar
2 cups coconut milk
½ cup chickpea miso paste
3 cups water
4–6 large portobello mushrooms, sliced into 1-inch strips
8 fresh basil leaves, thinly sliced

Must Do

1. Heat the onion in a medium sauté pan over medium heat and stir until fragrant, about 1 minute.

2. Add the coconut aminos, ginger, green curry paste, coconut nectar, and coconut milk and cook, stirring occasionally, until the spices are fragrant, about 2 minutes.

3. Add the miso paste to the water in a small bowl and stir to combine. Add this to the sauté pan and stir until incorporated.

4. Cover the pan and simmer for about 15 minutes. Add the mushrooms and let them simmer for another 5 minutes.

5. Serve over brown rice and top with the basil leaves.

SERVING SIZE: 1 CUP
Calories 80; Total Fat 2.2g; Protein 6.0g; Cholesterol 0.0g; Sodium 200mg; Fiber 6.0g; Sugars 2.5g; Total Carbohydrate 5.1g

Moroccan Stuffed Cabbage

MAKES 12 ROLLS

My mother hails from Eastern Europe and to keep her heritage holy, she has had to make stuffed cabbage for the last half century and then some. I never ventured into this culinary arena until recently because I always thought the cabbage had to be stuffed with meat. Now that I am so much the wiser, I decided to put a Moroccan spin on the filling and sauce. This is a wonderful holiday recipe, as it makes a lot of cabbage rolls and is very festive.

Must Have

1 large green cabbage (about 3-pounds), cored

FILLING
1 shallot, minced
½ cup coconut aminos
2 cups quinoa flakes
2 cups chopped cremini mushrooms
½ cup chopped Kalamata olives
¼ cup raisins
½ cup water

SAUCE
¾ cup apricot preserves
¼ cup coconut aminos
¼ cup green tea or water
2 tablespoons spicy mustard
2 cloves garlic, minced
2 teaspoons grated fresh ginger
1 teaspoon ground cumin

Must Do

1. Add the cored cabbage to a large pot of boiling water and blanch for about 10 minutes, or until the leaves start to separate. Drain in a colander, let cool, and separate the leaves. You should get 12 nice leaves.

2. To make the filling: Heat the shallot in a medium sauté pan over medium heat and stir until fragrant, about 1 minute.

3. Add the coconut aminos, quinoa flakes, mushrooms, olives, raisins, and water and cook, stirring occasionally, until the quinoa flakes are mushy, about 3 minutes.

4. Add the filling to a food processor. Pulse until the mixture is combined but still has texture.

5. To make the sauce: Heat the apricot preserves, coconut aminos, green tea, mustard, garlic, ginger, and cumin in a large saucepan over medium heat, stirring occasionally, until the ingredients are completely combined, about 1 minute.

6. Take a leaf of cabbage and fill the end closest to you with 1 to 2 tablespoons of the filling. Roll the cabbage leaf, while tucking in the sides as you go along, similar to a burrito. Do the same with the remaining cabbage leaves and filling.

7. Add the stuffed cabbage leaves to the sauté pan with the sauce, seam side down, and cover. Cook for about 15 minutes. Spoon some of the sauce from the pan over the cabbage halfway through cooking.

SERVING SIZE: 1 CABBAGE ROLL, 2 TABLESPOONS SAUCE
Calories 180; Total Fat 4.6g; Protein 4.9g; Cholesterol 0.0g; Sodium 200mg; Fiber 3.7g; Sugars 7.5g; Total Carbohydrate 33.1g

The Ultimate Boodle (Buddha Noodle) Bowl

SERVES 6

I have always found it ironic that a meal so healthful and weight management–friendly is named after a half-naked man with a huge belly. But no matter what the title, I love making and eating all sorts of bowls, any time of day, because there is no limit to what you can add to them. Although noodles are not a typical element, I add them because they lend comfort and tranquility and really bring this ultimate Buddha bowl home.

Must Have

BOWL

1 (8-ounce) package gluten-free spiral noodles
1 sweet potato, peeled and diced
1 pound Brussels sprouts, quartered
½ cup (8 tablespoons) coconut aminos, divided
1 large cauliflower (about 4 pounds), cut into florets
1 shallot, minced
1 clove garlic, minced
½ cup cherry tomatoes, chopped
1 serrano pepper, seeded and diced
2 cups sliced cremini mushrooms
1 red bell pepper, seeded and diced
1 teaspoon ground turmeric
½ teaspoon freshly ground black pepper
Avocado slices

CREAMY WASABI DRESSING

½ avocado, mashed
¼ cup rice vinegar
¼ cup coconut aminos
2 tablespoons mirin (Japanese rice cooking wine)
1 tablespoon coconut nectar
1 tablespoon wasabi powder (I use Hime brand; see Resources)

Must Do

1. Preheat the oven to 375°F. Line a 15 × 13-inch baking sheet with parchment paper.

2. To make the bowl: Prepare the noodles according to the package directions. Drain.

3. Spread the sweet potato and Brussels sprouts out in a single layer on the prepared baking sheet and drizzle with 3 tablespoons of the coconut aminos. Toss gently with your hands to coat.

4. Bake until the potatoes and Brussels sprouts are tender and slightly crisp, about 25 minutes. Toss halfway through baking so they brown evenly.

5. Add the cauliflower florets to a food processor. Pulse until the cauliflower looks like the consistency of rice.

6. Heat the shallot in a large sauté pan over medium heat, and stir until fragrant, about 2 minutes. Add the remaining 5 tablespoons coconut aminos, cauliflower, garlic, tomatoes, serrano pepper, mushrooms, bell pepper, turmeric, and black pepper and cook, stirring occasionally, until the spices are fragrant and the vegetables slightly tender, about 5 minutes.

7. Add the cooked noodles and stir to incorporate.

8. Distribute the cauliflower rice mixture among the bowls, dividing it evenly.

9. Top with the sweet potatoes and Brussels sprouts mixture and the avocado slices.

10. To make the dressing: Add the avocado, rice vinegar, coconut aminos, mirin, coconut nectar, and wasabi

powder to a food processor. Pulse until the mixture is completely smooth.

11. Drizzle over the Buddha bowls and serve.

SERVING SIZE: 2 CUPS

Calories 140; Total Fat 7.1g; Protein 4.9g;
Cholesterol 0.0g; Sodium 180mg; Fiber 7.7g;
Sugars 2.3g; Total Carbohydrate 19.1g

Inside Scoop: The dressing tastes better after refrigerating it overnight, so if you plan to make this recipe, just prepare the dressing in advance and you'll get the best flavor out of it.

Coriander Dal

SERVES 8

This nutrient-dense, delicious dish can be brought together very quickly for an easy week-night dinner, but it is festive enough that you can make it for guests. Although sliced avocado is not a traditional addition to this Indian meal, I like to top the dal with it, plus a squeeze of fresh lime juice. This acts as an antidote and refreshing twist to the pungent and aromatic spices.

Must Have

DAL

1 shallot, minced
¼ cup coconut aminos
3 cloves garlic, minced
2 serrano peppers, seeded and minced
1 tablespoon grated fresh ginger
2 teaspoons ground turmeric
2 teaspoons ground cumin
½ teaspoon cayenne pepper
¼ teaspoon ground coriander
2 cups red lentils, sorted and rinsed
3 cups No-Sodium Vegetable Broth (page 25)
2 cups coconut milk
1 cup chopped cherry tomatoes, with juice
½ cup packed chopped fresh cilantro

TOPPINGS

Avocado slices
Lime wedges
Cilantro

Must Do

1. **To make the dal:** Heat the shallot in a medium sauté pan over medium heat and stir until fragrant, about 1 minute.

2. Add the coconut aminos, garlic, serrano peppers, ginger, turmeric, cumin, cayenne, and coriander and cook, stirring occasionally, until the spices are fragrant, about 2 minutes.

3. Add the lentils, broth, coconut milk, and tomatoes, and bring to a boil. Lower the heat, cover the pan, and simmer until the lentils are soft and mushy, about 25 minutes.

4. Add the cilantro, stir to incorporate, and remove from the heat.

5. Serve immediately over rice, millet, or quinoa with the toppings and Caramelized Onion Naan (page 210) for dipping.

SERVING SIZE: 1 CUP

Calories 100; Total Fat 1.8g; Protein 6.1g; Cholesterol 0.0g; Sodium 135mg; Fiber 5.7g; Sugars 0.2g; Total Carbohydrate 14.8g

Spinach & Basil Dumplings

MAKES 18 DUMPLINGS

I think anything named "dumpling" is usually associated with something edible-y adorable and replete with doughy pleats. But not in this case. This dumpling is sans dough and dimples, but filled with gorgeous leafy greens, quinoa, pumpkin, and spices. It is so delicious in and of itself that you don't really need anything else. I included a sauce as an option for extra zing and awesomeness.

Must Have

DUMPLINGS
2 cups baby spinach
2 cups fresh basil leaves
½ cup quinoa flakes
½ yellow onion, chopped
1 serrano pepper, seeded and chopped
2 tablespoons pumpkin puree
1 tablespoon coconut nectar
1 teaspoon red pepper flakes
¼ teaspoon ground coriander
¼ teaspoon sea salt
¼ cup boiling water

SAUCE
1 small yellow onion, diced
¼ cup coconut aminos
2 cloves garlic, minced
1 serrano pepper, seeded and finely diced
1 tablespoon minced fresh ginger
1 tablespoon coconut nectar
2 teaspoons ground turmeric
1 teaspoon red pepper flakes
2 tablespoons tapioca flour
1 tablespoon cold water
3 cups coconut milk

Must Do

1. Preheat the oven to 350°F. Line a 15 × 10-inch rimmed baking sheet with parchment paper.

2. To make the dumplings: Add the spinach, basil, quinoa flakes, onion, serrano pepper, pumpkin, coconut nectar, red pepper flakes, coriander, and salt to a food processor and pulse to combine. While the machine is running, add the boiling water, 1 tablespoon at a time, until the mixture is smooth.

3. Take about 1 tablespoon of the mixture and shape it into a ball with wet hands. Place the ball on the prepared baking sheet. Repeat until you have used up all of the dumpling dough.

4. Bake the dumplings until they are a light golden brown, about 20 minutes. Turn the dumplings over after about 10 minutes.

5. To make the sauce: Heat the onion in a medium sauté pan over medium heat and stir until fragrant, about 1 minute.

6. Add the coconut aminos, garlic, serrano pepper, ginger, coconut nectar, turmeric, and red pepper flakes and cook, stirring occasionally, until the spices are fragrant, about 2 minutes.

7. Combine the tapioca flour and cold water in a small bowl, and stir until a paste forms. Whisk this mixture and the coconut milk into the pan.

8. Cover the pan and let simmer until the mixture thickens, about 4 minutes.

9. Transfer the ingredients from the pan to a high-speed blender. Puree until smooth.

10. Serve the dumplings and sauce immediately over rice, quinoa, or kasha. You can also serve them on top of the Palak Paneer (page 151) or Coriander Dal (page 159).

SERVING SIZE: 3 DUMPLINGS, ¼ CUP SAUCE

Calories 70; Total Fat 3.6g; Protein 1.3g; Cholesterol 0.0g; Sodium 200mg; Fiber 2.7g; Sugars 1.3g; Total Carbohydrate 9.5g

Tex-Mex Fakiin Bacon Burgers

MAKES 4 BIG BURGERS

Texans take their Tex-Mex very seriously. Just walking through an Austin airport gave me a Tex-Mex vibe that was a precursor to this recipe. Just so you know, a Tex-Mex flavor can be described by the spices. I use a taco seasoning that includes chili powder, cumin, garlic, and oregano. When combining this many spices, I think it's best to blend your own to minimize allergy issues. I also think it's fun to mix and match and, if necessary, eliminate one or two spices to customize to your taste and dietary restrictions. The mushrooms in these burgers act as the fakiin, as I describe in my Fakiin Bacon Crescent Rolls (page 48). They are the "meat" that makes these burgers truly memorable, and the spice kicks it up a notch.

Must Have

FAKIIN
2 cups sliced shiitake mushrooms
2 tablespoons coconut aminos

TACO SEASONING
2 teaspoons chili powder
2 teaspoons ground cumin
2 teaspoons smoked paprika
1 teaspoon dried oregano
¼ teaspoon garlic powder
¼ teaspoon sea salt

BURGERS
½ cup uncooked buckwheat groats
1 cup water
1 small Vidalia onion, diced
2 tablespoons coconut aminos
1 (15-ounce can) black beans, rinsed and drained
2 tablespoons taco seasoning (from above)
1 teaspoon vegan Worcestershire sauce

TOPPINGS (OPTIONAL)
Sliced avocado
Sautéed cremini mushrooms
Pickles
Lettuce
Sliced red onion

Must Do

1. Preheat the oven to 400°F. Line a 15 × 13-inch baking sheet with parchment paper.

2. To make the fakiin: Spread the shiitake mushrooms on the prepared baking sheet. Drizzle the coconut aminos on the mushrooms and toss them gently with your hands to coat. Bake until the mushrooms are slightly crisp, about 25 minutes.

3. To make the taco seasoning: Whisk together the chili powder, cumin, paprika, oregano, garlic, and salt in a small bowl.

4. To make the burgers: Toast the buckwheat groats in a medium pan over high heat for about 2 minutes. Add the water and bring to a boil. Lower the heat, cover the pot, and let simmer until the water is absorbed, about 8 minutes.

5. Once cooked, push the buckwheat groats to one side of the sauté pan and heat the onion on the other side, over medium heat, and stir until fragrant, about 1 minute.

6. Add the coconut aminos and cook, stirring occasionally, until the onion is translucent, about 2 minutes.

7. Add the black beans, roasted shiitake mushrooms (fakiin), taco seasoning, Worcestershire sauce, buckwheat groats, and onion to a food processor. Pulse until the mixture is combined but still has texture.

8. Lower the oven temperature to 375°F.

9. Divide the mixture evenly into 4 patties, and place them on the prepared baking sheet that you used for the mushrooms. Bake the burgers until they are firm and a little crispy on the outside, about 20 minutes. Flip the burgers over halfway through baking.

10. Transfer the pan from the oven to a wire rack and let rest for about 5 minutes.

11. Serve with desired toppings.

SERVING SIZE: 1 BURGER
Calories 70; Total Fat 0.4g; Protein 3.0g; Cholesterol 0.0g; Sodium 180mg; Fiber 3.1g; Sugars 0.7g; Total Carbohydrate 13.3g

Inside Scoop: I find that an easy way to flip the burgers is to place each on its own piece of torn parchment paper on the prepared baking sheet. When it's time to flip, lift the burger with the torn parchment paper underneath, turn it over onto the prepared baking sheet, and then remove the top piece of parchment paper. This reduces the chance of the burger falling apart when doing a somersault.

Krab Kakes

MAKES 16 KRAB KAKES

I really never thought I'd eat crab cakes again after eliminating animal protein from my diet. It didn't seem possible. But, after reading about how hearts of palm, with their stringy interior, can imitate lump crab, I was in. Once I knew that piece of the puzzle, I took the bait, and now I'm hooked. I make these krab kakes all the time and add them to salads, have them as a main course, or even eat as a krabwich with the works.

Must Have

SEASONING MIX
1 teaspoon ground ginger
1 teaspoon smoked paprika
1 teaspoon red pepper flakes
1 teaspoon dried dill
½ teaspoon celery salt
½ teaspoon freshly ground black pepper
¼ teaspoon ground nutmeg
¼ teaspoon ground cardamom
¼ teaspoon guar gum

KRAB KAKES
1 (14-ounce) can hearts of palm, rinsed and drained
1 shallot, minced
1 clove garlic, minced
1 celery stalk, finely diced
1 small red pepper, seeded and finely diced
¼ cup fresh parsley, finely chopped
1 tablespoon seasoning mix (from above)

BREADING
¾ cup ground gluten-free oats (I use a coffee grinder)
2 teaspoons seasoning mix (from above)

TOPPINGS
1 large lemon, sliced into wedges
Avocado slices
Prepared Horseradish (page 24)

Must Do

1. Preheat the oven to 375°F. Line a 15 × 13-inch baking sheet with parchment paper.

2. To make the seasoning mix: Whisk together the ginger, smoked paprika, red pepper flakes, dill, celery salt, black pepper, nutmeg, cardamom, and guar gum in a small bowl.

3. To make the krab kakes: Pull apart the insides of the palm as though it were string cheese. This is your lump crab. Chop it into ½-inch pieces and place in a large bowl. The outside of the palm doesn't shred, so you can chop this part into ¼-inch pieces.

4. Heat the shallot in a medium sauté pan over medium heat and stir until fragrant, about 1 minute.

5. Add the hearts of palm, garlic, celery, and red pepper and cook, stirring occasionally, until the vegetables are slightly tender, about 3 minutes.

6. Transfer the mixture from the sauté pan back to the large bowl.

7. Add the parsley and 1 tablespoon of the seasoning mix, and stir to combine.

8. To make the breading: Mix together the ground oats and remaining seasoning mix in a shallow dish.

9. Divide the krab kake mixture evenly into patties using approximately 1½ tablespoons each. Coat on both sides with the breading and place them on the prepared baking sheet.

10. Bake the krab kakes until they are a light golden brown around the edges, about 20 minutes.

11. Transfer the baking sheet from the oven to a wire rack, and let it sit for 10 minutes before removing the krab kakes gently with a spatula.

12. Serve with a wedge of fresh lemon and desired toppings.

SERVING SIZE: 2 KRAB KAKES
Calories 40; Total Fat 0.2g; Protein 0.9g; Cholesterol 0.0g; Sodium 110mg; Fiber 0.7g; Sugars 0.2g; Total Carbohydrate 1.6g

CHAPTER 9

The Side Show

Sometimes, the side show can be even more entertaining than the main event. This is not necessarily intentional on the part of the ringmaster, but things might just work out that way, beyond any-one's control or deliberation. I certainly didn't set out to outdo my entrée performers, but whenever I assemble the cast members in this list of sides, I start drooling just a little more than usual.

Green & Black Olive Tapenade

MAKES ABOUT 3 CUPS

One day I was in the grocery store, my home away from home, and I saw a jar of finely chopped olives and capers drenched in oil for the price of a first-class ticket to Greece. I knew it couldn't be that hard to make in a healthier way. So I went home and re-created what I saw in the jar, and it was not to be believed. I was delighted to learn that you just need to throw all the ingredients in a food processor, and in 5 seconds flat you have the most exquisite spread.

Must Have

1 cup pitted and chopped black Kalamata olives

1 cup pitted and chopped green olives

2 cloves garlic, minced

2 tablespoons capers, drained

1 tablespoon coconut nectar

2 medium carrots, steamed and diced

1 roasted red bell pepper (from a jar), sliced

1 teaspoon dried oregano

½ teaspoon dried thyme

Must Do

1. Add the black olives, green olives, garlic, capers, coconut nectar, carrots, red bell pepper, oregano, and thyme to a food processor. Pulse until the mixture is combined but still has some texture.

2. Serve with the Kalamata Rosemary Rustic Boule (page 216).

SERVING SIZE: ¼ CUP
Calories 30; Total Fat 1.6g; Protein 1.9g; Cholesterol 0.0g; Sodium 250mg; Fiber 1.7g; Sugars 1.0g; Total Carbohydrate 2.9g

Roasted Root Vegetable Hummus

MAKES ABOUT 5 CUPS

The great thing about never having gone to culinary school is that I am clueless in the kitchen. I don't know what culinary law I may or may not be breaking, so if it tastes good, is plant based, and is free of the top eight allergens, it goes in! That's why this hummus recipe may seem to have some nontraditional ingredients, but when it comes together, I don't think you'll go back to conventional hummus ever again.

Must Have

- 2 beets, peeled and chopped into 1-inch chunks
- 2 carrots, peeled and chopped into 1-inch chunks
- 1 rutabaga, peeled and chopped into 1-inch chunks
- ¼ cup coconut aminos
- 2 cloves garlic, minced
- 1 (15-ounce) can chickpeas, rinsed and drained
- 2 tablespoons Sunflower Seed Butter (page 20)
- ½ teaspoon chopped fresh rosemary
- ½ teaspoon ground cumin
- ½ teaspoon ground ginger
- ¼ teaspoon ground black pepper
- ¼ teaspoon cayenne pepper
- ⅛ teaspoon ground coriander
- ¼ cup freshly squeezed lemon juice
- 6 tablespoons water

Must Do

1. Preheat the oven to 400°F. Line a 15 × 10-inch baking sheet with parchment paper.

2. Spread the beets, carrots, and rutabaga in a single layer on the prepared baking sheet. Drizzle the coconut aminos evenly over the vegetables.

3. Bake until the vegetables are tender and slightly crisp, about 25 minutes. Toss halfway through baking so they brown evenly.

4. After they have cooled, add the roasted vegetables, garlic, chickpeas, sunflower seed butter, rosemary, cumin, ginger, black pepper, cayenne, and coriander to a food processor. Pulse to combine. While the machine is running, add the lemon juice and then the water, 1 tablespoon at a time, until the mixture is smooth.

5. Serve with pita chips or the Super Crunchy Seed Crackers (page 204).

SERVING SIZE: ¼ CUP

Calories 50; Total Fat 1.1g; Protein 2.9g; Cholesterol 0.0g; Sodium 54mg; Fiber 2.5g; Sugars 1.5g; Total Carbohydrate 8.0g

Everything Macaroni Salad

MAKES ABOUT 10 CUPS

If this recipe doesn't make you want to go on a picnic right about now, then I don't know what will. I love picnics and have the tricked-out basket to prove it. This macaroni salad contains all the foods you might find on a bruschetta buffet, and they mix and mingle so well with the macaroni that I can't help but smile (and drool) every time I make this.

Must Have

VINAIGRETTE

2 tablespoons chickpea miso paste

2 tablespoons apple cider vinegar

2 tablespoons mirin (Japanese rice cooking wine)

2 tablespoons Grade B maple syrup

2 cloves garlic, minced

⅓ cup chopped leeks

2 carrots, peeled and sliced

1 serrano pepper, seeded and chopped

1 teaspoon Hot Sauce (page 21)

¼ cup water

½ teaspoon freshly ground black pepper

MACARONI SALAD

1 pound gluten-free elbow macaroni

4 dill pickles, diced

3 celery stalks, diced

1 red bell pepper, seeded and diced

1 head radicchio, finely chopped (or red cabbage)

1 (8-ounce) can water chestnuts, sliced and chopped

1 (7.5-ounce) jar grilled artichokes, finely chopped

½ cup pitted and sliced Kalamata olives

½ cup pitted and sliced green olives

3 tablespoons finely chopped chives

3 tablespoons finely chopped dried dill

Must Do

1. To make the vinaigrette: Add the miso, apple cider vinegar, mirin, maple syrup, garlic, leeks, carrots, serrano pepper, hot sauce, water, and black pepper to a food processor. Pulse until the mixture comes together and is smooth.

2. To make the macaroni salad: Cook the macaroni according to the package instructions. Drain in a colander and rinse under cold water.

3. Transfer the macaroni to a large bowl and add the pickles, celery, red pepper, radicchio, water chestnuts, artichokes, black and green olives, chives, and dill.

4. Add the vinaigrette and toss to combine.

5. Place in the refrigerator to marinate for 1 hour or overnight, and serve chilled or at room temperature.

SERVING SIZE: ⅓ CUP

Calories 70; Total Fat 0.8g; Protein 2.4g; Cholesterol 0.0g; Sodium 100mg; Fiber 2.0g; Sugars 1.3g; Total Carbohydrate 13.0g

Sweet Potato Parsnip Fritters

MAKES 12 FRITTERS

I don't like to use food to bribe my son, but when desperation sets in, I stoop as low as a mom can go. So when my son refuses to read for the 20 minutes a day that is required by his teacher, I have to create an incentive. If it's not the latest Lego set, then it's these fritters. It works every time. When I say I'm going to make these for dinner if he reads, he cracks the spine of the latest kiddie best seller at lightning speed. These fritters are easy to make, offer all the essential nutrients, proteins, and beta-carotene you could ever ask for, feature a crisp and flavorful crust, and come with a chipotle lime avo-mayo dip to make it even more sublime. You really can't go wrong. I guess edible bribery isn't such a bad thing after all.

Must Have

FRITTERS

1 medium sweet potato, peeled and sliced

1 medium parsnip, peeled and sliced

¼ cup chopped fresh cilantro

2 teaspoons spicy mustard

¼ teaspoon sea salt

¼ teaspoon freshly ground black pepper

CRUST

½ cup sunflower seeds, roughly ground (I use a coffee grinder)

1 tablespoon nutritional yeast

1 teaspoon chipotle chili powder

CHIPOTLE LIME AVO-MAYO

1 medium avocado, peeled and pitted

¼ cup chopped fresh cilantro

¼ cup water

3 tablespoons freshly squeezed lime juice

1 teaspoon Grade B maple syrup

½ teaspoon chipotle chili powder

¼ teaspoon sea salt

¼ teaspoon freshly ground black pepper

Must Do

1. Preheat the oven to 400°F. Line a 15 × 10-inch baking sheet with parchment paper.

2. To make the fritters: Add the sweet potato and parsnip to a large pot of boiling water, lower the heat, cover the pot, and cook until fork tender, about 10 minutes.

3. Drain the potato and parsnip in a colander.

4. Add the potato, parsnip, cilantro, mustard, salt, and pepper to a food processor. Pulse until the mixture comes together but still has texture.

5. To make the crust: Whisk together the ground sunflower seeds, nutritional yeast, and chipotle chili powder in a small bowl.

6. Take about 2 tablespoons of the sweet potato and parsnip mixture and shape it into a patty. Dip the fritter into the crust mixture on both sides.

7. Place the fritter on the prepared baking sheet. Repeat this process until you have used up all the sweet potato and parsnip mixture.

8. Bake the fritters until they are a light golden brown and crisp, about 25 minutes. Flip the fritters over halfway through baking.

9. To make the mayo: Add the avocado, cilantro, water, lime juice, maple syrup, chipotle chili powder, salt, and black pepper to a food processor. Pulse until the mixture comes together and is smooth. Add more water if the avo-mayo is too thick.

10. Serve the fritters warm with a drizzle of the mayo and a side of Creamy Cabbage and Apple Slaw with a Kick (page 182).

SERVING SIZE: 2 FRITTERS, 1 TABLESPOON CHIPOTLE LIME AVO-MAYO

Calories 100; Total Fat 4.8g; Protein 2.9g; Cholesterol 0.0g; Sodium 110mg; Fiber 4.4g; Sugars 3.3g; Total Carbohydrate 16.1g

Kasha Varnishkes with Sriracha Broccoli

SERVES 8

To set the record straight, kasha is another name for roasted buckwheat groats. And buckwheat groats are seeds from a plant related to rhubarb. They contain no wheat, are gluten-free, and are in no way, shape, or form a grain. For many decades I was eating my mother's kasha varnishkes, never knowing their true identity. It was like a digestible mystery. So when I found out that kasha is made with groats, I was shocked; I felt stupid and elated all at once. So here, I re-create my mother's scrumptious dish with a fiery twist.

Must Have

KASHA VARNISHKES
8 ounces gluten-free bow tie noodles
1 Vidalia onion, diced
¼ cup coconut aminos
½ teaspoon salt
2 cups roasted buckwheat groats (or kasha)
4 cups green tea or water, at room temperature

SRIRACHA SAUCE
¼ cup Sriracha (page 22)
¼ cup coconut nectar
¼ cup coconut aminos
2 pounds broccolini (baby broccoli), chopped into ½-inch pieces

SERVING SIZE: 1 CUP
Calories 140; Total Fat 1.9g; Protein 4.9g; Cholesterol 0.0g; Sodium 180mg; Fiber 2.2g; Sugars 4.6g; Total Carbohydrate 26.8g

Must Do

1. Preheat the oven to 425°F. Line a 15 × 13-inch baking sheet with parchment paper.

2. **To make the kasha varnishkes:** Cook the pasta according to the package instructions. Drain.

3. Heat the onion in a large sauté pan over medium heat and stir until fragrant, about 1 minute. Add the coconut aminos, salt, and buckwheat groats and cook, stirring occasionally, until the onion becomes translucent, about 2 minutes.

4. Add the green tea and bring to a boil. Lower the heat, cover the pan, and let simmer until the liquid is absorbed, about 8 minutes.

5. **To make the Sriracha sauce:** Whisk together the Sriracha, coconut nectar, and coconut aminos in a large bowl.

6. Pour half of the sauce on the cooked buckwheat groats.

7. Add the broccolini to the large bowl and coat with the remaining sauce. Place the broccolini on the prepared baking sheet and bake until it is a little crispy, about 30 minutes.

8. Transfer the baking sheet from the oven to a wire rack, and then add the broccolini to the buckwheat groats mixture in the pan.

9. Add the cooked noodles and toss to incorporate. Serve immediately.

Smokin' Hot Mashed Yams

MAKES ABOUT 3 CUPS

You know why these yams are smokin' hot? Because I dressed them up that way. I would've put red spike heels on them, too, if they would let me. But even without the extra height, these girls are worth a spin around the dance floor. The extra heat from the hot sauce, the smooth charcoal accent from the liquid smoke, and, of course, the natural candied sweetness from the yam itself yield a mash you don't want to miss.

Must Have

3 medium yams (about 4 ounces each), peeled and sliced
½ cup nutritional yeast
¼ cup coconut aminos
1 tablespoon Hot Sauce (page 21)
1 teaspoon liquid smoke
½ teaspoon garlic powder
½ teaspoon sea salt
½ teaspoon freshly ground black pepper
¼ cup coconut milk

Must Do

1. Add the yams to a medium pot filled with boiling water and cook until fork tender, about 10 minutes.

2. Drain the yams in a colander. Add the yams, nutritional yeast, coconut aminos, hot sauce, liquid smoke, garlic powder, salt, and pepper to a food processor. Pulse until the mixture comes together but still has texture. While the machine is still running, add the coconut milk, 1 tablespoon at a time, until the mixture is smooth.

3. Serve immediately.

SERVING SIZE: ⅓ CUP

Calories 80; Total Fat 0.5g; Protein 2.6g; Cholesterol 0.0g; Sodium 200mg; Fiber 3.8g; Sugars 0.3g; Total Carbohydrate 17.2g

Lemon Orange Cauliflower

MAKES ABOUT 4 CUPS

A long time ago in a faraway place, I used to order lemon and orange chicken from my favorite Chinese restaurant. But after giving up animal protein and takeout, I wasn't quite sure how to quell my cravings for this dish. One day it came to me in the form of a cauliflower head. If I roasted cauliflower to make cauliflower steak, why not do the same to make cauliflower chicken? And while I'm at it, why not combine both of my favorite sauces into one and do lemon-orange? Eureka! You'll see.

Must Have

DREDGE MIXTURE
¾ cup tapioca flour
¼ teaspoon sea salt
¼ cup coconut milk

LEMON ORANGE SAUCE
2 cloves garlic, minced
1 tablespoon grated fresh ginger
½ cup freshly squeezed orange juice
¼ cup coconut aminos
¼ cup coconut nectar
¼ cup freshly squeezed lemon juice
2 tablespoons mirin (Japanese rice cooking wine)
2 teaspoons grated lemon zest
2 teaspoons grated orange zest

1 medium head cauliflower, cut into small florets
1 tablespoon red pepper flakes

Must Do

1. Preheat the oven to 400°F. Line a 15 × 10-inch baking sheet with parchment paper.

2. To make the dredge mixture: Whisk together the tapioca flour and salt in a medium bowl. Pour the coconut milk into a separate, small bowl.

3. To make the lemon orange sauce: Whisk together the garlic, ginger, orange juice, coconut aminos, coconut nectar, lemon juice, and mirin in a medium skillet over medium heat and cook, stirring occasionally, until the ingredients are thoroughly combined, about 3 minutes. Add the lemon and orange zests, and stir to combine. Turn off the heat and let the sauce cool a bit. Pour the sauce into a medium bowl.

4. Dredge the cauliflower florets in the tapioca flour mixture. Then dip them into the coconut milk and then into the lemon orange sauce.

5. Spread all the florets evenly in one layer on the prepared baking sheet and bake until the sauce on the florets turns a light golden brown, about 20 minutes.

6. Transfer the baking sheet from the oven to a wire rack and transfer the cauliflower to a serving bowl. Top with the red pepper flakes.

7. Serve immediately over brown rice or quinoa.

SERVING SIZE: ⅓ CUP
Calories 80; Total Fat 0.9g; Protein 2.3g; Cholesterol 0.0g; Sodium 100mg; Fiber 3.7g; Sugars 7.3g; Total Carbohydrate 17.7g

Creamy Cabbage and Apple Slaw with a Kick

MAKES ABOUT 6 CUPS

This coleslaw gets its creaminess from the oddest of places: a can of cannellini beans. I know, I know, it's pretty exciting stuff. No mayo, no oil, just pure protein with added spice, heat, and sweetness. This slaw will be your new go-to thing to bring to picnics and parties and your own table.

Must Have

DRESSING

1 (15-ounce) can cannellini beans, rinsed and drained
3 tablespoons apple cider vinegar
3 tablespoons coconut aminos
3 tablespoons mashed avocado
2 tablespoons prepared Horseradish (page 24)
2 tablespoons vegan, soy-free plain yogurt
1 tablespoon Grade B maple syrup
¼ teaspoon curry powder
¼ teaspoon sea salt
¼ teaspoon freshly ground black pepper
Juice of 1 lemon

SLAW

2 cups finely shredded red cabbage
2 cups finely shredded savoy or Napa cabbage
1 cup finely shredded baby bok choy
½ cup thinly sliced apple, with or without peel (I use Fuji)
¼ cup thinly sliced scallion
¼ cup finely shredded carrot
1 celery stalk, finely sliced
3 teaspoons caraway seeds

Must Do

1. **To make the dressing:** Add the cannellini beans, apple cider vinegar, coconut aminos, avocado, horseradish, yogurt, maple syrup, curry powder, salt, and black pepper to a food processor and pulse until the mixture comes together. Pour in the lemon juice, 1 tablespoon at a time, while the machine is running, and pulse until smooth.

2. **To make the slaw:** Add the red cabbage, Napa cabbage, bok choy, apple, scallion, carrot, celery, and caraway seeds to a large bowl.

3. Pour in as much dressing as you desire and toss until incorporated.

4. Refrigerate for at least 1 hour, or overnight, before serving. Store leftover dressing, if there is any, in an airtight container in the refrigerator for up to 7 days.

SERVING SIZE: ½ CUP

Calories 50; Total Fat 1.0g; Protein 1.9g; Cholesterol 0.0g; Sodium 140mg; Fiber 1.8g; Sugars 3.4g; Total Carbohydrate 8.0g

Spicy Sun-Dried Tomato Dip

MAKES ABOUT 2 CUPS

My husband's family came into town unexpectedly one weekend, and I needed food fast. I ran to the farmers' market, where I would normally only get the produce. In my haste, I purchased a sun-dried tomato dip that I bought on faith from the vendor, who swore it was good. When I served it with pita chips, my guests devoured it in less than two minutes. I re-create it here, but don't wait for guests to come over to make it because there won't be any left for you.

Must Have

1 (4-ounce) bag sun-dried tomatoes (not in oil), soaked in water for 20 minutes

1 cup fresh cilantro, chopped

½ cup fresh parsley, chopped

2 serrano peppers, seeded and diced

1 celery stalk, chopped

2 cloves garlic, minced

3 tablespoons freshly squeezed lemon juice

2 tablespoons Grade B maple syrup

1 teaspoon sea salt

1 teaspoon dried oregano

1 teaspoon dried basil

Must Do

1. Drain the sun-dried tomatoes and keep the soaking water.

2. Add the tomatoes, cilantro, parsley, serrano peppers, celery, garlic, lemon juice, maple syrup, salt, oregano, and basil to a food processor. Pulse until the mixture comes together but still has some texture.

3. While the machine is running, add the reserved soaking water, 1 tablespoon at a time, until the mixture is smooth. You should only need 2–3 tablespoons of the soaking water.

4. Place the dip in a container and refrigerate for at least 1 hour before serving.

SERVING SIZE: ¼ CUP

Calories 40; Total Fat 0.3g; Protein 1.4g; Cholesterol 0.0g; Sodium 250mg; Fiber 1.2g; Sugars 7.4g; Total Carbohydrate 1.4g

Nectarine Salsa

MAKES ABOUT 4 CUPS

One of the benefits of living in Southern California is the abundance of trees that bear all sorts of succulent fruit at different times of the year. As good luck would have it, some of these trees are in my backyard. The only bad thing is that when they bear fruit, it comes in HUGE quantities very quickly. And if you don't pick it right away, the squirrels eat it for you. So you're left either giving out care packages to the masses or putting the fruit in everything you cook, bake, broil, and puree. When our nectarine tree bore voluminous amounts of fruit last season, I quickly went to work strategically lodging it into every edible concoction I could think of. One of the things I made was this nectarine salsa. I had never made salsa with anything but tomatoes before (we have a lot of tomato vines, but that's another story), so this salsa was a revelation to me. It is tangy, sweet, and so refreshing. It was a massive hit with everyone who tasted it and complements any savory entrée beautifully.

Must Have

4 ripe medium nectarines, pitted and cut into ¼-inch slices

½ ripe avocado, diced

½ cup fresh cilantro, finely chopped

¼ cup red onion, finely chopped

¼ cup corn, freshly cut from the cob

1 serrano pepper, seeded and finely chopped

1 clove garlic, minced

2 tablespoons freshly squeezed lime juice

2 tablespoons grated fresh ginger

1 tablespoon coconut nectar

⅛ teaspoon fine sea salt

Must Do

1. Mix together the nectarines, avocado, cilantro, onion, corn, serrano pepper, and garlic in a medium bowl. Add the lime juice, ginger, coconut nectar, and salt, and stir to combine.

2. Let the salsa sit in the refrigerator for at least an hour or overnight to let the flavors blend before serving.

SERVING SIZE: ¼ CUP

Calories 50; Total Fat 2.0g; Protein 0.8g; Cholesterol 0.0g; Sodium 18.0mg; Fiber 2.4g; Sugars 3.6g; Total Carbohydrate 7.5g

Latkes

One of my favorite traditions of Hanukkah revolves around potato pancakes, otherwise known as latkes. They are usually made exclusively with russet potatoes, but I like to add in a sweet potato and some fresh herbs, which really lend a nice rustic and fragrant quality. The best part is: these are baked, not fried, and you get the same satisfying crispiness and flavor without the added oil and fat. It's a miracle!

Must Have

LATKES
1 medium sweet potato (about 6 ounces)
1 small yellow onion, diced
2 tablespoons coconut aminos
1 medium russet potato (about 5 ounces)
½ cup chopped fresh parsley
¼ chopped fresh cilantro
¼ cup chopped fresh dill
2 tablespoons chickpea miso paste
¼ teaspoon freshly ground black pepper

TOPPINGS
Applesauce
Prepared Horseradish (page 24)
Soy-free, dairy-free sour cream

Must Do

1. Preheat the oven to 425°F. Line a 15 × 13-inch baking sheet with parchment paper.

2. **To make the latkes:** Add the sweet potato to a small pot of boiling water, cover the pot, lower the heat, and cook until fork tender, about 10 minutes. Drain the sweet potato in a colander and let cool. Peel off the skin and mash the potato well with a fork.

3. Heat the onion in a medium sauté pan over medium heat and stir until fragrant, about 1 minute.

4. Add the coconut aminos and cook until the onion becomes translucent, about 2 minutes. Turn off the heat.

5. Peel the russet potato and grate it into a large bowl. Add the mashed sweet potato, parsley, cilantro, dill, miso, and black pepper, and stir to thoroughly combine.

6. Take about 3 tablespoons of the potato mixture, shape it into a small, flat pancake, and place it on the prepared baking sheet. Repeat until you have used up all the potato mixture.

7. Bake the potato latkes until they are a light golden brown, about 30 minutes. Flip the pancakes over halfway through baking.

8. Transfer the baking sheet from the oven to a wire rack, and let it sit for about 2 minutes before removing the latkes with a spatula. Serve immediately with desired toppings.

SERVING SIZE: 1 LATKE
Calories 40; Total Fat 0.1g; Protein 0.9g; Cholesterol 0.0g; Sodium 50mg; Fiber 0.8g; Sugars 0.2g; Total Carbohydrate 5.9g

Rainbow Quinoa & Portobello Pilaf

MAKES ABOUT 6 CUPS

I put this recipe in the "sides" chapter because it's only natural to think of food that has the semblance of a pilaf as an accompaniment to a protein-packed entrée. But the reality is, because this is made with quinoa and not rice, it contains all the protein you need, without adding a single thing. Either way, this dish is chock-full of robust flavor, hearty vegetables, and fungi, and a smoldering essence from the liquid smoke. So enjoy it as a side to an entrée or just on its own.

Must Have

- 1 medium red onion, chopped
- ½ cup coconut aminos
- 2 large portobello caps, chopped into ½-inch chunks
- 1 carrot, peeled and diced
- 1 tablespoon Grade B maple syrup
- ½ teaspoon liquid smoke
- 2 cups rainbow quinoa, rinsed (yellow or red quinoa is fine)
- 4 cups No-Sodium Vegetable Broth (page 25)
- 4 ounces kale, leaves deveined and finely chopped

Must Do

1. Heat the onion in a medium sauté pan over medium heat and stir until fragrant, about 1 minute.

2. Add the coconut aminos, portobellos, carrot, maple syrup, and liquid smoke and cook, stirring occasionally, until the vegetables are slightly tender, about 5 minutes.

3. Add the quinoa and broth, and stir to combine.

4. Bring to a boil, lower the heat, cover the pan, and simmer until the broth is absorbed, about 15 minutes.

5. Turn off the heat, add the kale, and stir to incorporate.

6. Serve immediately.

SERVING SIZE: 1 CUP

Calories 200; Total Fat 3.4g; Protein 8.6g; Cholesterol 0.0g; Sodium 180mg; Fiber 4.7g; Sugars 1.2g; Total Carbohydrate 41.1g

Kasha Knishes

MAKES 6 KNISHES

When I was living with my parents in Queens, many moons ago, every Friday night my mother would buy premade knishes at the local kosher market. These things were like suitcases. The knishes were as tasty as they were large—filled to the brim with salty mashed potatoes. Now that I am a somewhat civilized, health-conscious adult, I felt I should make a more petite and healthy version of the knishes I know and remember so well. So I substitute kasha for the filling and welcome in some warm spices. The result is a well-seasoned, mouthwatering circle of dough that is a great nosh or a perfect side to any meal, Friday night or otherwise.

Must Have

DOUGH
3 cups sorghum flour
1 cup tapioca flour
½ teaspoon xanthan gum
¼ teaspoon sea salt
1½ cups seltzer water
3 tablespoons pumpkin puree
1 teaspoon apple cider vinegar

FILLING
1½ cups medium roasted
   buckwheat groats (kasha)
4 cups water
1 small yellow onion, diced
½ cup coconut aminos

WASH
3 tablespoons molasses
1 tablespoon water
3 tablespoons nutritional yeast

DIPPING SAUCES
Spicy mustard
Prepared Horseradish (page 24)

Must Do

1. Preheat the oven to 350°F. Line a 15 × 13-inch baking sheet with parchment paper.

2. To make the dough: Whisk together the sorghum flour, tapioca flour, xanthan gum, and salt in a large bowl. Make a well in the middle.

3. Add the seltzer, pumpkin puree, and apple cider vinegar, and stir to combine until a dough forms. Flatten it into a disk and wrap it in plastic. Place in the fridge for about 15 minutes.

4. To make the filling: In a medium pot, cook the buckwheat groats (kasha) in the water over high heat. Bring it to a boil, lower the heat, and let simmer until all the water is absorbed, about 5 minutes.

5. Heat the onion in a medium sauté pan over medium heat and stir until fragrant, about 1 minute. Add the coconut aminos and cooked kasha, and stir to incorporate.

6. Take the ball of dough out of the fridge and divide it into 6 equal pieces. Then divide each of the 6 pieces in half so that you have 12 pieces of dough. Press out each piece, with your fingertips, into a circle about 3½ inches in diameter and ⅛ inch thick.

7. Fill the middle of 6 of the dough circles with about ¼ cup of the kasha mixture. Place the remaining dough circles on top of the filled ones and pinch around the perimeter to seal. Trim the edges using a pizza wheel or paring knife.

8. **To make the wash:** Whisk together the molasses, water, and nutritional yeast in a small bowl. Brush the tops and sides of each knish with the wash.

9. Place the 6 knishes on the prepared baking sheet. Bake until they are golden brown, about 30 minutes.

10. Transfer the pan from the oven to a wire rack, and let it sit for about 10 minutes. Serve with the desired sauces.

SERVING SIZE: 1 KNISH
Calories 300; Total Fat 2.3g; Protein 11.1g; Cholesterol 0.0g; Sodium 180mg; Fiber 9.0g; Sugars 2.5g; Total Carbohydrate 71.1g

Inside Scoop: Sometimes I add about 2 teaspoons of maple syrup to 3 tablespoons of spicy mustard to create a maple mustard dip. I highly recommend it.

Sea Vegetable & Cabbage Slaw

MAKES ABOUT 6 CUPS

Sea vegetables are just one of those perfect foods that give you so much and ask for very little in return. I think there is a tendency to shy away from seaweed because it looks a little slimy, if we're going to be truthful. But it really is quite yummy when prepared in just the right way. Also, sea veggies give us all 56 essential elements needed for human health, as well as trace elements such as selenium. I toss them with cabbage, cilantro, and bok choy in a light and fresh vinaigrette that brings out their best qualities.

Must Have

SLAW

1 (0.9-ounce) package mixed sea vegetables, soaked in water for 7 minutes and drained (I use SeaVegi's Seaweed Salad Mix; see Resources)

2 cups thinly sliced savoy or Napa cabbage

1 cup thinly sliced bok choy

¼ cup chopped fresh cilantro

DRESSING

5 tablespoons rice vinegar

2 tablespoons coconut aminos

2 tablespoons freshly squeezed lime juice

1 tablespoon coconut nectar

1 clove garlic, minced

2 tablespoons grated fresh ginger

TOPPING

2 tablespoons hemp seeds

Must Do

1. **To make the slaw:** Add the drained sea vegetables, cabbage, bok choy, and cilantro to a large bowl.

2. **To make the dressing:** Whisk together the rice vinegar, coconut aminos, lime juice, coconut nectar, garlic, and ginger in a small bowl. Pour it over the entire bowl of slaw and toss to combine.

3. Top the slaw with the hemp seeds.

4. Place in the refrigerator for an hour or overnight to allow the flavors to marinate. Serve cold. The slaw keeps in an airtight container for 3 days.

SERVING SIZE: 1 CUP

Calories 50; Total Fat 0.0g; Protein 1.4g; Cholesterol 0.0g; Sodium 110mg; Fiber 5.9g; Sugars 2.0g; Total Carbohydrate 8.8g

Krispy Kale Impaled Yams with Spinach-Artichoke Dip

MAKES 6 IMPALED YAMS

I must have been in a macabre mood when I created this recipe. There is a lot of impaling of potatoes and vegetables going on, but after the massacre, you get the most down-home, cozy, congenial side dish. I have always loved spinach and artichoke dip. And because the dip is usually in some edible container, like an artichoke, I just want to devour the whole kit and caboodle. I make that possible with the yam acting as the holding station and the kale impersonating a green, ruffled dress. You can dip in anything from raw veggies to cubes of bread, or just tear off pieces of the potato skin and use that as the delivery system for the spinach-artichoke mixture. Just rip and dip and have a party.

Must Have

YAMS
3 large yams (about 6½ ounces each)

SPINACH-ARTICHOKE DIP
1 small yellow onion, chopped
¼ cup coconut aminos
2 cloves garlic, minced
½ teaspoon ground nutmeg
1½ pounds spinach, chopped
¾ cup canned or jarred artichokes, chopped
¼ cup nutritional yeast
¼ cup coconut milk
1 teaspoon freshly ground black pepper

KRISPY KALE
6 large kale leaves, stemmed
2 tablespoons coconut aminos

Must Do

1. Preheat the oven to 350°F.

2. To make the yams: Add the yams to a pot of boiling water, cover the pot, lower the heat, and cook until fork tender, about 10 minutes. Drain the yams in a colander and let cool.

3. To make the dip: Heat the onion in a large sauté pan over medium heat and stir until fragrant, about 1 minute.

4. Add the coconut aminos, garlic, and nutmeg and cook, stirring occasionally, until fragrant, about 2 minutes.

5. Add the spinach, artichokes, nutritional yeast, and coconut milk, and cook until the spinach turns bright green and wilts a little, about 2 minutes. Turn off the heat and grind in the black pepper.

6. Cut the cooked yams in half widthwise and cut off the pointy tops on each to make a stable bottom. Scoop out the inside flesh of each yam, mash it, and add it to the spinach-artichoke dip. Stir well to incorporate.

7. Fill the inside of the yams with the dip.

8. To make the kale: Take each kale leaf and massage it with the coconut aminos until it starts to soften, about 1 minute. Wrap each yam half with a kale leaf and pin the kale onto the yam with 2 toothpicks.

9. Place the 6 yam halves in a small glass casserole dish and bake until the kale is slightly crisp, about 20 minutes.

SERVING SIZE: 1 KRISPY KALE IMPALED
YAM

Calories 100; Total Fat 0.6g; Protein 3.9g;
Cholesterol 0.0g; Sodium 180mg; Fiber 4.7g;
Sugars 1.7g; Total Carbohydrate 18.6g

Inside Scoop: If you have leftover dip
after stuffing the yams, bake it in a
separate dish while you bake the yams,
and you can have extra dip for a party or
yourself.

KALAMATA ROSEMARY RUSTIC BOULE
(SEE RECIPE ON PAGE 216)

CHAPTER 10

The Bread Basket

Back in the day, when food allergies and celiac disease had not yet taken up residence in our national conversation and lives, my family and I used to go out for dinner. The arrival of the bread basket was always the most anticipated moment of the meal. The different kinds of grains, seeds, textures, and shapes were a sight to behold and a taste to relish. Any mention of cross-contamination or gluten would have seemed like highfalutin scientific jargon. Those days are long gone, and in their stead, we have to consider these very issues. Here I propose a bread basket of a different kind. The ingredients have evolved as well as the taste, and the enjoyment of bringing the bread basket to the table has grown exponentially.

Soft Beer Pretzels

MAKES 8 PRETZELS

It's not like hot, soft, doughy pretzels need anything to make them taste better, but since beer and pretzels are meant for each other, I decided to infuse one with the other. Surprisingly, the gluten-free beer adds a malt-like flavor that is indescribably good. And if you want to take it even a step further, you can consummate the union by dipping the pretzels in spicy mustard. It's the kind of wedded bliss that you don't want to miss.

Must Have

DOUGH
1 (12-ounce) bottle gluten-free beer, warmed to about 108°F (I microwave for 30 seconds)
1 (2¼-teaspoon) packet active dry yeast
2 tablespoons coconut nectar
2 cups sweet white rice flour
1 cup sorghum flour
1 cup tapioca flour
1 tablespoon psyllium husk powder
½ teaspoon sea salt
2 tablespoons pumpkin puree

DIP
6 cups water
½ cup baking soda

GLAZE
1 tablespoon coconut milk
1 tablespoon coconut aminos

TOPPING
2 tablespoons Parmezan (page 24)

Must Do

1. Preheat the oven to 200°F and then turn it off. Line a 15 × 13-inch baking sheet with parchment paper.

2. To make the dough: Combine the warm beer and yeast in a small bowl. Add the coconut nectar and stir to combine. Let the yeast mixture sit for about 8 minutes, or until foamy.

3. Whisk together the sweet white rice flour, sorghum flour, tapioca flour, psyllium husk powder, and salt in a large bowl. Make a well in the middle.

4. Add the pumpkin to the yeast mixture, stir to combine, and then pour into the flour mixture. Mix together until a dough forms and shape it into a ball.

5. Divide the dough in half, and then in half again so that you have 4 pieces. Divide those 4 pieces in half to make 8 even pieces of dough. Roll out the first piece into a 15-inch rope.

6. Pull up the two ends into a U, cross them, and bring them down diagonally to the bottom of the U to form a pretzel. Repeat until you have done this with all 8 pieces of dough. Place the pretzels on the prepared baking sheet.

7. Cover the baking sheet with a clean dishtowel, place it in the oven, and allow the pretzels to rise for 1 hour.

8. Take the risen pretzels out of the oven, remove the dishtowel, and preheat the oven to 425°F.

9. To make the dip: Add the water to a medium pot over high heat and bring it to a boil. Add the baking soda and stir to dissolve. Remove the pot from the heat.

10. Place the pretzels, 2 at a time, into the hot-water dip until they float, about 30 seconds. Remove the pretzels

with a slotted spatula and place them on a paper towel to dry off. Place them back on the prepared baking sheet using the spatula.

11. **To make the glaze:** Combine the coconut milk and coconut aminos in a small bowl. Brush the pretzels with the glaze and top with the parmezan.

12. Bake the pretzels until they are golden brown and firm to the touch, about 15 minutes.

13. Transfer the baking sheet from the oven to a wire rack, and let it sit for 20 minutes before removing the pretzels.

14. Keep in an airtight container for up to 3 days or wrap and freeze for up to 3 months.

SERVING SIZE: 1 PRETZEL
Calories 320; Total Fat 1.5g; Protein 7.1g; Cholesterol 0.0g; Sodium 143mg; Fiber 5.7g; Sugars 2.5g; Total Carbohydrate 80.0g

Pumpernickel Bread

MAKES 1 LOAF, 9 SLICES

Pumpernickel bread is rye bread's tall, dark, and handsome brother. Mr. Pumpernickel gets his virile hue from the rye endosperm, which contains a darker pigment than the other parts of the rye seed. But since we're not using rye flour, due to its gluten content, we pump up the color with a little cacao and molasses. These are not merely coloring agents but also ways to infuse our bread with more minerals, vitamins, antioxidants, and flavor.

Must Have

1½ cups warm water, about 108°F
   (I microwave for 30 seconds)
1 (2¼-teaspoon) packet active
   dry yeast
2 tablespoons coconut nectar
2 cups sorghum flour
½ cup sweet white rice flour
¼ cup tapioca flour
2 tablespoons cacao powder
1 tablespoon psyllium husk
   powder
2 teaspoons caraway seeds
2 tablespoons pumpkin puree
1 tablespoon unsulfured molasses

SERVING SIZE: 1 SLICE

Calories 170; Total Fat 1.0g; Protein
4.3g; Cholesterol 0.0g; Sodium
1.2mg; Fiber 3.8g; Sugars 2.5g; Total
Carbohydrate 38.1g

Must Do

1. Preheat the oven to 200°F and then turn it off. Line a 9 × 5 × 2-inch loaf pan with parchment paper.

2. Combine the warm water and yeast in a small bowl. Add the coconut nectar and stir to combine. Let the yeast mixture sit for about 8 minutes, or until foamy.

3. Whisk together the sorghum flour, sweet white rice flour, tapioca flour, cacao powder, psyllium husk powder, and caraway seeds in a large bowl and make a well in the middle.

4. Add the pumpkin puree and molasses to the yeast mixture, stir to combine, and then pour into the flour mixture. Mix together until a dough forms. Transfer the dough to the prepared pan.

5. Cover the pan with a clean dishtowel, place it in the oven, and allow the dough to rise for 1 hour.

6. Take the risen dough out of the oven, remove the dishtowel, and preheat the oven to 425°F.

7. Place an 8 × 8-inch pan filled with ice cubes on the lower rack of the oven to help crisp up the crust.

8. Bake the bread until the crust turns a darker brown and is firm to the touch, about 40 minutes.

9. Transfer the loaf pan from the oven to a wire rack, and let it sit for 45 minutes before removing the bread for a complete cooldown. If you cut into the bread too soon it will be gummy, so please refrain from breaking bread too early.

10. Keep the bread in an airtight container for up to 3 days, or wrap and freeze for up to 3 months.

Super Crunchy Seed Crackers

MAKES 12 CRACKERS

Oh, how I love crispy seeded crackers. There is something so satisfying and satiating about the crunch and seedy savoriness of it all. In my quest to make the best crackers, I put my baking skills to the test. Crackers are a little bit more temperamental than cookies and strive to be really, really thin. Crackers are the original "skinny girls." So it's important that, before they go into the oven, they are as flat as flat can be. And when they come out of the oven, let them cool on the wire rack with only the parchment paper beneath them so no condensation can creep in. It's all worth it in the end, my friends, because this is no ordinary cracker. It's a super cracker.

Must Have

1 small carrot, peeled and diced
3 tablespoons water
⅔ cup pumpkin seeds
⅔ cup sunflower seeds
⅓ cup hemp seeds
¼ cup diced onion
1 tablespoon coconut aminos
1 tablespoon coconut nectar
¼ teaspoon guar gum
¼ teaspoon sea salt

Must Do

1. Preheat the oven to 300°F. Line a 9 × 9-inch square baking pan with parchment paper.

2. Add the carrot to a food processor and pulse. Add the water while the machine is running and process until the carrot is pureed.

3. Add the pumpkin seeds, sunflower seeds, hemp seeds, onion, coconut aminos, coconut nectar, guar gum, and salt, and pulse until the mixture comes together but still retains some texture.

4. Transfer the mixture to the prepared pan, place a piece of parchment paper on top, and press down evenly across, down, and into the corners, until the mixture is about ⅛ inch thick.

5. Bake the crackers until they turn a light golden brown, about 35 minutes. Rotate the pan from front to back halfway through baking.

6. Transfer the pan from the oven to a wire rack, and let it sit for 10 minutes before removing the crackers to cool completely.

7. Slice with a pizza slicer to divide into 12 individual rectangles.

SERVING SIZE: 1 CRACKER
Calories 60; Total Fat 3.6g; Protein 2.3g; Cholesterol 0.0g; Sodium 30mg; Fiber 8.9g; Sugars 1.7g; Total Carbohydrate 5.1g

Inside Scoop: You can also use the back of a wet spoon to smooth and flatten the mixture in the pan without placing parchment paper on top.

Jalapeño Cornbread Muffins

MAKES 12 STANDARD-SIZE MUFFINS

I believe cornbread should get a spicy kick in the pants. It wears it well, and let me tell you, cornbread doesn't need a holiday to be in fashion. And so it is with cornbread muffins. I revel in portion control, and I use my baking tins for this purpose. These muffins go well with soup, salad, and chili, and are good all on their own. They are so easy to make and they freeze well, so there is no excuse not to have them around at all times.

Must Have

¾ cup coconut milk

1 teaspoon apple cider vinegar

1½ cups All-Purpose Gluten-Free Flour Mix (page 20)

1 cup coarse-ground cornmeal

3 tablespoons nutritional yeast

2 tablespoons onion powder

2 teaspoons sodium-free baking powder

1 teaspoon baking soda

½ teaspoon xanthan gum

½ teaspoon sea salt

½ teaspoon smoked paprika

¼ teaspoon cayenne pepper

¼ cup pumpkin puree

¼ cup coconut sugar

¼ cup vegan, soy-free plain yogurt

1 jalapeño pepper, seeded and finely diced

½ cup corn kernels fresh off the cob, divided

Must Do

1. Preheat the oven to 350°F. Line a 12-cup standard-size muffin tin with paper baking cups.

2. Mix together the coconut milk and apple cider vinegar in a small bowl. This is your "buttermilk."

3. Whisk together the all-purpose flour, cornmeal, nutritional yeast, onion powder, baking powder, baking soda, xanthan gum, salt, smoked paprika, and cayenne in a large bowl. Make a well in the middle.

4. Add the pumpkin puree and coconut sugar, and stir to combine.

5. Add the "buttermilk" mixture and stir until the liquid is absorbed and the batter is smooth.

6. Add the yogurt, jalapeño, and ¼ cup of the corn kernels, and stir until well combined.

7. Pour the batter into the prepared muffin tin, dividing it evenly. Each cup should be almost full. Top the muffins with the remaining ¼ cup corn kernels.

8. Bake the muffins until they turn a light golden brown and bounce back slightly to the touch, about 18 minutes. Rotate the muffin tin from front to back halfway through baking.

9. Transfer the muffin tin from the oven to a wire rack, and let it sit for 10 minutes before removing the muffins to cool completely.

10. Keep in an airtight container for up to 3 days or wrap and freeze for up to 3 months.

SERVING SIZE: 1 MUFFIN

Calories 100; Total Fat 1.4g; Protein 3.2g; Cholesterol 0.0g; Sodium 95mg; Fiber 3.9g; Sugars 3.0g; Total Carbohydrate 21.1g

Banana Java Date Bread

MAKES 1 LOAF, 9 SLICES

I am a banana bread junkie. My addiction goes way back. I've attended support group meetings, hypnotherapy, and even tying myself up, but nothing holds me back from continuing to eat this sweet and delicious quick bread. And the sordid story that stands out the most from my long and dark path is the time I was escorted out the door of an all-you-can-eat smorgasbord on Long Island for sneaking some of the banana bread into my purse. That being my lowest moment, I decided I was going to learn how to make recipes that trumped any banana bread in a buffet line. So here is my best one yet, and I share it with you with a caveat. This banana bread is habit forming and makes you susceptible to eating more than one slice in any given sitting. Okay, you've been fairly warned.

Must Have

¼ cup pumpkin seeds

1¾ cups All-Purpose Gluten-Free Flour Mix (page 20)

¼ cup cacao powder

¼ cup hemp seeds

1½ teaspoons sodium-free baking powder

1 teaspoon baking soda

½ teaspoon guar gum

¼ teaspoon sea salt

½ cup coconut sugar

¼ cup applesauce

1 tablespoon gluten-free vanilla extract

2 very ripe medium bananas, mashed

5 Medjool dates, pitted and chopped into ¼-inch pieces

½ cup black coffee, at room temperature

Must Do

1. Preheat the oven to 375°F. Line a 9 × 5 × 2-inch loaf pan with parchment paper.

2. Add the pumpkin seeds to a small skillet over medium heat. Toast until they start to snap, crackle, and pop and turn a light golden brown, about 3 minutes. After the pumpkin seeds cool, give them a rough chop.

3. Whisk together the all-purpose flour, cacao powder, hemp seeds, baking powder, baking soda, guar gum, salt, and roasted pumpkin seeds in a large bowl. Make a well in the middle.

4. Add the coconut sugar, applesauce, vanilla, mashed bananas, and dates, and stir to combine. Add the coffee and stir to incorporate.

5. Pour the batter into the prepared loaf pan and bake until a toothpick inserted in the center of the bread comes out clean, about 45 minutes. Rotate the loaf pan from front to back halfway through baking.

6. Transfer the loaf pan from the oven to a wire rack, and let it sit for 20 minutes before removing the loaf to cool completely.

7. Keep in an airtight container for up to 3 days, or wrap and freeze for up to 3 months.

SERVING SIZE: 1 SLICE
Calories 150; Total Fat 1.7g; Protein 3.6g; Cholesterol 0.0g; Sodium 60mg; Fiber 4.3g; Sugars 12.0g; Total Carbohydrate 33.1g

Caramelized Onion Naan

MAKES 4 NAAN

Let's face it: naan's only purpose in life is to soak up all sorts of Indian food that might otherwise not be removed from its plate. I say, "No Indian food left behind." And don't be afraid about etiquette, good manners, or what the Buddha would do. Naan is a tool. Use it! This flatbread is different than most in that it is cooked in a skillet rather than the oven. I think that might make it less intimidating, as well as the fact that it's okay if you burn it a little bit. Now how many recipes can you say that about?

Must Have

1 small sweet onion, thinly sliced
2 tablespoons coconut aminos
1 cup warm water, about 108°F (I microwave for 30 seconds)
1 (2¼-teaspoon) packet active dry yeast
2 tablespoons coconut nectar
2 cups sorghum flour
1 cup tapioca flour
1 tablespoon psyllium husk powder
½ teaspoon sea salt
½ teaspoon garlic powder
¼ cup vegan, soy-free plain yogurt
2 tablespoons pumpkin puree

Must Do

1. Preheat the oven to 200°F and then turn it off.

2. Heat the onion in a large sauté pan over medium heat and stir until fragrant, about 1 minute. Add the coconut aminos and cook, stirring occasionally, until the onion is slightly translucent, about 2 minutes.

3. Remove most of the onion from the pan except for about 2 tablespoons and reserve in a small bowl.

4. Combine the warm water and yeast in a small bowl. Add the coconut nectar and stir to combine. Let the yeast mixture sit for about 8 minutes, or until foamy.

5. Whisk together the sorghum flour, tapioca flour, psyllium husk powder, salt, and garlic powder in a large bowl. Make a well in the middle.

6. Add the yogurt and pumpkin puree to the yeast mixture, stir to combine, and then pour into the flour mixture.

7. Form the dough into a ball. Place it in a bowl, cover it with a clean dishtowel, place it in the oven, and allow the dough to rise for 1 hour.

8. Take the risen dough out of the oven, remove the dishtowel, and divide the dough evenly into 4 pieces by cutting the ball of dough in half and then in half again.

9. Heat the sauté pan that contains the 2 tablespoons of onions over high heat.

10. Roll the first piece of dough out on a lightly floured piece of parchment paper with another piece of parchment paper on top of the dough until it's an oblong shape or the shape of a teardrop, about ¼ inch thick. If the dough

is sticky, flour the top before you place the parchment paper on top of it.

11. Transfer the dough to the sauté pan using a spatula, and place it over the caramelized onions. Let the dough cook by putting the lid on the sauté pan until the bottom side turns a light golden brown and the onions are slightly burnt, about 2 minutes. Flip over the dough and cook for another 2 minutes.

12. Remove the naan from the pan and place it on a plate.

13. Repeat this process with the remaining pieces of dough, placing about 2 tablespoons of the reserved sautéed onions in the pan each time, until you have 4 naan with onions on one side.

14. Serve with the Palak Paneer (page 151) or the Coriander Dal (page 159).

SERVING SIZE: 1 NAAN
Calories 300; Total Fat 2.1g; Protein 8.5g; Cholesterol 0.0g; Sodium 280mg; Fiber 7.0g; Sugars 3.5g; Total Carbohydrate 80.0g

Stromboli

SERVES 8

Stromboli is actually a small island off the north coast of Sicily where there is an active volcano. And because of this, the word *stromboli* has come to mean "small explosion." Well, that's exactly how I feel about this overstuffed Italian turnover. It's an eruption of spices, herbs, and flavors. It's quite exciting to taste and even more so to look at. Its appearance can be a little intimidating if you don't know how it is done. But in the instructions below, I tell you exactly how, and you'll be amazed that it is so easy.

Must Have

FILLING
1 shallot, finely sliced
¼ cup coconut aminos
3 cloves garlic, minced
1 teaspoon dried oregano
½ teaspoon dried basil
¼ teaspoon sea salt
1 cup sliced cremini mushrooms
1 cup deveined and roughly
  chopped kale
1 medium heirloom tomato,
  seeded and diced

DOUGH
1 cup warm water, about 108°F (I
  microwave for 30 seconds)
1 (2¼-teaspoon) packet active
  dry yeast
2 tablespoons coconut nectar
1¾ cups sweet white rice flour
⅔ cup sorghum flour
1 tablespoon psyllium husk
  powder
½ teaspoon sea salt
2 tablespoons pumpkin puree

GLAZE
2 tablespoons coconut nectar
2 tablespoons coconut milk
2 tablespoons nutritional yeast

TOPPING
Hemp seeds

Must Do

1. Preheat the oven to 200°F and then turn it off. Line a 15 × 13-inch baking sheet with parchment paper. Lightly flour the entire area.

2. **To make the filling:** Heat the shallot in a large sauté pan over medium heat and stir until fragrant, about 1 minute. Add the coconut aminos, garlic, oregano, basil, salt, mushrooms, kale, and tomatoes and cook, stirring occasionally, until the spices and herbs are fragrant and the kale is a bright green, about 2 minutes.

3. **To make the dough:** Combine the warm water and yeast in a small bowl. Add the coconut nectar and stir to combine. Let the yeast mixture sit for about 8 minutes, or until foamy.

4. Whisk together the sweet white rice flour, sorghum flour, psyllium husk powder, and salt in a large bowl. Make a well in the middle.

5. Add the pumpkin puree to the yeast mixture, stir to combine, and then pour into the flour mixture. Mix together until a dough forms.

6. Form the dough into a ball, place it on the prepared baking sheet, and place another piece of parchment on top. If the dough is sticky, flour the top before you place the parchment paper on top of it. Roll out the dough to make a rectangle about 8 × 6 inches and about ¼ inch thick.

7. Spread the vegetable mixture evenly over the entire area, leaving about a 1-inch border around the perimeter.

8. Roll the dough from the long side closest to you upward with the help of the parchment paper.

9. Turn the stromboli seam side down on the parchment paper. Seal the ends by pinching the dough together. Cut four 1-inch slits with a paring knife into the dough across the top.

10. Cover the stromboli with a clean dishtowel and place in the oven for 1 hour.

11. Take the risen dough out of the oven, remove the dishtowel, and preheat the oven to 400°F.

12. **To make the glaze:** Whisk together the coconut nectar, coconut milk, and nutritional yeast in a small bowl. Brush the entire stromboli with the glaze. Sprinkle the hemp seeds on top.

13. Place an 8 × 8-inch pan filled with ice cubes on the lower rack of the oven to help crisp up the crust.

14. Bake the stromboli until the crust is a light golden brown and firm to the touch, about 30 minutes.

15. Transfer the baking sheet from the oven to a wire rack, and let it sit for 20 minutes before removing the stromboli for a slight cooldown.

16. Cut it with a serrated knife into 8 slices.

SERVING SIZE: 1 SLICE
Calories 250; Total Fat 0.9g; Protein 5.3g; Cholesterol 0.0g; Sodium 70mg; Fiber 3.7g; Sugars 3.7g; Total Carbohydrate 60.0g

Challah

Challah is braided bread served on the Sabbath and Jewish holidays. Traditionally, this bread is made with a lot of eggs, so it was never a consideration as something I would make for my egg-allergic son. But after I received numerous requests from my bakery customers to "figure it out," I became inspired. My revelatory moment came when I finally decided to include chickpea flour in the recipe. Chickpea flour has an egg-like flavor and makes this conventional egg bread taste more authentic. All I can say is *challah-lujah!*

Must Have

DOUGH

1 cup warm water, about 108°F (I microwave for 30 seconds)
1 (2¼-teaspoon) packet active dry yeast
2 tablespoons coconut nectar
2 cups sorghum flour
¾ cup tapioca flour
½ cup chickpea flour
½ cup sweet white rice flour
1 tablespoon psyllium husk powder
1 teaspoon sea salt
¼ cup pumpkin puree
½ cup coconut milk

GLAZE

2 tablespoons coconut milk
1 tablespoon molasses

TOPPING

2 teaspoons chia seeds

Must Do

1. Preheat the oven to 200°F and then turn it off. Line a 15 × 13-inch baking sheet with parchment paper.

2. **To make the dough:** Combine the warm water and yeast in a small bowl. Add the coconut nectar and stir to combine. Let the yeast mixture sit for about 8 minutes, or until foamy.

3. Whisk together the sorghum flour, tapioca flour, chickpea flour, sweet white rice flour, psyllium husk powder, and salt in a large bowl. Make a well in the middle.

4. Add the pumpkin puree and coconut milk to the yeast mixture, stir to combine, and then pour into the flour mixture. Mix together until a dough forms.

5. Transfer the dough onto the prepared baking sheet, and divide the dough evenly into three 12-inch-long strands. Pinch the strands together at one end. Cross the ends in the middle one at a time to make a simple braid, and then pinch the ends together on the other side.

6. Cover with a clean dishtowel and place the braided dough in the oven for 1 hour to rise.

7. Take the risen dough out of the oven, remove the dishtowel, and preheat the oven to 375°F.

8. **To make the glaze:** Mix together the coconut milk and molasses in a small bowl. Brush the challah with the glaze, and sprinkle the top with the chia seeds.

9. Place an 8 × 8-inch pan filled with ice cubes on the lower rack of the oven to help crisp up the crust.

10. Bake the challah until the crust turns golden brown and it feels firm to the touch, about 40 minutes.

11. Transfer the baking sheet from the oven to a wire rack, and let it sit for 30 minutes before removing the challah for a complete cooldown.

12. Keep in an airtight container for up to 3 days or wrap and freeze for up to 3 months.

SERVING SIZE: 1 SLICE
Calories 170; Total Fat 1.5g; Protein 4.9g; Cholesterol 0.0g; Sodium 150mg; Fiber 4.6g; Sugars 2.5g; Total Carbohydrate 37.7g

Kalamata Rosemary Rustic Boule

MAKES 1 LOAF, 8 SLICES

A big, bloated boule is not my style, so I decided to make this one oblong, as I find it easier to slice. I add Kalamatas because there is nothing more worthy of human consumption than those plump, dark purple, smooth, meaty olives. And life just doesn't get much better than lodging them into bread. To make matters even more gluttonous, I highly suggest you top this bread with the Green & Black Olive Tapenade on page 168. This will make your existence complete.

Must Have

DOUGH

1¼ cups warm water, about 108°F (I microwave for 30 seconds)

1 (2¼-teaspoon) packet active dry yeast

2 tablespoons coconut nectar

1½ cups sorghum flour

½ cup sweet white rice flour

½ cup tapioca flour

½ cup ground buckwheat groats (I use a coffee grinder)

1 tablespoon psyllium husk powder

¼ teaspoon sea salt

½ cup pitted and chopped Kalamata olives

2 tablespoons chopped fresh rosemary

2 tablespoons pumpkin puree

GLAZE

2 tablespoons coconut milk

Must Do

1. Preheat the oven to 200°F and then turn it off. Line a 9-inch round cake pan with parchment paper.

2. To make the dough: Combine the warm water and yeast in a small bowl. Add the coconut nectar and stir to combine. Let the yeast mixture sit for about 8 minutes, or until foamy.

3. Whisk together the sorghum flour, sweet white rice flour, tapioca flour, buckwheat groats, psyllium husk powder, salt, Kalamata olives, and rosemary in a large bowl. Make a well in the middle.

4. Add the pumpkin puree to the yeast mixture, stir to combine, and then pour into the flour mixture.

5. Mix the dough together and form it into an oval about 7 inches long, 4 inches wide, and 2 inches high. Place the dough in the prepared cake pan. Cover the pan with a clean dishtowel, place it in the oven, and allow the dough to rise for 1 hour.

6. Take the risen dough out of the oven, remove the dishtowel, and preheat the oven to 425°F.

7. Cut four ¼-inch slits on top of the dough with a paring knife.

8. To make the glaze: Brush the top with the coconut milk, and place in the oven.

9. Place an 8 × 8-inch pan filled with ice cubes on the lower rack of the oven to help crisp up the crust.

10. Bake the bread until the crust turns golden brown and feels firm to the touch, about 45 minutes.

11. Transfer the cake pan from the oven to a wire rack, and let it sit for a half hour before removing the bread for a complete cooldown. If you cut into the bread too early, it will be gummy, so please refrain from breaking bread prematurely.

12. Keep the bread in an airtight container for up to 3 days, or wrap and freeze for up to 3 months.

SERVING SIZE: 1 SLICE
Calories 150; Total Fat 1.5g; Protein 3.3g; Cholesterol 0.0g; Sodium 80mg; Fiber 3.3g; Sugars 1.9g; Total Carbohydrate 31.9g

Buttery Garlic Twists

MAKES 30 TWISTS

You have to admit that when you're at an Italian restaurant, the delivery of the garlic knots, garlic rolls, or any incarnation of garlic and dough to the table is one of the highlights of the meal. So here I re-create this highly anticipated addition to the bread basket.

Must Have

TWISTS

1 cup warm water, about 108°F (I microwave for 30 seconds)
1 (2¼-teaspoon) packet active dry yeast
1 tablespoon coconut nectar
1 cup sorghum flour
½ cup tapioca flour
½ cup sweet white rice flour
1 tablespoon psyllium husk powder
½ teaspoon sea salt
2 tablespoons pumpkin puree

GARLIC BUTTER SAUCE

5 cloves garlic, minced
2 tablespoons minced fresh parsley
2 tablespoons dried oregano
¼ cup coconut milk
2 tablespoons coconut aminos

Must Do

1. Preheat the oven to 200°F and then turn it off. Line a 15 × 13-inch baking sheet with parchment paper.

2. **To make the twists:** Combine the warm water and yeast in a small bowl. Add the coconut nectar and stir to combine. Let the yeast mixture sit for about 8 minutes, or until foamy.

3. Whisk together the sorghum flour, tapioca flour, sweet white rice flour, psyllium husk powder, and salt in a large bowl. Make a well in the middle.

4. Add the pumpkin puree to the yeast mixture, stir to combine, and pour into the flour mixture. Mix together until a dough forms.

5. Form the dough into a ball, place it on a lightly floured piece of parchment paper, and place another piece of parchment on top. If the dough is sticky, flour the top before you place the parchment paper on top of it. Roll out the dough to make a rectangle about 15 × 8 inches.

6. Divide the dough in half, widthwise, with a pizza slicer, and then cut it lengthwise into fifteen 1-inch strips. Repeat with the other half of dough.

7. To twist the dough, take a strip of it, roll it between the palms of your hands to form a rope, and twist the ends together. Repeat with the remaining strips of dough.

8. Place the twists on the prepared baking sheet, cover with a clean dishtowel, and place in the oven to rise for 1 hour.

9. After the twists have risen, remove the dishtowel and preheat the oven to 375°F.

10. **To make the garlic butter sauce:** Add the garlic, parsley, oregano, coconut milk, and coconut aminos to a small bowl and stir to combine.

11. Brush the twists with the garlic butter sauce and bake them until the edges are golden brown and the twists are firm to the touch, about 20 minutes.

12. Transfer the baking sheet from the oven to a wire rack, and let it sit for 15 minutes before removing the twists.

13. Keep in an airtight container for up to 3 days or wrap and freeze for up to 3 months.

SERVING SIZE: 1 TWIST
Calories 30; Total Fat 0.5g; Protein 0.4g; Cholesterol 0.0g; Sodium 40mg; Fiber 0.9g; Sugars 0.6g; Total Carbohydrate 6.1g

Rye Bread Focaccia

MAKES 1 SQUARE LOAF, 6 SLICES

There's something about rye bread that I find seductively alluring. I didn't realize what quality it was about this handsome Jewish deli loaf that drew me until I tried to re-create it without gluten. After careful sleuthing I discovered that the caraway seeds are the attribute that most enchants me. I was amazed at how one aromatic element can fake out your taste buds so thoroughly. Other inherent aspects of rye bread DNA include a touch of dried dill, whole-grain flours, and earthy cacao powder. And when all put together, they create a gluten-free rye bread even your *bubbe* (grandmother) would be proud to call her own.

Must Have

DOUGH

1¼ cups warm water, about 108°F (I microwave for 30 seconds)

1 (2¼-teaspoon) packet active dry yeast

2 tablespoons coconut nectar

1½ cups sorghum flour

½ cup tapioca flour

½ cup sweet white rice flour

1 tablespoon psyllium husk powder

1 tablespoon caraway seeds

1 tablespoon dried dill

1 teaspoon dried thyme

1 teaspoon dried rosemary

½ teaspoon sea salt

2 tablespoons pumpkin puree

¼ cup coconut milk

GLAZE

1 tablespoon coconut milk

1 tablespoon coconut aminos

TOPPING

1 teaspoon dried oregano

Must Do

1. Preheat the oven to 200°F and then turn it off. Line a 9 × 9-inch square baking pan with parchment paper.

2. To make the dough: Combine the warm water and yeast in a small bowl. Add the coconut nectar and stir to combine. Let the yeast mixture sit for about 8 minutes, or until foamy.

3. Whisk together the sorghum flour, tapioca flour, sweet white rice flour, psyllium husk powder, caraway seeds, dill, thyme, rosemary, and salt in a large bowl. Make a well in the middle.

4. Add the pumpkin puree and coconut milk to the yeast mixture, stir to combine, and pour into the flour mixture.

5. Mix together until a dough forms. The dough will have the consistency of a loose batter.

6. Pour the dough into the prepared pan. With wet fingertips, press evenly across, down, and into the corners.

7. Cover the pan with a clean dishtowel, place it in the oven, and allow the dough to rise for 1 hour.

8. Take the risen dough out of the oven, remove the dishtowel, and preheat the oven to 425°F.

9. To make the glaze: Combine the coconut milk and coconut aminos in a small bowl. Brush the top of the dough with the glaze, sprinkle the oregano evenly over the top, and place it back in the oven while it preheats.

10. Place an 8 × 8-inch pan filled with ice cubes on the lower rack of the oven to help crisp up the crust.

11. Bake the bread until the crust turns a light golden brown and feels firm to the touch, about 40 minutes.

12. Transfer the pan to a wire rack, and let it sit for 30 minutes before removing the bread for a complete cooldown.

13. Cut the focaccia into thirds, and then cut each piece in half, to make 6 pieces that measure 3 × 4½ inches.

14. Keep the bread in an airtight container for up to 3 days, or wrap and freeze for up to 3 months.

SERVING SIZE: 1 SLICE
Calories 225; Total Fat 1.2g; Protein 5.3g; Cholesterol 0.0g; Sodium 190mg; Fiber 3.7g; Sugars 2.5g; Total Carbohydrate 48.9g

Inside Scoop: Because the dough is very delicate before it is baked, I usually brush the glaze on the dough with my fingertips instead of a brush.

Cinnamon Raisin Bread

MAKES 1 LOAF, 9 SLICES

This is the kind of bread that begs to be slathered. All sorts of spreadables qualify, depending on your preference, allergies, and dietary allowances. For some it may be almond butter; others, sunflower seed butter; and even others, just plain butter. But no matter what you disperse on top of it, this cinnamon raisin bread needs to be recognized for her own sweet and swirly attributes. No matter which way you cut it, she shows off her curves in the most seductive and acrobatic way. Let's face it: she's a show-off. And in keeping with her teasing ways, she's easy. So easy you may not believe it at first. But when you do it once, you'll realize I am right. So give it a whirl and you'll be rewarded with a loaf that's easy to fall in love with.

Must Have

DOUGH
1 cup warm water, about 108°F (I microwave for 30 seconds)
1 (2¼-teaspoon) packet active dry yeast
2 tablespoons coconut nectar
2 cups sorghum flour
¾ cup sweet white rice flour
1 tablespoon psyllium husk powder
2 tablespoons ground cinnamon
¼ teaspoon sea salt
¼ cup coconut milk
3 tablespoons applesauce
2 teaspoons apple cider vinegar

FILLING
½ cup coconut sugar
2 tablespoons ground cinnamon
⅓ cup raisins

GLAZE
2 tablespoons coconut nectar

Must Do

1. Preheat the oven to 200°F and then turn it off. Line a 9 × 5 × 2-inch loaf pan with parchment paper.

2. To make the dough: Combine the warm water and yeast in a small bowl. Add the coconut nectar and stir to combine. Let the yeast mixture sit for about 8 minutes, or until foamy.

3. Whisk together the sorghum flour, sweet white rice flour, psyllium husk powder, cinnamon, and salt.

4. Add the coconut milk, applesauce, and apple cider vinegar to the yeast mixture, stir to combine, and then pour into the flour mixture. Mix together until a dough forms. Form the dough into a ball with your hands.

5. Roll out the dough on a lightly floured piece of parchment paper, with another piece of parchment paper on top of the dough, until it is an 8 × 6-inch rectangle. If the dough is sticky, flour the top before you place the parchment paper on top. Make sure the shorter side of the rectangle is facing you.

6. To make the filling: Mix together the coconut sugar and cinnamon in a small bowl.

7. Sprinkle the coconut sugar–cinnamon mixture evenly over the entire rectangle, leaving a 1-inch border around the perimeter. Top with the raisins.

8. Starting from the 6-inch side of the rectangle, roll up the dough, and then pinch the edges together to seal.

9. Place the dough in the prepared pan, sealed side down, cover it with a clean dishtowel, place it in the oven, and allow the dough to rise for 1 hour.

10. Take the risen dough out of the oven, remove the dishtowel, and preheat the oven to 350°F.

11. Place an 8 × 8-inch pan filled with ice cubes on the bottom rack of the oven. This helps crisp up the crust.

12. **To make the glaze:** Brush the top of the dough with the coconut nectar and bake until the top is golden brown and firm to the touch, about 1 hour.

13. Transfer the loaf from the oven to a wire rack, and let it sit for 45 minutes before removing the loaf from the pan for a complete cooldown. If you cut into the bread too early, it will be gummy, so please refrain from breaking bread prematurely.

14. Keep the bread in an airtight container for up to 3 days, or wrap and freeze for up to 3 months.

SERVING SIZE: 1 SLICE
Calories 200; Total Fat 1.2g; Protein 4.7g; Cholesterol 0.0g; Sodium 63mg; Fiber 4.0g; Sugars 5.0g; Total Carbohydrate 42.1g

NYC Deli–Style Flatbread

MAKES 18 FLATBREADS

When you're originally from New York City you take your flatbread pretty seriously. My idea of this ideal breadstuff is that it is shaped like a runway, has toppings like an "everything" bagel, and is a bit crisp around the edges, with a slight softness in the middle. This flatbread, luckily, lends itself to being just that. I usually have mine with the Spicy Sun-Dried Tomato Dip on page 185, but you can also serve it as an accompaniment to salads, soups, and hummus.

Must Have

DOUGH

1 cup amaranth flour
1 cup sorghum flour
¾ cup tapioca flour
¼ cup sunflower seeds, ground (I use a coffee grinder)
2 teaspoons onion powder
1 teaspoon sodium-free baking powder
1 teaspoon sea salt
1 teaspoon garlic powder
1 teaspoon dried rosemary
1 teaspoon dried thyme
½ teaspoon dried oregano
½ teaspoon xanthan gum
½ teaspoon smoked paprika
1 cup water
2 tablespoons pumpkin puree
1 teaspoon coconut sugar

GLAZE

2 tablespoons coconut milk

TOPPING

1 tablespoon caraway seeds
1 tablespoon dried oregano

Must Do

1. Preheat the oven to 400°F. Line a 15 × 13-inch baking sheet with parchment paper. Lightly flour the entire area.

2. **To make the dough:** Whisk together the amaranth flour, sorghum flour, tapioca flour, ground sunflower seeds, onion powder, baking powder, salt, garlic powder, rosemary, thyme, oregano, xanthan gum, and smoked paprika in a large bowl. Make a well in the middle.

3. Add the water, pumpkin puree, and coconut sugar, and stir to combine until a dough forms.

4. Place the dough on the prepared baking sheet with another piece of parchment paper on top of the dough. If the dough is sticky, flour the top before you place the parchment paper on top of it.

5. Roll out the dough until it is a 12 × 9-inch rectangle, about ⅛ inch thick. Remove the top piece of parchment paper and, with a pizza slicer, cut 9 long rectangles 1 inch across, and then slice the long rectangles in half, keeping the dough together.

6. **To make the glaze:** Brush the dough with the coconut milk. Top with the caraway seeds and oregano. You may have to press them in to stick.

7. Bake the flatbreads until they are a light golden brown and firm to the touch, about 30 minutes. For the last 5 minutes of baking, break apart the flatbreads where you sliced them with the pizza cutter, so they have a chance to toast evenly around the perimeters.

8. Transfer the baking sheet from the oven to a wire rack, and let it sit for 10 minutes before removing the flatbreads for a complete cooldown.

9. Keep in an airtight container for up to 3 days, or wrap and freeze for up to 3 months.

SERVING SIZE: 1 FLATBREAD
Calories 80; Total Fat 1.7g; Protein 2.8g; Cholesterol 0.0g; Sodium 90mg; Fiber 2.9g; Sugars 0.2g; Total Carbohydrate 15.1g

TIRAMISU CUPCAKES
(SEE RECIPE ON PAGE 237)

CHAPTER 11

A Feast of Sweets

There's something about dessert that makes people feel guilty and then confess their sins. So folks who know I own a bakery, but do not know about the inherent health benefits of my baked goods, usually enlist me at parties as an off-the-rack psychotherapist. I am always pleased to tell them that desserts, particularly mine, are not always evil, this list included. Although these might sound rich and unhealthy, they are actually filled with ultra-nutritious nuggets of whole foods that add hearty value and delicious decadence.

Dark Chocolate Cherry Rugelach

MAKES 16 RUGELACH

In Yiddish, *rugelach* means "little twists," and these crescent-shaped cookies are filled with jams, cinnamon, currants, chocolate—you name it. I prefer to stuff them with dried cherries and chocolate, because like any hot-blooded woman, I cherish chocolate-covered cherries. Traditionally, the dough contains cream cheese, so I created a faux version that adds just the right texture and taste. When it all comes together, it's the perfect, twisted pastry.

Must Have

CREAM CHEEZE
½ cup sunflower seeds, soaked in boiling water for 15 minutes
2 tablespoons vegan, soy-free plain yogurt
1 tablespoon chickpea miso paste
1 tablespoon freshly squeezed lemon juice
1 tablespoon coconut milk

DOUGH
1½ cups All-Purpose Gluten-Free Flour Mix (page 20)
1 cup coconut sugar
½ cup cacao powder, plus extra for dusting
¼ cup pumpkin puree

FILLING
¼ cup coconut sugar
½ cup dried cherries, finely chopped
½ cup sugar-free, dairy-free chocolate chips (I use Lily's brand; see Resources)

TOPPING
2 tablespoons coconut milk
2 tablespoons coconut sugar
2 tablespoons sugar-free, dairy-free chocolate chips

Must Do

1. Preheat the oven to 325°F. Line a 13 × 9-inch baking sheet with parchment paper. Dust the entire area with cacao powder.

2. **To make the cream cheeze:** Drain the sunflower seeds in a small sieve. Add the sunflower seeds, yogurt, miso, lemon juice, and coconut milk to a food processor. Pulse until the mixture comes together but retains some texture. Scrape down the sides a couple of times because the sunflower seeds will initially fly high.

3. **To make the dough:** Add the all-purpose flour, coconut sugar, cacao powder, and pumpkin puree to the food processor with the cream cheeze. Pulse until the dough comes together into a ball. It will do this all on its own.

4. Divide the dough evenly into 2 balls. Flatten the balls into disks, wrap in plastic wrap or parchment paper, and refrigerate for about 10 minutes.

5. Take out one disk from the fridge, place it on the prepared baking sheet, and place another piece of parchment on top. If the dough is sticky, flour the top with cacao powder before you place the parchment paper on top.

6. Roll out the dough to make an 8-inch circle about ⅛ inch thick.

7. **To make the filling:** Sprinkle half of the coconut sugar evenly all over the top of the dough. Spread half of the cherries on top of the coconut sugar and sprinkle half of the chocolate chips on top.

8. Cut the dough into 8 even wedges with a pizza slicer by cutting the dough in half, then cutting the halves in half, and then cutting those pieces in half.

9. Roll each triangle up from the longest side to the point. Place on the prepared baking sheet.

10. Repeat these steps with the second disk of dough and the remaining filling ingredients.

11. To make the topping: Brush the rugelach with the coconut milk and then generously sprinkle the coconut sugar on top of each. Dot the tops with the chocolate chips.

12. Bake the rugelach until your kitchen smells like chocolate and they are firm to the touch, about 18 minutes. Rotate the baking sheet halfway through baking.

13. Transfer the baking sheet from the oven to a wire rack, and let it sit for about 10 minutes before removing the rugelach to cool completely.

14. Keep the rugelach in an airtight container for up to 3 days or wrap and freeze for up to 3 months.

SERVING SIZE: 1 RUGELACH
Calories 100; Total Fat 4.0g; Protein 2.9g; Cholesterol 0.0g; Sodium 30mg; Fiber 2.6g; Sugars 5.0g; Total Carbohydrate 15.2g

Apple Cobblers

MAKES 6 COBBLERS

The beginning of fall is usually christened with the arrival of apples on trees, in grocery stores, and at farmers' markets. Aside from just taking a bite out of one, the best way I know to enjoy apples is in cobblers. I give some suggestions below as to what apples to use, but really any kind will do. The oat and seed crust is as easy as pie to make, unlike piecrust, which can get tricky. The sunflower seed butter incorporated into the crust gives it a peanut-buttery flavor. The strategic use of ramekins for serving gives you your very own cobblette, so you have permission not to share.

Must Have

CRUST

1 cup gluten-free oats, ground (I use a coffee grinder)

½ cup pumpkin seeds, ground (I use a coffee grinder)

1 tablespoon Sunflower Seed Butter (page 20)

1 teaspoon ground cinnamon

2 tablespoons coconut nectar

½ cup green tea or water

FILLING

6 medium sweet apples, cored, peeled, and chopped into ¼-inch pieces (Pink Lady, Gravenstein, and Braeburn are good choices)

3 tablespoons freshly squeezed lemon juice

¼ cup coconut sugar

2 tablespoons tapioca flour

1 teaspoon ground cinnamon

TOPPING

1¼ cups gluten-free oats, ground (I use a coffee grinder)

½ cup coconut sugar

¼ cup unsweetened shredded coconut

¼ cup coconut milk

1 teaspoon ground cinnamon

SERVING SIZE: 1 RAMEKIN

Calories 200; Total Fat 3.9g; Protein 2.9g; Cholesterol 0.0g; Sodium 5mg; Fiber 6.5g; Sugars 15.5g; Total Carbohydrate 40.1g

Must Do

1. Preheat the oven to 350°F. Place six 6-ounce ramekins on a 15 × 10-inch baking sheet.

2. To make the crust: Add the ground oats and pumpkin seeds to a medium bowl. Add the sunflower seed butter, cinnamon, coconut nectar, and green tea, and stir until combined.

3. Spoon about ¼ cup of the crust mixture into each ramekin, dividing it evenly. Press the mixture firmly into the bottom of each ramekin and slightly up the sides.

4. Bake the crusts until they are a light golden brown, about 9 minutes.

5. To make the filling: Add the apples and lemon juice to a medium bowl and stir to coat. Add the coconut sugar, tapioca flour, and cinnamon, and stir until all the ingredients are thoroughly combined.

6. Spoon the filling mixture into the ramekins, dividing it evenly.

7. To make the topping: Add the oats, coconut sugar, shredded coconut, coconut milk, and cinnamon to a small bowl, and stir to combine. Cover each cobbler completely with the topping, dividing it evenly.

8. Bake the cobblers until the topping turns a toasty golden brown, about 25 minutes.

9. Transfer the baking sheet from the oven to a wire rack, and let it sit for about 10 minutes before serving.

10. Top with vegan, soy-free ice cream or coconut cream, if desired.

Chocolate Pudding Pie with Seed Crust

MAKES 12 MINI PIES

I don't know if you remember this, but many years ago, I'm talking the '70s, I think every mom in America was required to make her children chocolate pudding in a graham cracker crust and slather it with whipped cream. This was actually something I really loved to eat. Of course, I had to figure out a healthy, allergy-free version of it for my son (and for myself, who am I kidding?). The best part is there is no need to bake it. Just assemble the parts and put it in the freezer. The avocado hiding out in the chocolate pudding adds a boost of potassium, a rich creaminess, and a smooth texture that makes it taste like custard.

Must Have

CRUST
¾ cup sunflower seeds
¼ cup pumpkin seeds
2 tablespoons hemp seeds
6 Medjool dates, pitted and soaked in water for 20 minutes, then drained

PUDDING
¾ cup green tea or water, at room temperature
10 Medjool dates, pitted and soaked in water for 20 minutes, then drained
¼ cup cacao powder
¼ cup Sunflower Seed Butter (page 20)
¼ cup mashed avocado

WHIPPED CREAM TOPPING
1½ cups coconut cream or any nondairy whipped cream
1 tablespoon maple syrup

SERVING SIZE: 1 PIE

Calories 180; Total Fat 10.1g; Protein 5.7g; Cholesterol 0.0g; Sodium 2mg; Fiber 3.7g; Sugars 9.0g; Total Carbohydrate 15.1g

Must Do

1. Line a standard 12-cup muffin tin with paper baking cups.

2. To make the crust: Add the sunflower and pumpkin seeds to a medium sauté pan over low heat and toast, stirring occasionally, until the seeds turn a light golden brown, about 5 minutes.

3. Add the toasted sunflower seeds, toasted pumpkin seeds, hemp seeds, and drained dates to a food processor. Pulse until the mixture comes together but retains some texture.

4. Add about 1½ tablespoons of the crust mixture to each of the prepared cupcake wells. Press down to make an even layer. You don't need to go up the sides.

5. To make the pudding: Add the green tea, drained dates, cacao powder, sunflower seed butter, and avocado to a food processor. Pulse until the mixture comes together and is very smooth.

6. Spoon about 3 tablespoons of the pie mixture on top of the crust mixture, dividing it evenly among the tins.

7. To make the whipped cream topping: Whisk together the coconut cream and maple syrup in a small bowl. Place in the refrigerator.

8. Place the pudding pies in the freezer for 2 hours or overnight. Peel off the cupcake liners and top each pie with the whipped cream. Serve immediately.

9. Keep in an airtight container for up to 3 months in the freezer.

Cookie Dough Cupcakes

MAKES 12 STANDARD-SIZE CUPCAKES

I consider this the "great experiment." I never had cookie dough anything before I tried to make it on my own, but according to everyone in the world, cookie dough is something to get really excited about. My curiosity got the best of me, and I'm very grateful it did. Now I'm hooked. And since it's called cookie dough, I made it into cupcakes. This way you can get a double dose of the cookie dough: one in the filling and one in the frosting. Makes sense, right? And with no raw eggs to worry about, it's safe for everyone—everyone in the world who loves cookie dough.

Must Have

COOKIE DOUGH FILLING

1 cup All-Purpose Gluten-Free Flour Mix (page 20)
⅛ teaspoon fine sea salt
¼ cup coconut nectar
3 tablespoons applesauce
¼ cup sugar-free, dairy-free chocolate chips (I use Lily's brand; see Resources)

CUPCAKES

1 cup coconut milk
1 teaspoon apple cider vinegar
1¾ cups All-Purpose Gluten-Free Flour Mix (page 20)
⅓ cup cacao powder
1¼ teaspoons sodium-free baking powder
1 teaspoon baking soda
½ teaspoon guar gum
¼ teaspoon fine sea salt
¼ cup applesauce
¼ cup coconut nectar
2 teaspoons gluten-free vanilla extract
⅜ teaspoon stevia powder
⅓ cup vegan, soy-free plain yogurt

COOKIE DOUGH FROSTING

1¼ cups All-Purpose Gluten-Free Flour Mix (page 20)
½ cup powdered erythritol (I use confectioner's Swerve brand; see Resources)
¼ cup coconut nectar
½ cup unsweetened coconut milk
½ cup sugar-free, vegan, soy-free chocolate chips

Must Do

1. Preheat the oven to 325°F. Line a 9 × 9-inch square baking pan with parchment paper. Line a standard 12-cup muffin tin with paper baking cups.

2. To make the cookie dough filling: Whisk together the flour and salt in a medium bowl. Make a well in the middle. Add the coconut nectar, applesauce, and chocolate chips. Stir to combine.

3. Divide the dough into 12 balls using a melon baller. Place the balls in the prepared baking pan and freeze for about 30 minutes.

4. To make the cupcakes: Mix together the coconut milk and apple cider vinegar in a small bowl.

CONTINUED ON NEXT PAGE

5. Whisk together the all-purpose flour, cacao powder, baking powder, baking soda, guar gum, and salt in a large bowl. Make a well in the middle.

6. Add the applesauce, coconut nectar, vanilla, and stevia, and stir to combine. Next add the coconut milk mixture and stir until the liquid is absorbed and the batter is smooth. Stir in the yogurt until well combined.

7. Pour the batter into the prepared muffin tin, dividing it evenly. Each cup should be about two-thirds full.

8. Take the baking sheet out of the freezer and place a frozen ball of cookie dough in the middle of each cupcake.

9. Bake the cupcakes until they bounce back slightly to the touch, about 16 minutes. Rotate the muffin tin from front to back after 10 minutes of baking.

10. Transfer the muffin tin from the oven to a wire rack, and let it sit for 10 minutes before removing the cupcakes to cool completely.

11. To make the frosting: Mix together the all-purpose flour and powdered erythritol in a medium bowl. Make a well in the middle. Add the coconut nectar, coconut milk, and chocolate chips, and stir to combine.

12. Frost the completely cooled cupcakes. Keep unfrosted cupcakes in an airtight container for up to 3 days, or wrap and freeze them for up to 3 months. Leftover frosting keeps in the fridge for about 1 week if stored in an airtight container, but if I were you, I'd eat it off a spoon way before then.

SERVING SIZE: 1 CUPCAKE
Calories 150; Total Fat 2.1g; Protein 4.0g; Cholesterol 0.0g; Sodium 50mg; Fiber 4.9g; Sugars 6.0g; Total Carbohydrate 29.1g

Tiramisu Cupcakes

MAKES 12 STANDARD-SIZE CUPCAKES **(SEE PHOTO ON PAGE 226)**

The Italian translation of *tiramisu* is "pick-me-up." This is an understatement, since eating one slice of these espresso-and-coffee-crammed cupcakes can send you reeling into outer space from all the caffeine. But this is a good thing, and I wouldn't have it any differently. I love the way the coffee syrup seeps into the cake, rendering it moist and even more coffee flavored than it already is. I guess you really have to be a java addict to appreciate this. The frosting features an unusual ingredient but I promise no one will ever know unless you kiss and tell. Cauliflower. Steamed and then pureed with the dates, coffee, and sunflower seeds, the cauliflower delivers an incredibly satisfying and sweet topping to a dessert that's a real pick-me-up in every sense of the idiom.

Must Have

FROSTING

8 ounces cauliflower (about 20 small florets), roughly chopped

¼ cup strong black coffee, at room temperature

2 cups sunflower seeds, soaked in water for 15 minutes, then drained

12 Medjool dates (about 1 cup), pitted and soaked in water for 20 minutes, then drained

¼ teaspoon fine sea salt

COFFEE SYRUP

½ cup black coffee, at room temperature

2 tablespoons coconut sugar

1 teaspoon gluten-free vanilla extract

CUPCAKES

¾ cup black coffee, at room temperature

1 teaspoon apple cider vinegar

2 cups All-Purpose Gluten-Free Flour Mix (page 20)

2 tablespoons instant espresso powder

1½ teaspoons sodium-free baking powder

1 teaspoon baking soda

½ teaspoon guar gum

¼ teaspoon fine sea salt

¼ cup applesauce

¼ cup coconut nectar

1 teaspoon coffee extract

⅜ teaspoon stevia powder

⅓ cup vegan, soy-free plain yogurt

TOPPING

Instant espresso grounds

Chocolate shavings

12 espresso beans

Must Do

1. Preheat the oven to 325°F. Line a standard 12-cup muffin tin with paper baking cups.

2. To make the frosting: Add the cauliflower to a small pot of boiling water and cook until very soft and tender, about 10 minutes. Drain the cauliflower.

3. Add the cauliflower, coffee, drained sunflower seeds, drained dates, and salt to a high-speed blender. Pulse until the mixture comes together and is very smooth.

4. Transfer the frosting to a large bowl, cover, and refrigerate for at least 1 hour.

5. To make the coffee syrup: Add the coffee, coconut sugar, and vanilla to a small sauté pan over medium heat. Bring to a boil, lower the heat, and let simmer until the mixture reduces down, about 10 minutes. Pour the mixture into a small bowl.

CONTINUED ON NEXT PAGE

6. To make the cupcakes: Mix together the coffee and apple cider vinegar in a small bowl.

7. Whisk together the flour, espresso powder, baking powder, baking soda, guar gum, and salt in a large bowl. Make a well in the middle.

8. Add the applesauce, coconut nectar, coffee extract, and stevia, and stir to combine.

9. Add the coffee–apple cider mixture and stir until the liquid is absorbed and the batter is smooth. Stir in the yogurt until well combined.

10. Pour the batter into the prepared muffin tin, dividing it evenly. Each cup should be about two-thirds full.

11. Bake the cupcakes until they bounce back slightly to the touch, about 15 minutes. Rotate the muffin tin from front to back after 10 minutes of baking.

12. Transfer the muffin tin from the oven to a wire rack, and let it sit for 10 minutes before removing the cupcakes to cool completely.

13. After the cupcakes are cool, brush the top of each with the coffee syrup. Then frost the completely cooled cupcakes.

14. To make the topping: Sprinkle the top of each cupcake with the espresso grounds and chocolate shavings, and place an espresso bean in the center.

15. Keep the cupcakes in an airtight container for up to 3 days or wrap and freeze for up to 3 months.

16. The frosting can be frozen as well (it actually tastes great that way) for up to 3 months.

SERVING SIZE: 1 CUPCAKE
Calories 150; Total Fat 3.1g; Protein 4.7g; Cholesterol 0.0g; Sodium 95mg; Fiber 6.7g; Sugars 9.0g; Total Carbohydrate 20.1g

Chocolate-Covered Graham Crackers

MAKES 18 GRAHAM CRACKERS

I used to have two reasons for eating chocolate-covered graham crackers. They tasted like hopes and dreams, and my friends would come over knowing I was dealing them for a fair price: a penny each. Now that I'm older, I believe these taste like love and light, but I don't charge my friends. I'm a different person now. I just make a big stash for myself and hide them in the freezer where no one can find them but me. Yes, I hoard them. I am ashamed of myself, but after you make this recipe, you'll totally get it.

Must Have

COOKIES

1 cup ground buckwheat groats (I use a coffee grinder)
1 cup sorghum flour
½ cup cacao powder
½ teaspoon xanthan gum
¼ teaspoon sea salt
½ cup coconut milk, warmed
½ cup coconut sugar
¼ cup applesauce
2 tablespoons mashed avocado
1 tablespoon molasses
1 tablespoon gluten-free vanilla extract
¼ cup warm water

CHOCOLATE DIP

8 ounces unsweetened 100% cacao bar
¾ cup coconut nectar
½ teaspoon stevia powder
⅛ teaspoon sea salt

Must Do

1. Preheat the oven to 350°F. Line two 15 × 13-inch baking sheets with parchment paper. Lightly flour each baking sheet with cacao powder.

2. To make the cookies: Whisk together the ground buckwheat groats, sorghum flour, cacao powder, xanthan gum, and salt in a large bowl. Make a well in the middle.

3. Add the coconut milk, coconut sugar, applesauce, mashed avocado, molasses, vanilla, and water, and stir until the liquid is absorbed and the ingredients are thoroughly combined.

4. Form the dough into a ball and cut it in half, dividing it evenly. Place one ball on one of the prepared baking sheets and place a piece of parchment paper on top of the ball. If the dough is sticky, flour the top with cacao powder before you place the parchment paper on top.

5. Roll the dough out as thin as possible, about ⅛ inch, and shape it into a 9 × 9-inch square. Repeat these steps with the second ball of dough.

6. Cut the dough into nine 3-inch squares using a pizza slicer. Poke holes in the middle of each square using fork prongs in any design that expresses your true self.

7. Bake the cookies until they are crisp, about 18 minutes. Rotate the baking sheets from top to bottom and vice versa, halfway through baking.

8. Transfer the baking sheets from the oven to a wire rack, and let them sit for about 10 minutes before removing the cookies to cool completely.

9. **To make the chocolate dip:** Chop the chocolate into chunks, place them in a medium microwave-safe bowl, and microwave for 30 seconds at a time until the chocolate melts.

10. Add the coconut nectar, stevia, and salt, and stir to combine.

11. Dip each graham cracker into the melted chocolate and set it down on parchment paper. Let the chocolate set at room temperature, or put the graham crackers in the fridge.

12. Keep in an airtight container in the fridge for up to 3 days, or wrap and freeze for up to 3 months.

SERVING SIZE: 1 GRAHAM CRACKER
Calories 80; Total Fat 0.7g; Protein 2.2g; Cholesterol 0.0g; Sodium 30mg; Fiber 2.2g; Sugars 4.7g; Total Carbohydrate 18.6g

Hamantaschen

MAKES ABOUT 13 HAMANTASCHEN

This three-cornered jam-packed cookie is traditionally eaten during the Jewish holiday of Purim. The filling can be something other than jam, though. These cookies can be filled with prunes, chocolate, caramel, poppy seeds—really almost anything. I fill mine with chia seeds, as they lend extraordinary texture as well as invaluable nutrients, very few calories, and lots of fiber and flavor. These cookies freeze dramatically well, so I end up eating them quite often, holiday or no holiday.

Must Have

FILLING
¾ cup chia seeds
½ cup coconut milk
½ cup coconut nectar
2 tablespoons pumpkin puree
1 teaspoon orange juice
¼ teaspoon orange extract

DOUGH
2¼ cups All-Purpose Gluten-Free Flour Mix (page 20)
½ teaspoon baking soda
¼ teaspoon sea salt
¼ teaspoon guar gum
¼ cup applesauce
¼ cup coconut nectar
6 tablespoons water
1 teaspoon gluten-free vanilla extract

SERVING SIZE: 1 HAMANTASCHEN

Calories 120; Total Fat 4.6 g; Protein 5.6g; Cholesterol 0.0g; Sodium 50mg; Fiber 4.3g; Sugars 3.4g; Total Carbohydrate 18.2g

Must Do

1. Preheat the oven to 325°F. Line a 15 × 13-inch baking sheet with parchment paper.

2. To make the filling: Add the chia seeds, coconut milk, coconut nectar, pumpkin puree, orange juice, and orange extract to a sauté pan over medium heat and cook, stirring occasionally, until the mixture starts to thicken, about 8 minutes. Remove from the heat.

3. To make the dough: Whisk together the all-purpose flour, baking soda, salt, and guar gum in a large bowl. Make a well in the middle.

4. Add the applesauce, coconut nectar, water, and vanilla, and stir to combine.

5. Form the dough into a ball and roll it out to about ¼-inch thickness. Cut out circles with a biscuit cutter or 3-inch-diameter jar or glass. Collect the scraps of dough and roll them out again to cut out more cookies.

6. Put about 1½ teaspoons of filling in the middle of each circle. Fold the left and right sides of the circle in, pinch the top to make a point, and then fold the bottom up to form a triangle. Pinch the right and left triangle points. It helps to have wet fingertips when you do this.

7. Bake the hamantaschen until the dough is a light golden brown around the edges, about 12 minutes. Rotate the baking sheet from front to back after 9 minutes of baking.

8. Place the cookie sheet on a wire rack, and let it sit for about 15 minutes before removing the cookies to cool completely.

9. Keep in an airtight container for 3 days or individually wrap and freeze for up to 3 months.

Caramel Macchiato Sandwich Cookies

MAKES ABOUT 10 SANDWICH COOKIES

There is a certain coffee chain—I'm sure you've never heard of it—that serves a Caramel Macchiato Espresso. It is really decadent and sweet and qualifies as liquid therapy in my book. And like all foods or drinks that I fall in love with, I like to reincarnate them as a cookie. I make the caramel filling with a combination of sunflower seed butter and dates, and the cookie itself contains ground espresso powder. Man, what a buzz. Sometimes I have this with my morning coffee, and I usually get a lot done on those days.

Must Have

COOKIES
1 cup amaranth flour
½ cup sunflower seeds, ground (I use a coffee grinder)
½ cup cacao powder
1 tablespoon espresso powder
¼ teaspoon baking soda
¼ teaspoon guar gum
¼ teaspoon sea salt
¼ cup applesauce
¼ cup coconut nectar
¼ cup coconut sugar
1 teaspoon gluten-free vanilla extract
6 tablespoons brewed espresso

CARAMEL ESPRESSO FILLING
6 Medjool dates, pitted and soaked in hot water for 15 minutes, then drained
¼ cup Sunflower Seed Butter (page 20)
2 tablespoons brewed espresso

Must Do

1. Preheat the oven to 325°F. Line a 15 × 13-inch baking sheet with parchment paper.

2. To make the cookies: Whisk together the amaranth flour, ground sunflower seeds, cacao powder, espresso powder, baking soda, guar gum, and salt in a large bowl. Make a well in the middle.

3. Add the applesauce, coconut nectar, coconut sugar, vanilla, and brewed espresso, and stir until combined.

4. Take about 1 tablespoon of the dough and shape it into a ball. Place the ball on the prepared pan. Repeat until you have used up all the dough.

5. Press down gently on each ball to flatten slightly.

6. Bake the cookies until the kitchen smells like chocolate and they are firm to the touch, about 11 minutes. Rotate the baking sheet from front to back after 8 minutes of baking.

7. Transfer the baking sheet from the oven to a wire rack, and let it sit for about 10 minutes before removing the cookies to cool completely.

8. To make the caramel filling: Add the drained dates and sunflower seed butter to a food processor. Pulse until the mixture comes together and forms a paste. Add the brewed espresso, 1 tablespoon at a time, until the mixture becomes very smooth.

9. To make the sandwich cookies, place about 1½ teaspoons of the mixture on top of the flat side of the

cookies, and repeat until you have added filling to half of the baked cookies. Close the sandwich with the remaining cookies by placing the flat side of the unfilled cookies on top of the filled ones.

10. Keep in an airtight container for up to 3 days, or wrap and freeze for up to 3 months.

SERVING SIZE: 1 SANDWICH COOKIE
Calories 140; Total Fat 3.9g; Protein 3.8g; Cholesterol 0.0g; Sodium 30mg; Fiber 3.2g; Sugars 10.0g; Total Carbohydrate 25.0g

Inside Scoop: Freeze the sandwich cookies so the filling will harden and taste like caramel fudge. I love eating them this way.

Candy Bar Cookies

MAKES ABOUT 13 COOKIES

When I was a kid, my favorite candy bar was a trifecta of caramel, chocolate, and peanuts. It was the epitome of bliss. Freezing the bars was euphoria. As an adult, I still crave that combination of flavors, but without the allergens and in the form of a cookie. I felt this recipe fit the bill, and, of course, I prefer these cookies frozen.

Must Have

CARAMEL SAUCE
¼ cup coconut nectar
2 tablespoons Sunflower Seed Butter (page 20)
⅛ teaspoon sea salt

CHOCOLATE SAUCE
1 tablespoon coconut nectar
2 tablespoons cacao powder
⅛ teaspoon stevia powder
⅛ teaspoon sea salt
3 teaspoons warm water

COOKIES
½ cup gluten-free oats, ground (I use a coffee grinder)
½ cup All-Purpose Gluten-Free Flour Mix (page 20)
½ cup amaranth flour
¼ cup quinoa flour
¼ teaspoon baking soda
¼ teaspoon guar gum
¼ teaspoon sea salt
¾ cup coconut sugar
¼ cup applesauce
¼ cup Sunflower Seed Butter (page 20)
1 teaspoon gluten-free vanilla extract
7 tablespoons water

Must Do

1. Preheat the oven to 325°F. Line a 15 × 13-inch baking sheet with parchment paper.

2. To make the caramel sauce: Mix together the coconut nectar, sunflower seed butter, and salt in a small bowl until well combined.

3. To make the chocolate sauce: Mix together the coconut nectar, cacao powder, stevia, and salt in a small bowl, and stir until smooth. Add the water, 1 teaspoon at a time, until the sauce loosens up a bit.

4. To make the cookies: Whisk together the oats, all-purpose flour, amaranth flour, quinoa flour, baking soda, guar gum, and salt in a large bowl. Make a well in the middle.

5. Add the coconut sugar, applesauce, sunflower seed butter, vanilla, and water, and stir to combine.

6. Take about 1½ tablespoons of the dough, shape it into a ball, and place it on the prepared baking sheet. Repeat until you have used up all the dough, placing the balls about 2 inches apart on the baking sheet. Flatten each ball gently using your fingertips dipped in water, so they don't stick to the dough. Put a small indentation in the middle of the dough with your finger.

7. Pour about 1 teaspoon of caramel sauce into each indentation.

8. Bake the cookies until they are a light golden brown around the edges, about 16 minutes. Rotate the baking sheet from front to back halfway through baking.

9. Transfer the baking sheet from the oven to a wire rack, and let it sit for about 10 minutes before removing the cookies to cool completely.

10. Drizzle the chocolate sauce over each cookie.

11. Keep in an airtight container for up to 3 days, or wrap individually and freeze for up to 3 months.

SERVING SIZE: 1 COOKIE
Calories 80; Total Fat 1.2g; Protein 2.5g;
Cholesterol 0.0g; Sodium 88mg; Fiber 2.9g;
Sugars 3.5g; Total Carbohydrate 15.1g

Inside Scoop: The doughnuts rise a little more and get more rounded on top if you let them sit in the doughnut pan for 10 minutes before baking them.

Chocolate Rosemary Doughnuts

MAKES 6 DOUGHNUTS

Doughnuts: any kind, any size, any flavor, any topping, any glaze, any filling, brings grown children to their knees. That would be me. I don't know what it is about these hole-y doughy circular desserts that hold such power. And I know I'm not alone. So to break the chains of doughnut slavery I created a baked version, which takes this fudge-y dunker with exquisite accents of rosemary to a whole new level.

Must Have

DOUGHNUTS
½ cup All-Purpose Gluten-Free Flour Mix (page 20)
½ cup cacao powder
¼ cup amaranth flour
¼ cup tapioca flour
1 tablespoon finely chopped fresh rosemary
1½ teaspoons sodium-free baking powder
¼ teaspoon sea salt
¼ teaspoon guar gum
¼ teaspoon baking soda
½ cup pumpkin puree
½ cup coconut sugar
1 tablespoon gluten-free vanilla extract
¼ teaspoon stevia powder
1 cup coconut milk

FUDGE FROSTING
3 tablespoons cacao powder
1 tablespoon coconut nectar
½ cup powdered erythritol (I use confectioner's Swerve brand; see Resources)
⅛ teaspoon fine sea salt
3–4 tablespoons water

TOPPING
Sugar-free, dairy-free chocolate chips (I use Lily's brand; see Resources)

Must Do

1. Preheat the oven to 325°F.

2. **To make the doughnuts:** In a medium bowl, mix together the all-purpose flour, cacao powder, amaranth flour, tapioca flour, rosemary, baking powder, salt, guar gum, and baking soda. Make a well in the middle.

3. Add the pumpkin puree, coconut sugar, vanilla, stevia, and coconut milk, and stir to combine.

4. Spread the batter evenly into a nonstick, 6-well doughnut pan, filling it to the top of each well.

5. Bake the doughnuts until they bounce back slightly to the touch, about 15 minutes. Rotate the pan halfway through baking.

6. Transfer the doughnut pan from the oven to a wire rack, and let it sit for 10 minutes before removing the doughnuts to cool completely.

7. **To make the fudge frosting:** Add the cacao powder, coconut nectar, powdered erythritol, and salt to a small bowl, and stir to combine. Add the water, 1 tablespoon at a time, until the frosting becomes smooth and spreadable.

8. Frost the completely cooled doughnuts and place them on the wire rack to set.

9. Keep in an airtight container for up to 3 days, or wrap individually and freeze for up to 3 months.

SERVING SIZE: 1 DOUGHNUT
Calories 150; Total Fat 4.2g; Protein 3.8g; Cholesterol 0.0g; Sodium 100mg; Fiber 3.5g; Sugars 3.0g; Total Carbohydrate 27.1g

Glazed Lemon Wonuts

MAKES 6 WONUTS

I love every incarnation of doughnut. That's why, when I bought a waffle iron in the middle of my midlife crisis (see the intro to Blueberry Buckwheat Waffles, page 28), I couldn't wait to hot press this recipe and make wonuts, or waffle doughnuts. The crispy edges and chewy center appealed to me instantly, as well as the way the glaze wiggles and waggles in and out of those grooves. And this particular lemon glaze is so refreshing and sweet it does a number on your endorphins. Since this hybrid is part waffle, you can even have these for breakfast with no guilt whatsoever. Just call them doffles.

Must Have

WONUTS

1 cup All-Purpose Gluten-Free
   Flour Mix (page 20)
½ cup amaranth flour
½ cup sweet white rice flour
½ cup coconut sugar
½ teaspoon sodium-free baking
   powder
¼ teaspoon sea salt
1 teaspoon grated lemon zest
¼ cup applesauce
¼ cup coconut nectar
½ teaspoon gluten-free vanilla
   extract
½ teaspoon lemon extract
½ cup unsweetened coconut milk

GLAZE

½ cup powdered erythritol (I use
   confectioner's Swerve brand;
   see Resources)
6 tablespoons freshly squeezed
   lemon juice

Must Do

1. Preheat your waffle iron according to the manufacturer's instructions.

2. **To make the wonuts:** Whisk together the all-purpose flour, amaranth flour, sweet white rice flour, coconut sugar, baking powder, salt, and lemon zest in a large bowl. Make a well in the middle.

3. Add the applesauce, coconut nectar, vanilla, and lemon extracts, and stir to combine.

4. Add the coconut milk and stir until it is absorbed and the batter is smooth.

5. Pour about ⅓ cup of the batter onto each waffle grid, close the lid, and iron the wonuts until they are golden brown and do not stick to the waffle grid, about 4 minutes. Repeat with the remaining batter.

6. **To make the glaze:** Whisk together the powdered erythritol and lemon juice in a small bowl until fully incorporated.

7. Drizzle the glaze on the wonuts and serve.

8. Keep in an airtight container for up to 3 days, or wrap individually and freeze for up to 3 months.

SERVING SIZE: 1 WONUT

Calories 170; Total Fat 2.2g; Protein 4.8g; Cholesterol 0.0g;
Sodium 95mg; Fiber 3.8g; Sugars 5.0g; Total Carbohydrate 34.1g

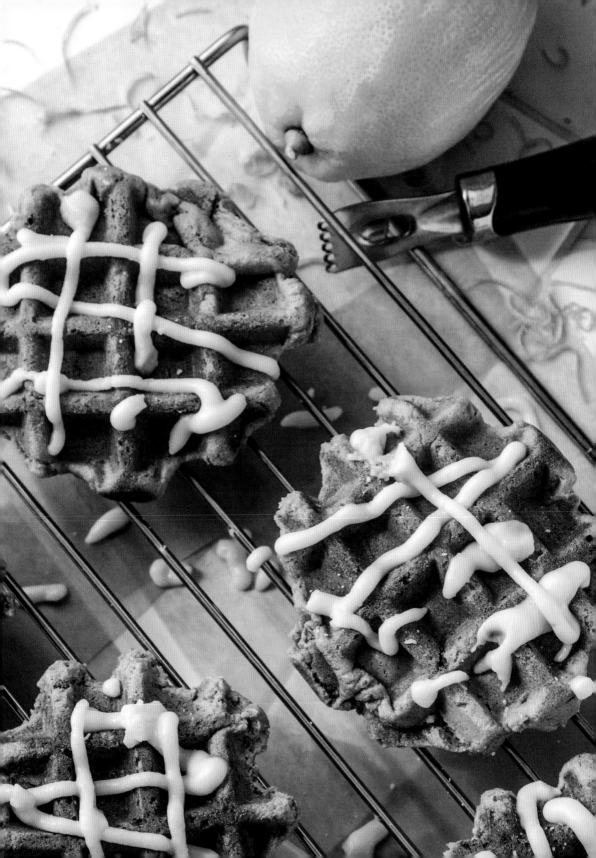

Rosemary & Fig Galette-lets

MAKES 4 GALETTE-LETS

I love fig season. But it is very short and sweet, so I always run to the farmers' market on the two or three Sundays that they have fresh figs and grab whatever is available. I usually can't finish them all, so I end up making these galette-lets, and they are such a treat. They are so easy to make, as the crust comes together quickly in a food processor, and then you just strategically dole out your figs and you're off to the races. The rosemary lends an earthiness, which really brings it home.

Must Have

CRUST
5 Medjool dates, pitted and soaked in 1 cup water for 20 minutes
1½ cups All-Purpose Gluten-Free Flour Mix (page 20)
½ cup gluten-free rolled oats
¼ cup applesauce
¼ cup Sunflower Seed Butter (page 20)
2 tablespoons coconut sugar
¼ teaspoon sea salt

FILLING
10 fresh Black Mission figs, cut into quarters
¼ cup coconut sugar
1 teaspoon finely chopped fresh rosemary
1 teaspoon gluten-free vanilla extract

TOPPING
3 tablespoons coconut milk
2 tablespoons coconut sugar

Must Do

1. Preheat the oven to 350°F. Line a 15 × 13-inch baking sheet with parchment paper.

2. To make the crust: Drain the dates and reserve the soaking water.

3. Add the dates, flour, oats, applesauce, sunflower seed butter, coconut sugar, and salt to a food processor. Pulse to combine until the mixture has a crumbly consistency. While the machine is running, add the reserved soaking water, 1 tablespoon at a time, until the dough comes together and is very smooth and moist, about 5 tablespoons.

4. Form the dough into a ball and divide it into 4 equal pieces by cutting it in half and then in half again. Form the 4 pieces of dough into balls and place them on the prepared baking sheet.

5. Press down the dough balls with your hands to make flat circles that are about 5 inches wide and ¼ inch thick.

6. To make the filling: Add the figs, coconut sugar, rosemary, and vanilla to a medium bowl, and stir to combine.

7. Place the fig mixture in the middle of each of the disks, dividing it evenly, and leaving about a ½-inch border around the perimeter. Fold over the dough border, or just pinch the dough up to create a rim.

8. To make the topping: Brush the dough rims with the coconut milk. Sprinkle the coconut sugar around the rims and a little on top of the figs.

9. Bake the galette-lets until the rims are golden brown, about 20 minutes.

10. Transfer the baking sheet to a wire rack, and let it sit for about 10 minutes. Serve immediately or at room temperature.

11. Keep in an airtight container for up to 3 days, or wrap individually and freeze for up to 3 months.

SERVING SIZE: 1 GALETTE-LET
Calories 300; Total Fat 4.1g; Protein 11.0g; Cholesterol 0.0g; Sodium 143mg; Fiber 0.9g; Sugars 32.0g; Total Carbohydrate 70.1g

Inside Scoop: If fresh figs are not in season, feel free to use dried figs.

Inside Scoop: Unlike most of the other baked goods in this chapter, these pie-lets do not freeze well. So eat them within a week from the fridge, which shouldn't be hard to do.

Pumpkin Pie-lets

MAKES 12 PIE-LETS

I live on these little pie-lets. I love the seeded crust that forms the crisp seat for the smooth pumpkin filling. True to form, I prefer them in individual portions, but if you're so inclined, you can make a 9-inch pie with the same ingredient amounts. This is a perfect dessert to make for the holidays, and a little coconut-whip topping makes it even more perfect.

Must Have

CRUST
¾ cup gluten-free oats
½ cup sunflower seeds
½ teaspoon ground cinnamon
8 Medjool dates, pitted and soaked in water for 20 minutes, then drained
3 tablespoons water

FILLING
1 (15-ounce) can pumpkin puree
¼ cup coconut milk
¼ cup coconut nectar
2 tablespoons tapioca flour
2 teaspoons pumpkin pie spice
1 teaspoon gluten-free vanilla extract

STREUSEL
¼ cup gluten-free oats, ground (I use a coffee grinder)
¼ teaspoon ground cinnamon

Must Do

1. Preheat the oven to 325°F. Line a standard 12-cup muffin tin with paper liners.

2. To make the crust: Add the oats, sunflower seeds, cinnamon, and dates to a food processor. Pulse until the mixture comes together but retains some texture. Add the water, 1 tablespoon at a time, until the mixture is moist and a little smoother.

3. Add about 2 tablespoons of the crust mixture to each cupcake liner and press down to make an even layer. Press up the sides of the walls just a little bit.

4. To make the filling: Mix together the pumpkin puree, coconut milk, and coconut nectar in a large bowl. Add the tapioca flour, pumpkin pie spice, and vanilla, and stir to combine.

5. Spoon about 3 tablespoons of the filling on top of the crust mixture in the cupcake wells, dividing it evenly.

6. To make the streusel: Mix together the ground oats and the cinnamon in a small bowl.

7. Lightly cover each pie-let with a little of the streusel.

8. Bake the pie-lets until the streusel is toasted and the middle is firm to the touch, about 25 minutes.

9. Transfer the muffin tin to a wire rack, and let it sit for about 30 minutes before placing in the refrigerator for 3 hours to set completely.

10. Keep in an airtight container in the fridge for up to 7 days.

SERVING SIZE: 1 PIE-LET
Calories 180; Total Fat 9.1g; Protein 5.3g; Cholesterol 0.0g; Sodium 2mg; Fiber 4.5g; Sugars 7.4g; Total Carbohydrate 19.9g

Trail Mix Macaroons

MAKES ABOUT 18 MACAROONS

These macaroons are not to be confused with the colorful and poufy French pastry *macaron* or the macaroons that you get during Passover in the tin cans. These are gourmet, granola macaroons that are held together not with eggs or egg substitutes but by sheer will and sunflower seed butter. The trail mix on the inside and on the chocolate drizzle over the outside make this a perfect dessert for any occasion, like a midhike snack or even a midlife crisis.

Must Have

MACAROONS

3 cups unsweetened shredded coconut

½ cup All-Purpose Gluten-Free Flour Mix (page 20)

2 tablespoons Sunflower Seed Butter (page 20)

⅛ teaspoon fine sea salt

½ cup coconut milk

⅓ cup coconut nectar

1 teaspoon gluten-free vanilla extract

¼ teaspoon stevia powder

⅓ cup Trail Mix Granola (page 47)

DRIZZLE

¼ cup cacao powder

⅛ teaspoon sea salt

⅛ teaspoon stevia powder

3 tablespoons coconut nectar

3 teaspoons water

TOPPING

¼ cup Trail Mix Granola (page 47)

Must Do

1. Preheat the oven to 325°F and line a 15 × 13-inch baking sheet with parchment paper.

2. To make the macaroons: Whisk together the shredded coconut, all-purpose flour, sunflower seed butter, and salt in a large bowl. Make a well in the middle.

3. Add the coconut milk, coconut nectar, vanilla extract, and stevia, and stir to combine.

4. Add the granola and stir to incorporate.

5. Carve out balls of macaroon dough with a 2-inch ice cream scoop and place them on the prepared baking sheet. Dip the utensil in water in between scoops.

6. Bake the macaroons until they are a light golden brown, about 18 minutes. Rotate the baking sheet halfway through baking.

7. Transfer the baking sheet from the oven to a wire rack, and let it sit for about 10 minutes before removing the macaroons to cool completely.

8. To make the drizzle: Mix together the cacao powder, salt, and stevia in a small bowl and stir to combine. Add the coconut nectar and stir to incorporate. Add the water, 1 teaspoon at a time, until the drizzle has a smooth consistency.

9. Top the macaroons with the drizzle and the granola.

10. Keep in an airtight container for up to 3 days, or wrap and freeze for up to 3 months.

SERVING SIZE: 1 MACAROON

Calories 120; Total Fat 7.2g; Protein 2.0g; Cholesterol 0.0g; Sodium 30mg; Fiber 2.9g; Sugars 7.0g; Total Carbohydrate 10.1g

Resources

Ancient Harvest

WWW.ANCIENTHARVEST.COM

This company makes a wide variety of gluten-free products that are non-GMO and organic. I like to use their hot cereal quinoa flakes in particular. You can buy them on the Ancient Harvest website or at Whole Foods, as well as on Amazon.

Bragg

WWW.BRAGG.COM

This health-conscious company serves up gluten-free, salt-free, sugar-free nutritional yeast (nooch) that is beyond compare. It is easily found online, at Amazon, and in many health food stores.

Coconut Secret

WWW.COCONUTSECRET.COM

This company makes the best-tasting coconut nectar and coconut aminos in the country, as far as I'm concerned. And I've tasted most of them. Luckily, these products are becoming more readily available and can be found online at Amazon and at some health food stores.

Dynamic Health

WWW.DYNAMICHEALTH.COM

Dynamic Health makes the pomegranate juice concentrate that I use for my Raisin Bran Scones with Pomegranate Icing. They make a promise that no yeast, corn, wheat, gluten, soy, dairy, fish, animal derivatives, preservatives, artificial colors, or artificial flavors are added to their products. The products are also gluten-free and sugar-free.

Edward and Sons

WWW.EDWARDANDSONS.COM

This company has a line of sauces called the Wizard's Organic Saucery. I use their vegan Worcestershire sauce for the recipes that call for Worcestershire. They also make a wheat-free version for gluten-intolerant customers.

Frontier Co-Op

WWW.FRONTIERCOOP.COM

In order for the bread recipes in this book to soar in terms of taste and texture, you need to use psyllium husk powder. The best is from Frontier Co-Op, which sells it from their own website. I have also bought it on Amazon. The powder comes in a 1-pound bag.

Great Eastern Sun

WWW.GREAT-EASTERN-SUN.COM

I get the most delicious chickpea miso paste, Miso Master, from this company. Their products are organic and non-GMO certified, and you can find them at Whole Foods or order directly from the company online.

Hime

Hime makes a wasabi powder that you mix with water to produce wasabi paste. It is sold on Amazon and at many grocery stores, including Whole Foods.

Lily's Sweets

WWW.LILYSSWEETS.COM

Lily's makes sugar-free, dairy-free chocolate chips that are really something to write home about. All their chocolate is non-GMO and contains only Fair Trade–certified cacao. To top that off, they are certified gluten-free. You can find their products in many grocery stores around the country and on Amazon.

Living Harvest

WWW.LIVINGHARVEST.COM

Because tofu is made with soy, I couldn't use it in any of my recipes until this amazing company thought to make tofu with hemp seeds. It works like a charm and tastes great. You can find it, under the brand name Tempt, at health food stores where they keep the regular tofu. It comes in 8-ounce packages.

Lotus Foods

WWW.LOTUSFOODS.COM

I love the line of organic rice ramen noodles this company makes. The flavors they offer are forbidden rice, jade pearl rice, and organic millet & brown rice. Their products are free of gluten and wheat, and they remove toxic agrochemicals from the soil in which they grow their rice. You can find these products at Whole Foods or online at their website or on Amazon.

SeaSnax

WWW.SEASNAX.COM

SeaSnax makes all things seaweed. I use their SeaVegi Seaweed Salad Mix for my Sea Vegetable & Cabbage Slaw (page 195), and you can buy directly from them online, on Amazon, or at Whole Foods.

So Delicious Dairy Free

WWW.SODELICIOUSDAIRYFREE.COM

I religiously use the So Delicious Dairy Free coconut milk plain yogurts and the unsweetened coconut milk exclusively for all the recipes in this book that require yogurt or nondairy milk. Luckily, this brand is in practically every grocery store nationwide, so you shouldn't have a problem finding it. I have to say this is one of the nicest companies in terms of customer service and listening to what the consumer really wants and needs.

Spicely Organics

WWW.SPICELY.COM

I get all my spices from this company. Their products are certified gluten-free, vegan, organic, kosher, and non-GMO verified. They also make the promise that no peanuts, soybeans, milk, eggs, fish, crustaceans, tree nuts, wheat, MSG, artificial colors, preservatives, artificial sweeteners, cornstarch, or hydrogenated oils are in their products. These spices can be found in cute little boxes in Whole Foods or on Amazon.

Star Anise Foods

WWW.STARANISEFOODS.COM

This company makes gluten-free, non-GMO Vietnamese brown rice spring roll wrappers that you can buy on Amazon or at Whole Foods.

SweetLeaf

WWW.SWEETLEAF.COM

It's very hard to find a stevia powder that doesn't have an aftertaste, is organic, and is gluten-free. SweetLeaf stevia fits the bill and delivers on all of the above. The taste is really great, and I use it exclusively. You can buy this online at Amazon or at Whole Foods.

Swerve

WWW.SWERVESWEETENER.COM

In my quest to find an alternative to powdered sugar, along came confectioners'-style Swerve to save the day. Don't get the granulated Swerve because that won't work for the purposes of the recipes in this book. The confectioners' Swerve is basically powdered erythritol, an all-natural sweetener derived from fruits and vegetables. Swerve is kosher, certified non-GMO, gluten-free, and vegan. The best part of all? It has zero calories. You can find confectioners'-style Swerve online at Amazon or at Whole Foods.

Teff Company

WWW.TEFFCO.COM

Ivory teff flour is an ingredient of the All-Purpose Gluten-Free Flour Mix (page 20) that I use at my bakery and at home. It is milder in taste than brown teff and lighter in texture. You can buy ivory teff flour on this company's website or on Amazon.

Thai Kitchen

WWW.THAIKITCHEN.COM

It's a wonderful thing when a company is aware and diligent enough to provide up-to-date allergen information on all their products and on their website. That's why I feel secure in using Thai Kitchen's green curry paste. They provide an allergen spreadsheet on their website that indicates this paste is gluten-free, dairy-free, vegan, nut-free, and fish-free. Thai Kitchen products can be found at most grocery stores nationwide.

Acknowledgments

To my parents, Rachel and Leo, who show me by example what it means to live with integrity and love unconditionally.

To my brother, Barry, who is the best and most caring brother a big sister can have.

To my agent, Lisa Ekus: I am forever in awe of your steadfast belief in me, your enduring guidance, and your tireless efforts on my behalf.

To my oh so talented food photographer, Carl Kravats, who always makes my recipes look like gorgeous movie stars.

To my brilliant food stylist, Cindy Epstein, who knows how to dress a meal and a table in the most fashionable and stunning ways.

To Joni Wilhelm, who did a superb job re-creating my recipes for their close-ups.

To Glenn Yeffeth, for recognizing the need for a book like this, and my outstanding team at BenBella Books, including Leah Wilson, Alicia Kania, Heather Butterfield, Adrienne Lang, Monica Lowry, Rachel Phares, Lindsay Marshall, and Sarah Dombrowsky. I am so grateful to all of you for your sage suggestions, profound wisdom, and tremendous support.

To my outstanding editor, Karen Levy, thank you for your incredible attention to detail and your overall editorial genius.

To my BFF Elissa, whom I am so lucky to have in my life. Your friendship means the world to me.

To my husband, who is my true North Star, the special someone on whom I can always depend, and who demonstrates his love daily with his actions and with his being.

Index

About the Author

Debbie Adler is the owner of the nationally renowned, vegan, allergy-free, gluten-free, sugar-free bakery Sweet Debbie's Organic Cupcakes, located in Los Angeles, California.

In addition, Debbie is the author of the critically acclaimed cookbook *Sweet Debbie's Organic Treats: Allergy-Free & Vegan Recipes from the Famous Los Angeles Bakery*. It was named a "Best Gluten-Free Cookbook" by *Delicious Living* magazine, a "Favorite Book" by *Gluten Free & More* magazine, and a "Best Vegan Cookbook" by the blog *Green Vegan Living*.

Debbie has been interviewed on NBC's *Nightly News*, ABC-7's *Eyewitness News*, CBS Los Angeles News, KTLA's *Health Smart*, WISH-TV's *Indy Style*, the nationally syndicated WGN's *Lunchbreak*, and Fox 7's *Good Day Austin*.

She has been featured in the *Los Angeles Times* and on NPR's radio show *Here and Now*. Her recipes have been published in national magazines such as *Allergic Living, Living Without, Simply Gluten-Free, Delight Gluten-Free, Pilates Style, Where Women Cook*, and *Low Sugar Living;* on popular websites and blogs such as *Fox News Magazine, Parents, Self, Glamour, The Chalkboard, The Kitchn*, and *Epicurious Community Table;* and on the websites for food companies such as So Delicious Dairy Free, Sambazon, and Navitas Naturals.

Debbie speaks at conferences nationwide and is a regular guest presenter at hospitals and medical schools, where she talks to doctors, residents, interns, and medical students about the health benefits of a plant-based diet.

Please visit www.debbieadler.tv for more information.